Modern Theories of Language

Sound and Meaning

The Roman Jakobson Series

in Linguistics and Poetics

C. H. van Schooneveld,

Series Editor

Modern Theories of Language

The Empirical Challenge

Mortéza Mahmoudian

Duke University Press

Durham and London 1993

© 1993 Duke University Press

Printed in the United States of America

on acid-free paper ∞

Library of Congress Cataloging-in-Publication Data

appear on the last printed page of this book.

Contents

Contents **vii**

List of Figures and Tables

Preface

Is it possible to take stock of our current knowledge of language? I think it is, and this book is based on this belief. Moreover I not only think it possible to make such an assessment, I am convinced it can be done without the complacent optimism which would praise this discipline to the skies, say, as a pilot discipline, and without the excessive pessimism which would bring linguistics and all its achievements spiraling down.

This preface has not been written to announce to the reader what one will find in this work; the synopsis at the beginning of each chapter should suffice to satisfy this need. The aim here is quite different: to explain my approach to language and the way I examine the problems language raises.

As shown by its title, this book examines modern theories of language. Its endeavor is to evaluate theories on the strength of their empirical adequacy. Such an examination should consist neither of juxtaposed accounts of the various positions about language nor of the evaluation of theories on the basis of principles acknowledged by one particular linguistic thought. I have tried therefore to avoid the two extremes of dogmatism and eclecticism. The former would lead us to a dead end by imprisoning us in a preconceived system. The problem is not that research has as its starting point hypotheses *a priori;* such *a prioris* are unavoidable. Dogmatism arises when one's theses are placed beyond the reach of all empirical or even theoretical argument; if this occurs, there is a danger of losing control over the initial hypotheses and of obstructing any chance of readjusting and renewing the hypotheses. One criticism of eclecticism is that by borrowing fragments of theories from here and there, the resulting theory is likely to be a mass of ideas not linked in any way to build a whole (i.e., something that could be called a theoretical construction). Clear debate requires well-defined notions and precise terminology; without them, one risks that any discussion will be about rather vague theses leading to multiple, or even contradictory, interpretations with no idea as to which to accept and which to leave aside. I am not myself free from this paradox, but I have tried to resolve it. In order to ensure clarity of discussion, I have defined the concepts I use and have found terms to correspond to them; in order to avoid dogmatism, I have not assumed *a priori* the validity or efficiency of these concepts. I have made a special effort to clarify the concepts without worrying too much about terminology and its elegance and connotations, since, after all, if the object of the debate is clearly presented, the choice of terminology is of little importance. Instead, other choices—for a start, the presentation of acquired knowledge common to the various theoretical discourses—seem more important to me and, I feel, should be pointed out. Sketching an outline of what is generally accepted and presenting the conceptual relationship of the various schools of thought is not a simple thing to do: it presumes that notions and terminologies are interpreted and that a decision is made about what is essential and what is contingent in order to conclude that two concepts—for example, the articulations of Saussurian linguistics and the creativity of the generativists—are one and the same. In all this, the exegete's responsibility—in this case mine—is involved.

A linguistic presentation can focus on the point of view of the language user or the point of view of the describer. In the one case the question is "what does the native speaker do with his language?" In the other, it is "what does the linguist do, or what should he do, to account for the way in which the native speaker uses his language?" Although it is indeed possible to transpose to one point of view a problem considered initially from the other, this transposition is in itself a fastidious exercise that I have tried to avoid. I have restricted myself to a single perspective: that of the language user. I believe that from this angle, the object under study becomes more immediate, which in my opinion has a certain advantage: empirical verification is understood by everyone to constitute a kind of ultimate test of validity.

As to the status of linguistic theory, my starting point is the idea that the aim of linguistic research is to examine and understand the nature of language; a theory is just a tool to attain this goal. Consequently, as long as a theory leaves much to be desired in its ability to explain the object in question, it can be justified by its intrinsic qualities only (such as coherence, simplicity, elegance, sophistication, exhaustiveness, etc.). By failing to be properly concerned with the explanatory power of theory, many linguists deprive linguistics of its empirical task, with the result of delegating to others (e.g., psychologists, psycholinguists, sociolinguists, et al.) the duty of confronting linguistic hypotheses with the data; I consider this unacceptable since linguistic reflection thus loses enriching feedback.

If one is interested in empirical adequacy (i.e., the power to explain), one soon realizes that any linguistic phenomenon cloaks both psychic and social aspects. Certainly one may want, out of a desire for objectivity, to confine oneself to the observation of linguistic phenomena and the behavioral responses which are linked to them. Even then, subjective elements slip in: the link between speech and behavior cannot be grasped by direct observation. There is always someone who creates the link. This someone may be the linguist himself, or it may be one or more speakers of the language. I preferred this last solution for several reasons, among them to avoid being both judge and defendant. The reason is that the data used to support the theses are neither neutral nor anonymous; they issue from specific speakers and are collected under specific conditions. That is to say, social class and psychic conditions have an influence on the observed object. Hence, the work is resolutely engaged in the evaluation of the empirical adequacy of linguistic theories by recourse to the psychical and social dimensions of linguistic phenomena. The inconvenience of this approach is that the hypotheses cannot be deemed confirmed once and for all; their validity remains linked to a particular social group and specific conditions of observation. My conviction is that without this prudence—which is dictated by the complexity of language itself—the dangers are great: the formal, general regularities (that is to say, those valid for a whole language community under all conditions of observation) that are sought will more than likely come up against a mass of counterexamples or be reduced to generalities without contributing anything really new.

If it is a sin for the linguist to support theses tainted with psychological or sociological arguments, I have sinned, and I must say so explicitly. To justify this standpoint I will invoke two arguments. Firstly, in principle, one may ask where the line should be drawn between linguistics and sociology or between linguistics and psychology. It is impossible to provide an answer to this question that is not *ad hoc*. Furthermore, factual convergences between these disciplines can be noted. On the one hand, there is a convergence in terms of their object: when a sociologist—for instance, Bourdieu—inquires about the qualifiers people are inclined to use to describe their home, what is he seeking to establish? The type of habitat each of the social classes believes is ideal, certainly. But at the same time, does he not reveal that the semantic value of words depends on social class? (c.f. Bourdieu, 1982, p. 18). On the other hand, there is a convergence in terms of method: the techniques that are used to confront hypotheses with data by a linguist like Labov or a psychologist like Rosch offer few differences, at least in their main outlines.

The subtitle, *The Empirical Challenge*, emphasizes the place of experimental data in this work. It should be noted that only one type of experimentation is examined in depth: namely, the survey. But this does not mean that other techniques of observation and experimentation are rejected in principle. The reasons for my choice, which are closely related to each other, are that I wanted to show, on the one hand, that a survey has more extensive applications than are generally thought, and on the other, that it enables a dialectic connection to be established between theoretical reflection and empirical research. Moreover, as instrumental techniques, and in particular their validity, have not been the subject of serious thought, their scope and limits do not seem to me to give adequate guarantees with respect to the conclusions that might be drawn; the sophisticated tools that are used multiply the hazards and thus increase the risk of unfounded interpretation.

A different title, *Language in Mind and Society*, was considered, but I rejected this alternative in order to avoid a possible misunderstanding: the reader could expect to find in it long theoretical discussions about the relationship of linguistics with psychology or sociology.

I also hope that the work's title, *Modern Theories of Language*, does not give the impression that I am addressing only theoreticians qualified in linguistics. I am aiming at a wider audience. My goal has been to present as simply as possible what has been achieved in linguistics and the residual problems that remain unsolved. In my presentation, I address myself first to the question of the properties of the object, and given these properties, I seek to discover which analytical approaches are adequate. I hope that I have succeeded in making the problems of linguistics accessible to nonlinguists, at least in Part One. In contrast, in Part Two, discussions of analysis and related procedures have been undertaken in order to highlight the importance accorded to theoretical divergences; but even then, the language user's point of view is never abandoned. Even someone who rejects boring formalism and vacuous discussion will find something that concerns and interests him. He will certainly have to arm himself with patience during the terminological "clearing up" to see the actual object of debate revealed; but at no moment is an excessive effort of memorization imposed on him to store a lot of heavy technical apparatus (terms, formulae, diagrams, etc.).

I did not adopt this approach so as to produce a best-seller. My choice is based on an established fact: too often, specialized terminology serves as a protective cocoon that allows those in the know to fall back on their positions and to defend themselves against the intrusion of outsiders. I am convinced that the structure of language is — as many have said—simple in its broad outline and that it can be presented simply, in accessible terms. I have often noticed that the "naive," "innocent" questions of the layman concern fundamental problems; terminological apparatus should not be used as protection by the linguist in distress.

Incidentally, clearing up the terminology and making the concepts explicit allow us to think that the current status of linguistics is not far from that of a "normal" science, in Kuhn's sense. Indeed, a growing majority holds to the same paradigm—that is, its members share a common platform of received knowledge and common research prospects.

Before ending this preface let me say a word about the theories mentioned in this book. The list is far from being exhaustive; it does not even include all the "classics" in the field. (It would in any case be illusory to aim today at exhaustivity, especially if one considers the mass of publications produced every year!) Nor have I attempted to cite the latest fashion. I set myself the task of showing the problems one comes across within one or another theoretical framework when one applies oneself to treating a linguistic phenomenon (sometimes general, sometimes more specific). With this as my starting point, I have dedicated my efforts to the search for a solution which may find support in empirical data. In discussing the theses, I have cited various authors to make the problems and debates more concrete so that I do not give the impression of tilting at windmills.

I hope that this debate will be received as a discussion about ideas and not as a polemic between people or a war of words. I owe a lot to certain people whose theses I criticize. I have sometimes defended the thesis of an author I do not know personally. Is it permitted, is it possible for the researcher to accomplish his task as the workman of science he is expected to be, and to do so honestly, without his relationships of friendship and partiality being drawn in? I believe it is, and on this basis I have written the book now before you.

Acknowledgments

For this book, I owe much to many. I would like to thank all of the following people for their help and invaluable assistance: to my students first, for the discussions they allowed and the remarks they formulated, which worked as an incentive in the preparation of this work; to numerous colleagues and friends who helped and encouraged me, in particular Sandor Hervey, Rémi Jolivet, Thomas Lahusen, Georges Mounin and Henry Schogt; to Yvan Cruchaud and Jennifer Mountford, who translated certain chapters that had been written in French; to Jacqueline Perez, who typed the first chapters; to Elizabeth Ashley, who revised the final version of the manuscript; to the Faculté des lettres of Lausanne University and to the Fondation Chuard-Schmid for their financial support.

Parts of this book have already been published as articles in reviews. They have been freely used and modified here. Sections VI.1–VI.9 are reprintings—with minor changes—of "Structure du signifié et fonction de communication," published in *La linguistique*, vol. 21, pp. 251–274 (with the kind permission of the Presses Universitaires de France). Section VII.2 is a rewrite of "Objectivité et subjectivité dans la connaissance du langage," slightly modified and abridged, published in *Tranel*, no. 11, 1986, pp. 7–20, brought out by the Institut de linguistique de l'Université de Neuchâtel.

Modern Theories of Language

PART ONE

In this part, my aim is to present a broad view of the main problems of today's linguistics. This account has a twofold aim. On the one hand, vulgarization: by not delving too deeply into technical details, the account remains accessible to the noninitiate and provides him with a clear view on the object and methods of linguistics. On the other hand, I am presenting the state of the art: Part One sums up the acquired knowledge and the most fundamental issues of our field and outlines the direction my work will take in Part Two.

1 The Unity of Linguistics

I.0 Synopsis

If we consider linguistic thought over the last few decades, we will be struck by the controversies and the polemics opposing different theoretical currents and tendencies. However, we will also notice that some principles have been commonly agreed upon and generally admitted. With a reasonable dose of optimism, we could consider these principles as common features of today's linguistics as a whole. In this chapter, I shall discuss six such features, namely: 1. system versus unit, 2. rule and class, 3. formal versus random, 4. linguistic universals, 5. signifiant (form, expression) and signifié (meaning, content), and 6. the frame of analysis.

A difference in terminology seems to be one of the main reasons these features do not at first glance appear common to different theories. To put it in other words, terminology is a nut whose shell we shall crack to find what is inside. In fact, some comments and interpretations are needed to show the common purport of such principles as syntactic rules (e.g., rewriting rules) and the concept of combination or compatibility in Martinet's work.

I.1 System versus Unit

A feature common to all linguistics in the twentieth century is the admission that a linguistic unit is only definable within the system to which it belongs; that is, it cannot be defined in isolation. Thus, the linguistic unit must not be confused with its positive, physical properties. We therefore arrive at an abstract conception of units. The abstractness of units can be based on the principle of pertinence or relevance, as is the case for the Prague School or the Copenhagen School. But it may also be based on the principle of abstraction, as in transformational grammar. For instance, a phoneme is not considered as the sum of its phonetic properties: its definition is based on those sound features which oppose and link it to the other phonemes of the same language. Let us take a classic phonological example: consider French /b/ in /bō/ *bon* 'good'. It can be adequately defined as 'bilabial', 'voiced', and 'oral' (or 'non-nasal'). Each of these features is necessary to distinguish it from some other unit in the French phonemic system. Should 'bilabiality' be left out, /b/ would be confused with /d/ (as in /dō/ *don* 'gift'), /g/ (as in /gō/ *gond* 'hinge'), and so on. If we leave out the feature 'voiced', we would be unable to differentiate /b/ from /p/ (as in /pō/ *pont* 'bridge'). If we leave out 'orality', /b/ will no longer contrast with the nasal phoneme /m/ (as in /mō/ *mont* 'mountain'). Yet, the phonetic features of /b/ are far more numerous and complex than can be listed here. If we seek to give an accurate account of the phonetic makeup of /b/, we must also state that it is a 'nonaspirate', 'weak', 'stop', and so on. But such features have no separate relevance in French phonology, as there is no 'voiced' phoneme that is not 'nonaspirate'. In the same way, in Korean phonology we would need to mention if a phoneme is 'weak' or 'strong', but not in the French phonemic system, where a 'weak' phoneme cannot be opposed to a 'strong' one. The units are thus conceived of as the sum of their relevant features; consequently, they are abstract entities insofar as many of the characteristics effectively present in their realizations are put aside.

I should like to insist on one point: in my view, the two principles—idealization and relevance—are not equivalent and do not entail the same implications. Yet both lead us to consider the linguistic unit as an abstract entity. If we have to choose, I prefer the principle of relevance, which not only gives abstract units but also to a certain extent constrains the abstraction on functional grounds and makes its limits explicit.

I.2 Rule and Class (cf. also V.1)

What should we retain of the controversy over taxonomic linguistics? Personally, I think that certain ambiguities have made this issue unclear, in particular those I discuss below.

(a) Taxonomy: necessary or sufficient?

It has taken a long time to clear up the confusion between two conceptions of taxonomy either as a necessary component in language description, and hence in its functioning, or as a sufficient one. In the latter case, the job of the descriptive linguist would be finished as soon as he had established classes. By this reasoning, all that transcends the setting up of classes of linguistic units would be beyond the field of linguistics.

It seems to me that the structuralists of the classical era, especially distributionalists, argued for the necessity of the concept of class, but in fact, they viewed classification as the final aim of linguistic description, that is to say, as sufficient.

(b) The foundations of classification

Classification could be conceived of as a wholly arbitrary operation undertaken by a describer. Such a thesis is not worthy of serious consideration or discussion.

However, we may want to base classification on theoretical grounds. For example, we could question whether a linguistic structure without any taxonomic component could function as ordinary languages do. If this is not possible, then the necessity of the notion of class seems to be demonstrated.

(c) Taxonomy versus explanation

Another ambiguity lies in the so-called opposition between taxonomy and explanation, and those who criticize taxonomy start from the often implicit idea that classes are *ad hoc*. But why should there be such an opposition if the classes are not *ad hoc* and if they constitute a necessary element of the functioning of language? Under such conditions, taxonomy could help us in the explanation of language structure. For example, classification could theoretically be motivated by the economy it provides. If the notion of economy is clearly defined, we will be able to say which of the possible classifications corresponds best to language functioning and why.

Incidentally, I know of no linguist who has ever supported both taxonomy and the arbitrariness of classes. Even Harris justified his distributional classes on the basis of simplicity. But the concept of simplicity was itself neither justified nor explicit enough in his writings and was therefore open to criticism. Yet those who opposed taxonomy, ironically enough, maintained the criterion of simplicity.

I.3   Formal and Random (cf. also II.7, V.2)

Following Carnap (1968), we consider as formal a system in which units and their interrelations can be replaced by symbols. Beyond its practical import, which is secondary, this definition implies that units and their relations are absolute (discontinuous or discrete, etc.)—that is, they are subject to the logic of "yes or no" or to the law of "all or none" (the law of excluded middle).

The application of this concept entails that: (i) a language has a limited number (perhaps a finite number) of units and rules; and (ii) the most interesting types of research are those devoted to the study of structure or competence and not of usage or performance.

Independently of my personal position, I must admit that neither of these theses is currently supported by a wide range of linguists, not even any longer among transformational linguists. On the one hand, the absoluteness of linguistic phenomena was questioned by Lakoff (1969), Ross (1972, 1973), Carden (1973), and others around the beginning of the 1970s. On the other hand, the works of Labov, De Camp, and others show how interesting the study of usage (or performance) might be as a way of gaining insight into aspects of structure.

Most nontransformational linguists have always shown their interest in the study of the use of language and have sometimes been unduly criticized for this interest. However, their ideas show some inconsistencies that I shall discuss later. Some linguists view the formal character of language structure as the basis of creativity. But creativity does not entail the formal character of language; creativity is a consequence of one's explanatory attitude toward language. If one considers that the sentences of a language are infinite in number and therefore that it is not possible to learn them one by one, then the speakers and hearers must possess a more efficient way of producing and understanding sentences. If this is what is meant by creativity (as according to Postal, 1968), then creativity is virtually equivalent to Martinet's principle of articulation.

If we reject the formal character of language phenomena, we have to admit that they are random, and as such could be usefully studied by means of statistical methods and tools.

I.4 Linguistic Universals

Is linguistic structure arbitrary? And if so, can we therefore drop the notion of language universals? I am almost tempted to answer this question both yes and no. Yet I do not feel that I am giving a noncommittal answer. I think, on the one hand, that by reducing variants to constant units, the linguist takes account of some constraints that arise due to man's physical and social makeup, and on the other hand, that these constraints do not operate similarly in all cases. For example, under given conditions, we find it justified to subsume [i] and [j] as allophones of a phoneme but not [ŋ] and [h]. Such a description may be motivated by perceptual and phonatory constraints. Owing to such constraints, the nasal phoneme or archiphoneme is realized as [ŋ] when followed by a homosyllabic /k/ or /g/. This is the case in many languages (French, English, German, Farsi, etc.) but not in Russian. Now, should we aim at establishing linguistic universals or not? If so, what do we do with the exceptions? If not, how do we reduce variants to units without ad hoc arguments? I believe that the defenders and opponents of universals do not hold such diametrically opposed positions as it might appear at first glance.[1] They both have a principle as their point of departure and admit the existence of a number of exceptions to that principle. The problem is that the distinction between rule and exception is a matter of taste. A solution seems impossible without recourse to a statistical dimension. Here again we see an instance where our theoretical position can be usefully shaped by consideration of factors that are random.

I.5 Signifié and Signifiant

One of the problems that has long divided linguists into different camps is the status of the signifié. There was a temptation in the 1930s and 1940s to exclude the study of the signifié from the field of linguistics (cf. Harris, 1954). I think that by now this thesis has lost its attraction; nobody would consider a linguistic description as complete without at least one chapter on semantics.

Another way of conceiving of the signifié was to include it in the linguistic field and to consider its structure as isomorphic with the structure of the signifiant. The term isomorphism reminds us of Hjelmslev and his glossematic school. In his view (cf. Hjelmslev, 1953), isomorphism implies that signifié and signifiant have a parallel organization, that is, they both have the same levels of analysis, the same types of unit and relation; and in both, analysis would bring up a limited number of ultimate elements, namely phonemes on the one hand and relevant semantic features (which he conceived of as minimal semantic units and called morphemes) on the other. The idea of parallelism between the two structures—signifiant and signifié—is found in other linguistic theories, though formulated in different terms.[2]

This isomorphism—and especially the postulation of a limited number of relevant semantic features—creates problems that we shall discuss later (cf. III.6, VI.14). Sometimes the principle is implicit; for example, all those who analyze monemes on the content plane into relevant semantic features suppose that they will obtain a limited number of items by doing so. Otherwise, the analysis of the signifié into features would turn out to be merely an intralanguage translation, a kind of paraphrase. What could possibly be the interest of describing the French word *bruit* as '*sorte de son* kind of sound' and the word *son* 'sound' as '*sorte de bruit* kind of noise'? I hardly exaggerate!

The isomorphism between the structure of expression and the structure of content is increasingly questioned by linguists, for instance by all those who conceive of the signifié in relation with human experience and therefore take into account a cognitive aspect in semantic studies; this is the case for Mounin (1972), Frédéric François (1977), Lakoff (1969), McCawley (1968), and others. Another example, though less obvious: in his extended standard theory, Chomsky (1977) admits that surface structure has a certain relevance for semantic interpretation, while the semantic component has no bearing on phonological interpretation. In my view, this is a case of a break in the parallelism between signifié and signifiant and leads apparently to abandoning the postulation of a limited or finite number of relevant semantic features.

I.6 Frame of Analysis

Most structuralists have adopted the principle that the sentence should be the maximal frame for syntactic analysis. Some have gone so far as to say that there is nothing in language that we could not find in the sentence, for example, Benveniste (1966, p. 131). This limitation of the frame of analysis has given rise to a great deal of discussion—perhaps more than it should—and is generally no longer recognized as being valid for either theoretical or empirical reasons.

On a theoretical level, it is admitted that the object of a science has no natural boundaries; the researcher decides which domain interests him, that is, any definition of an object of study is necessarily arbitrary. The adequacy of the resulting study is the only criterion which permits us to choose one delimitation rather than another.[3]

On an empirical level, it has been observed that regularities are not limited to the sentence, and that certain regularities can be found in units beyond the sentence, for instance, in discourse, dialogue, narrative, and so on. If by structure we mean that the assembly of simple parts to construct complexes conforms to regularities, then we should admit that these segments—larger than sentences—are structured.

We should be cautious in our criticism of classical structuralism. The choice of structuralists may have been only a tactical and not a theoretical one; that is, they may have merely found it preferable, in a given state of knowledge, to give precedence to one frame over others.

In conclusion it must be said that linguistic reflection has reached a point where more and more convergences appear between approaches, once abstraction is made of terminological differences. This could be promising: to recognize common factors could make for a fruitful exchange between schools of thought and may shed new light on differences. It is dangerous to ignore the contribution of other schools, if for no other reason than to avoid a waste of time and effort in rediscovering what others had already discovered decades earlier.

II Experimentation in Linguistics

II.0 Synopsis
My purpose in this chapter will be to illustrate the value of experimentation in linguistics and expose some of its problems. Experimentation requires as its basis the setting up of models within the framework of a theory.

Taking communicative function as a point of departure, I hope to illustrate the consequences of experimentation for our conception of language structure. On the one hand, if we follow this approach, we will find that linguistic phenomena should be deemed more complex (heterogeneous, hierarchized, etc.) than is usually conceived of. On the other hand, certain remaining problems will be put on a new basis, which will result in a more satisfactory solution, as we will see later.

II.1 Necessity of Experimentation
The point of departure of this chapter is Karl Popper's idea concerning the necessity of inductive evidence in our quest for knowledge: without such evidence we run the risk of confusing the schizophrenic who takes himself for a fish with the rational person (Popper, 1972). I will present no case for induction; I couldn't possibly do it better than Popper did. I shall come back to this issue later (cf. VII,1–2); however, I will not insist on some points, such as the necessity of adopting a scientific method, the advantage of an axiomatic construction, and so forth.

I will restrict myself to two remarks, as follows.

(i) I agree with G. G. Granger (1967) when he says that one can distinguish three types of conceptual thinking: idealistic, realistic and transcendental. In idealistic thinking, the form is taken for the object and is confused with it. In realistic thinking, the notion becomes a tool, and science tends to be a technique. In transcendental thinking, the theory defines its structure-object and the conditions of its validity. I imagine that Harris's methods (1951) can qualify as realistic, mechanistic. I support the idea that Hjelmslev's (1953) method could be called formalistic, idealistic. The danger of idealism is its formalism. Realism involves the risks of positivistic physicalism, mechanism.

(ii) If we adopt the transcendental point of view, science has to make the definition of its object and the conditions of its validity explicit. This is done partly by the theory, but the definition of the object on a theoretical level is too general and therefore not explicit enough for experimental purposes, and models are needed to link theory and empirical data. A model can be conceived of as a relatively autonomous construction (with restricted scope) within the framework of a theory (Granger, 1967). Let us return to phonology. A theory can affirm the existence of phonemes in every language. It is incumbent on the model(s) to determine the precise conditions of such an existence. For instance, on a theoretical level the signifiant is to be regarded as being composed of phonemes. Is this the case for all signifiants? Are some signifiants exceptions to this general rule? And when a signifiant is a sequence of phonemes, how can we show the reality of these phonemes experimentally? To answer these questions, we have to construct models. For example, we could assume that linguistic units (among them phonemes) have a psychic reality, and that we can attain this by observing the language user's introspection. We will thus have good grounds for describing the phonemes of a language by taking into consideration the speaker's linguistic consciousness (or knowledge, or intuition). This model is compatible with the theoretical principle of phonemic articulation. See, for instance, Martinet's second articulation (Martinet, 1960) or Bloomfield's Assumption 6[4] (Bloomfield, 1926). But it is not the only possible model within these theoretical frameworks; one could also put forward the hypothesis that phonemes correspond to behavioral reality. Hence the relative autonomy of models with regard to theory.

To mention one or two examples in this respect, what Bloomfield expounds in his *Set of Postulates* (1926) is theory, while his work on

Menomini morphophonemics (1939) is a model. Likewise, Martinet's definition of a language (1960, §1.14) is theory, and his survey on French phonology (Martinet, 1945) is a model.

II.2 Problems of Experimentation
In my view, the main difference between theory and model is like that between a general statement and a particular, restricted one. In other words, a single theory allows the setting up of a number of models, which are necessary supplements in order to elucidate and make explicit different aspects of this theory.

By the relative autonomy of models it is meant that not each of the statements a model implies is equally valid for any given collection of data. Refuting a model does not mean the refutation of the underlying theory; hence, the models are autonomous with respect to each other and with respect to the theory.

On the other hand, models are more or less adequate with respect to data; they are not true or false, but good, better, less good, worse, and so on.

Scientific research aims at supplying us with a more precise knowledge of the object. Its point of departure is thus a certain state of our knowledge. Any scientific progress could be considered as a passage from states of lesser knowledge to states of more advanced knowledge (Piaget, 1967, p. 7).

Models are therefore evaluated in a relative manner: the greater the distance between the new state of knowledge and the prior one, the better the model.

II.3 Implications of Communicative Function
It is generally admitted that language has a communicative function. What is meant by communication? Prieto (1968) defines it as the intentional transmission of information. I would add that this information is about an experience which is not necessarily common to both speaker and hearer. In this respect, Bloomfield's example of Jack and Jill illustrates my purpose well: the experience took place in Jill only. Jack was nonetheless informed of Jill's hunger (cf. Bloomfield, 1933, §2).

If language permits communication, this is due to the fact that signifiant and signifié are associated with each other. This association is necessarily located somewhere in the language user, let us say in his mind or his nervous system or whatever we call it. On the other hand, communication is possible if and only if the association signifiant/signifié is valid for both speaker and hearer. Imagine what the functioning of a language would be were this not the case.

We can find a good example in Ionesco's *Présent passé. Passé présent* (1968). Josette, a character in this novel, says: *je ne regarde pas la chaise en mangeant mon oreiller* 'I don't look at the chair while eating my pillow'. Any normal French speaker would fail to understand what she means, unless he knew the conventions she had made with her father. According to them, *chaise* and *oreiller* have meanings different from their accepted ones (respectively 'chair' and 'pillow'). In this case, French *chaise* means 'window' and French *oreiller* means 'bread'.

To recapitulate, the success of a communicative act is subject to two conditions: signa must have a psychological (or mental) aspect (or dimension) and a social one.

Before going on in my argument, I would like to emphasize that there is no heresy in wanting to integrate a mentalistic dimension into linguistic research. Even if we keep to structuralistic principles, the relevance of psychic and social dimensions in linguistic studies follows directly from the concept of communication.

With respect to models, the crucial problem is, can we gain access to these dimensions of signa, and if so, how? Bloomfield's answer (1933, §2) to the question seems, for instance, to be oversimplified: the study of behavior—however useful it may be—is not always possible, is not the only way of accessing semiotic reality, and, last but not least, is not the easiest way.

In their search for objectivity, linguists suggested restricting the linguistic study of meaning to the practical events preceding and/or following the speech act. These are certainly of great help, for instance in finding out what John means when he cries out *it is snowing!* Actually the relation between such an utterance and certain atmospheric conditions might well give us clues to grasp some features of the meaning. But the association of practical events (atmospheric conditions) and linguistic units (*snow*), however frequent it may be, is not always accessible to our observation. The same linguistic sequence *it is snowing!* could be uttered in July or in equatorial areas, that is, detached from those practical events it refers to; nonetheless, it keeps its meaning. Moreover, certain linguistic units or utterances have only displaced uses (*unicorn, god,* or, for most normal people, *spacelab).* This is why language offers the possibility of conveying lies, fictions, untruth, and so forth.

Moreover, if we are able to find out the meaning of displaced speech (Bloomfield, 1933, §2.5, 4), this implies that recourse to practical stimuli and reactions is not the only possible way. Just as we learn the traffic code by use of language (e.g., red light means 'stop'), in the same way, we can grasp the meaning of a linguistic unit with the help of other units. For example, *snow* can be described as 'atmospheric vapor frozen into ice crystals'.

Finally, a behavioristic procedure for defining meaning is not the easiest way. One could easily imagine how difficult it would be if we tried to learn the traffic code without the use of language resources.

Oddly enough, Bloomfield himself did not observe behavior but based his study on what he imagined this might be.

II.4 Access to the Data

To come back to my question, I take it for granted that the answer will be affirmative—that we can observe the mental and social dimensions of communicative processes, even if all that is conceivably possible cannot be actualized at present. Given that we can gain access to these data, I will discuss only how we can do so. We could be tempted to study the mental aspect of language phenomena by observing the physical processes that take place in man's nervous system while using language. But this—if ever realizable—is merely a very remote possibility. On the other hand, in order to gain insight into neurological processes, specialists use evidence provided by language behavior; that is, in our present state of knowledge, linguistic phenomena are more easily observable than neurological ones.

Now, if one admits the necessity of examining the psychical aspect and rules out the possibility of directly observing neurological processes, to what else can we look?

As far as I know, two solutions have been proposed: observing what the language user does with his language and observing what he believes he does with it. The first is known as the behavioristic or sociological approach and the second as the psychological, psycholinguistic, or mentalistic approach. Before discussing these two approaches, two remarks are in order.

The first concerns the autonomy of linguistics as a discipline. Reacting against the excesses of psychologism or sociologism, the young structuralist linguistics of the 1940s and 1950s looked forward to establishing its proper methods and defining its specific object. In my opinion this mistrust of other sciences was tactically justified. In search of rigorous scientific methods, linguistics could not rely on neighboring disciplines which were still less advanced scientifically. Often the linguists' lack of arguments was supplemented by recourse to psychology or to hypothetical psychical evidence. Discussing the gender of ship names, a French grammar (Wagner and Pinchon, 1962, §35.2) concludes as follows: if one thinks of a masculine generic noun (*vaisseau* 'vessel', *croiseur* 'cruiser'), then one would say *Le Liberté, Le Normandie, Le Vengeance;* on the contrary, if one thinks of a feminine generic noun (*corvette* 'corvette', *frégate* 'frigate', *pinasse* 'pinnace'), then the feminine gender will be used: *La Liberté, La Normandie, La Vengeance.* How can these grammarians know the language user's thoughts? Of course, this is an extreme case, but such assertions thirty years after Bloomfield's criticism show that he was tactically right. Yet such a prejudice should not constitute a theoretical principle: it is not impossible to observe the language user's intuition or feeling (or at least some aspects of these).

The second remark is relative to the discrepancy between declared principles and actual practice. One might be willing to set aside psychological aspects of linguistic elements, declare this in theoretical discussion, and yet consider them in one's descriptive practice.

II.5 Corpus

Bloomfield's distrust of the psychological aspect led him to exclude all recourse to the linguist's or speaker's introspection, whatever the purpose of this solicitation: to produce linguistic material, to judge the possibility of some schema in that language, or to determine the sense of a linguistic form. From this came the idea of a corpus, which was supposed to provide us with raw data. It is worth asking some questions, as follows.

(i) Are the data contained in a corpus as "untouched by human hands" as it would appear at first sight? It does not seem so to me, at least for one reason: the observer's language habits have an influence on data collection. It is a well-known fact now that one easily perceives the phonological distinctions one practices oneself; moreover, one is inclined to find one's own sound distinctions in the usage of others. Martinet (1945, p. 10, n. 1) reports the case of an informant from Orne, Normandy, who pronounced differently French *mot* 'word' and *mots* 'words', respectively /mɔ/ and /mo/. He was convinced that this distinction was general and declared having heard it in the pronunciation of three other French speakers who themselves believed they did not make it. The implication is that the transition from the sounds (as physical events) to the phonemes (as linguistic units) is based on the describer's and/or user's intuition.

(ii) To what extent do the results of the study of a corpus show the structural properties of the language? In other words, what is legitimate extrapolation? In a study on French syntax (Mahmoudian, 1970), it was observed that the corpus had only a very limited number of nominal phrases with partitive articles in the function 'subject', such as *du vin ne me conviendrait pas* 'wine would not suit me'. It was therefore not possible to state which nominal subclasses could be combined with 'partitive' and which ones could not. On the basis of the data obtained from the corpus, one should make the same statement for proper nouns (*du Paul, du Paris*) and the names of things (*du beurre* 'butter', *du raisin* 'grapes'), and so on, which is obviously unsatisfactory. In this respect, any extrapolation is either unjustified or founded on data outside the corpus. For some other units and constructions, for example, definite or indefinite articles, the same corpus allowed satisfactory extrapolations (cf. Jolivet, 1981).

It seems obvious to me that the study of a corpus would have very little bearing on linguistic structure if the results were valid exclusively in the corpus itself; were that the case, the only interest in describing the materials contained in a corpus would be to assure that in given circumstances such linguistic phenomena have been uttered. Linguistic description would thus be lacking in generality, and therefore the criticisms against the use of a corpus would seem to be justified. But I continue to believe that these criticisms were too severe and that some experimental value should be attributed to the study of corpuses.

Consider, for instance, *Français parlé* by Denise François (1974), which is the description of a Parisian's idiolect. The results are valid not only for the usage considered in her work: it has been shown empirically (cf. Jolivet, 1981) that a considerable number of syntactic features are common to different usages of French.

II.6 Survey

Adoption of the psychological approach justifies considering the user's beliefs concerning his language as criteria. But here again there must be some reservations, among them the following.

(i) How can we be sure that the user is aware of what he does with language? I may walk miles every day without knowing the mechanisms of walking—which muscles enter into the action, which bones are involved, and so on. Even if the user knew something about the use he makes of his language, would he tell us the truth, or would he declare what he thinks suitable for his social status? To what extent is it legitimate to solicit intuitive judgments about language? Does this solicitation not distort or modify the psychological phenomena that we want to discover?

(ii) What generalizations can we make on the basis of the intuitive reactions of one or several informants?

We shall discuss this in greater detail later (cf. II.7 and IV). Briefly, I would say that on the one hand one cannot give complete credence to users' intuitive reactions. But if we find that under similar conditions (e.g., in other users) similar reactions are produced, we must admit that users' intuition has some regularity; it is somehow structured.

If we put the same question—for instance, on the pronunciation of *lac* 'lake' and *laque* 'lacquer' (Martinet, 1945, p. 39)—to French speakers, and if almost all the Southerners declare they pronounce them differently while the non-Southerners say the contrary, then we shall conclude that the users' intuition is structured. If, moreover, the repetition of this survey brings up analogous results (Reichstein, 1960, Deyhime, 1967, et al.), the existence of structure is well established.

Hjelmslev's position is very interesting in this respect: he retained neither the mental nor the social aspects of linguistic phenomena (Hjelmslev, 1943, §14 and passim). I fear that such an attitude would endanger our quest for objective knowledge—that is, it spells the danger of idealistic formalism.

It should be pointed out that this criticism is valid only for the descriptive studies Hjelmslev carried out and not for the theoretical program he proposed (Hjelmslev, 1953, §5).

II.7 Relativity of Structure: Hierarchy and Fuzziness

I have tried to show that within given limits the use of either a corpus or a survey allows regularities to be established in certain domains but leads to less structured or even completely unstructured results in others.

What should one do under such circumstances? Should one reject the methods of corpus and/or survey and search for new techniques? Such a rejection would leave the observer's intuition as the sole basic source of data. In my view, recourse to the describer's judgment is not a better solution. My suggestion is to admit that linguistic structure is not formal but random, not homogeneous but hierarchized, containing different layers. Relevance must then be deemed to have different degrees and not just two values, plus or minus. Given a feature, the problem will not be to decide whether it is relevant or not but to what degree it is relevant. From this point of view, descriptive practice closely resembles physical measurement (such as length, weight, etc.), and a descriptive technique should be considered to be a means of measurement. Every time we measure something, we admit to a certain inaccuracy. The degree of precision of our measurement is a function of what our aim is. We don't use the same instrument for weighing a diamond and a truckload of potatoes. The instrument appropriate in one case is not so in the other. It is the same for descriptive techniques: each of them has its utility and its field of application. There are some descriptive techniques appropriate for fine measurement and others for gross measurements, just as we can look at things with the naked eye or through an electron microscope.

The scope of experimentation is not restricted to what we discussed above. Other experimental perspectives are open, and some methods are currently practiced especially in some areas of interdisciplinary research. I shall mention some of them later.

The essential problem is to know whether it is justified to stick to the classical conception of relevance or better to redefine our notion of relevance and envisage degrees of relevance.

If we consider the history of the sciences that have reached maturity, this evolution of linguistics seems normal. In fact, during the nineteenth century, the natural sciences underwent an evolution in which global systems led to restricted models (cf. Granger, 1967, pp. 199–200). In my opinion, this evolution is also positive in linguistics: we will not jeopardize what has been gained throughout the last decades, but we will probably acquire a more precise knowledge of language phenomena, and this precision might modify to some extent certain aspects of our views on language structure.

II.8 Implications of Relativity

The conception of a language as a relative system is considerably different from that of classical structuralism. A language cannot be deemed to have a homogeneous structure; different layers of structure can and must coexist in it. What are the implications of this multilayer (hierarchized) conception?

Let us return to the communicative function of language. If a language has a homogeneous structure (i.e., is invariable in its social and mental dimensions), then the communicative function would be absolute too. Thus linguistic units and constructions should enable every member of a speech community to convey his experience to any other. Empirical evidence suggests, however, that this is not the case. For example, it is easier for a Parisian French speaker to understand another Parisian than for a French speaker from the north of France to understand someone from the south (say, Lille and Marseilles). Numerous reliable studies show that intercomprehension may range from zero to the highest possible degree.

The relative structure of linguistic systems enables us to explain this. When the protagonists share only the higher layers of linguistic phenomena, the communicative possibilities are restricted. These possibilities increase insofar as the speaker and the hearer have in common the lower layers. In other words, rudimentary communication makes use only of the resources of the most central layers, while for more nuanced, more elaborate communications, recourse to the more marginal (lower) layers—hence more subtle phenomena—is necessary. That is the reason the communicative act is a very delicate adjustment in certain cases (for instance, in poetry).

Relativity of structure has other implications. Consider the diachronic aspect of language: an outstanding feature of linguistic evolution is that it is continuous in a language throughout its history, and yet its synchronic functioning is not perturbed to any great extent. This is due to the fact that linguistic changes, considered over a short period, do not affect the higher layers of a system, and only the lower ones are more or less touched or reorganized. If we examine the appropriateness of data collection procedures, we will find that the question "what technique is appropriate?" is wrongly put. Nothing allows us to assume that a single procedure can be applied to the whole range of data. A technique appropriate for the higher layers could be inefficient for the lower ones. Conversely, the lower layers need refined techniques which could be unduly complicated for the higher layers. Moreover, for some layers, more than one procedure could be appropriate and yield the same results. The use of the speaker's introspection (including the describer's intuition) is therefore justified as long as the higher layers are involved. A description of the lower layers requires, on the contrary, more elaborate tools. For instance, the possibility of a syntactic structure like *This table is red* and its semantic implications in "normal" situations can be judged by almost any English speaker. This is not the case for the possibility of constructions such as:

I want it washed
It needs washing
I want it washing
It needs washed.

Table 1 Schema of a multilayer conception of a linguistic structure. (Each layer can be attributed properties according to the following point of view.)

	Hierarchy	Synchronic functionning	Social extension	Diachronic change	Adequacy of descriptive technique
Layer (a)	high (central)	rudimentary communication	widespread in speech community	subject to evolution only over a long period	elementary and/or multiple techniques
Layer (b)					
Layer (c)					
. . .					
Layer (n)	low (marginal)	nuanced communication	restricted on socio-geographic scale	subject to evolution over shorter periods too	elaborate and/or specific techniques

Whether a speaker accepts one or another of these or not depends on the region he comes from—the south of England, the Midlands, the north of Scotland (cf. Hughes and Trudgill, 1979). The same applies for the semantic interpretation of *can I lend a bike?* Another example: is there a way of saying in English "he must not do it" in the past or future? What is the meaning of constructions like the following?

> *He hasn't to do it*
> *He's not got to do it*
> *He hasn't got to do it*

Do they mean 'he wasn't allowed to do it', 'he mustn't do it', or something else?

In such cases, data collection involves accessing the social dimensions in order to bring to light the regularities and limits of these linguistic phenomena. The mere questioning of a native speaker would not be conclusive. Therefore more elaborate techniques are indispensable. This is summed up by the schema given in table 1. We will see later that the same applies to the mental dimension and complicates the understanding of linguistic phenomena and their structure.

III On Some Syntactico-Semantic Problems

III.0 Synopsis

In this chapter my aim is to show the complexity of syntax and semantics. I shall begin with an illustration of some interrelations between syntax and semantics. In the next step, I will expose some problems from the syntactic and semantic domains for which any formal solution seems to be *ad hoc*. I shall support the position that phonological and semantic analyses are not totally symmetrical and suggest considering the levels of linguistic phenomena to be hierarchized in the following order: phonology, morphology, syntax, and semantics, progressing from the most to the least rigorous structure. It is worth noting that this hierarchy is distinct from the hierarchy inherent in each level.

In previous chapters I have tried to outline the state of the art in linguistics, to point out what we know about language structure, and to draw attention to some remaining questions. In this chapter I will consider in more detail the problems that arise when we study the phenomena of syntax and semantics.

To highlight the lacunae in linguistics, I have to examine prior works fairly and squarely, remembering that most of the criticisms I am going to make could also be directed at my own research.

III.1 Syntax, Semantics, and their Relations

Let us begin with some terminological conventions. I shall use the term syntax to designate all phenomena connected with the identity and combination of linguistic signs, whatever their size: moneme (morpheme), word, or syntagm (phrase). I suggest restricting the domain of syntax to the study of signs as wholes. What we obtain by splitting the sign into signifiant and signifié will thus be outside the scope of syntax. The study of signifiant as such should be subsumed under morphology and that of the signifié under semantics. I shall not consider phenomena beyond the limits of the sentence. This division could be represented as follows:

Field	Its object
Syntax	Linguistic sign
Morphology	Signifiant
Semantics	Signifié

Let us consider *John started yesterday*. From the syntactic point of view we shall examine such problems as:

—How many significant units (monemes) are contained in this utterance (*John, start, -ed* and *yesterday*)?
—According to what rules can these units be combined (for example, *-ed* cannot be combined either with *John* or with *yesterday*, etc.)?

On the morphological level, we have to answer questions like:

—What realizations has the signifiant of the moneme "past" (for example: /-d/ in *tried*, /-id/ in *wanted*, /-t/ in *walked*, and so on)?
—Is the sequence *start* the only realization of the signifiant of the moneme *start*, or has it other realizations too?
—and so forth

As for the semantic level, one should state the meaning of *start* and the way it varies according to extralinguistic situations or linguistic contexts such as:

John started the book
John started the dinner
John started to walk
this started me coughing.

What creates problems is the mutual conditioning of the three fields separated by the above definitions. Consider the constitution of a verbal syntagm, for example, *start* in *we start to work*.

At least two descriptions are possible here:

(i) one could analyze this syntagm into the following monemes:

— lexeme (lexical moneme) *start*

— present tense

(ii) one could also consider that *start* is the only moneme of this verbal syntagm.

The first solution is almost that of traditional grammar and has been adopted by transformational generative grammar. The second corresponds to the solution generally accepted by structural linguistics.

In my view, no convincing argument exists for the choice of one solution rather than the other. For the moment, my concern is to show what the choice of either syntactic solution entails for the levels of semantics and morphology, whatever the reasons on which the choice is based.

If we adopt the first solution, we will be led to set up the following statements in terms of morphology: the signifiant of the moneme 'present tense' is zero (= zero morph) in *we start*; the same moneme is represented by the /-s/-*s* in *he starts,* by /-z/-*s* in *he begins.*

I won't linger on the implications of the second solution for morphology. Let it suffice that the problem would be to determine to which signifiant the sequence -*s* belongs and under which contextual conditions it appears.

On a semantic level, the same syntactic descriptive solution (i.e., solution (ii) will have the following implications:

(a) We must have among our language universals a statement such as the following:

If to the expression of an event no tense expression is associated, then the event is likely (or most likely) to be related to the present moment.

(b) We must also determine under which conditions the lack of expression for 'tense' can refer to a moment, on the axis of time, other than the present—for example, *I was out walking the other day, when there I am suddenly surrounded by hundreds of cows.* Assumption (a) does not

sound implausible and can be paralleled with man's nonlinguistic behavior. As Goffman (cf. Goffman, 1959) observed, if you ask somebody
to shut the door or open the window, you won't consider that he has
satisfied your request if two months later he closes the door or opens
the window. Yet utterances like *shut the door* or *open the window* do
not carry any mention of time. What makes the issue complex is the fact
that this principle—let us call it the principle of unmarked present—is
not absolute. In certain languages, such as Arabic or Persian, the present
is marked and the past unmarked, as can be seen from the following
examples:

> Farsi: /neveʃt/ 'he (or she) wrote'
> /minevisad/ 'he (or she) writes'
> Arabic: /kataba/ 'he wrote'
> /jaktubu/ 'he writes',

where an approximate way of deciding on the marked form could be
by a phoneme count.

All I want to conclude from the above is that: (1) any syntactic analysis has repercussions on the morphological and semantic levels and
vice versa (I shall refer to this interrelation later; cf. V.1,3,5; VI.10–13;
VII.3(iii)); and (2) strictly speaking, the boundaries of syntax (with morphology on the one hand and semantics on the other) cannot be set
unless they are based on language universals (conceived of as general
tendencies, like (a) or (b), and not a condition *sine qua non*).

III.2 Should We Drop the Syntactic Component?

The justification of a syntactic component is not obvious to all linguists.
In some theoretical currents, doubts have been clearly expressed about
the theoretical foundation of syntax; examples could be cited from the
classical era of structuralism (Hjelmslev) to the post-transformational
one (Fillmore), with Prieto between the two. Hjelmslev's and Prieto's
theses can be summarized as follows.

A linguistic sign is the combination of a signifiant and a signifié. The
signifiant is not the sound, nor the signifié the meaning. Among sound
features, only those which contribute to establishing meaning are relevant, that is, constitutive of the signifiant. Conversely, from the whole
range of meaning features, we retain as parts of the signifié only those

whose presence or absence may change the signifiant. For instance, the sound feature "voiced" is relevant in /b/ (*bill, bad,* etc.). If it is replaced by another sound feature, say "voiceless," we obtain /p/ (*pill, pad,* etc.), whose meanings are quite different. On the meaning plane, the French verbal syntagm *a fait* has among its meaning features the indicative (mood). And this feature is relevant, because its replacement by subjunctive (mood) would entail a change in the phonic form (*ait fait* vs. *a fait*). Compare:

Je ne dirai pas qu'il l'a fait exprès
'I won't say he did it on purpose' and
Je ne dirai pas qu'il l'ait fait exprès
'I won't say he did it on purpose'.[5]

Even if the English verbal syntagm *did* had exactly the same meaning as French *a fait,* the meaning feature 'indicative (mood)' could not be considered as relevant, hence not as part of the signifié.

The test which allows us to determine the relevance of a feature is called commutation. According to a certain definition, relevance and commutation are based on the relation that links the plane of signifiant to the plane of signifié. Therefore it is not possible to apply these concepts to the linguistic sign as a whole (cf. Prieto, 1964, §1; also Hjelmslev, 1953, 1966).

From a theoretical point of view, we can note that the whole of linguistic analysis is based—according to both—on the commutation test, and for the definition of commutation they stick too closely to Prague school phonological practice. But relevance is susceptible to a more general definition, such as the one proposed by Jan Mulder, according to which a feature is functional or relevant if it plays a separate role in the purpose of the whole of which it is a part (Mulder, 1977). In this case the concept of relevance, and hence the commutation test, is not only valid in its Praguean type of application but also allows us to determine the relevance of items and relations in any complex linguistic phenomena. The complex phenomenon that we examine can be a signifiant: in this case the signifié will be used as the criterion for identification. Conversely, we will use the signifiant to identify the relevant features when the complex considered is a semantic phenomenon. The complex under study can be a sequence of signs as well. Here, its constitutive parts can be determined according to their contribution to the purport of the whole. And this will be syntax as we defined it above (cf. III.1 above).

As for American linguistics, I would like to remark at the outset that the distinction between deep structure and surface structure is an attempt to give more place to semantic aspects in the description of syntactic structure. The whole discussion about deep structure, its shape, and its place in linguistic analysis brings to light—explicitly or not—the existence of a gradual transition with multiple gradients between syntax and semantics. If more than one decade of debate has not led to a clarification of this problem, then this must be a hint that a sharp distinction between syntax and semantics cannot be made.

Besides, within certain theoretical currents, the expectation was to find some formal solution to syntactic problems. Where an adequate analysis seemed to lead to random (statistical) solutions, one of two attitudes was adopted: either the existence of a deep structure or syntactic component was put into doubt, or the formal character of linguistic structure was questioned.

I think that the elimination of the syntactic component (or some part of it) does not resolve any problems. It is just a way of putting off to a later phase the explanation of some embarrassing phenomena. This is the case, for instance, when one refuses to consider certain phenomena and puts them in a residual class for which no solution is put forward. Examples of this can be found in Fillmore's case theory or in the literature on generative semantics. The other attitude toward the border area of syntax and semantics seems preferable and allows for a more precise insight into the structure and the use of language.

So much for theoretical arguments. On an empirical level, it should be remarked that without recourse to the level of the sign it would not be possible to explain analogic changes, popular etymology, homonymic or synonymic attraction, analogic processes (in ontogenesis), or some synchronic problems of morphology. I shall discuss these later.

Let us give an example of the first type of phenomenon cited above: analogic change. If a moneme has more than one realization on the level of the signifiant, and if it belongs to a class of which the majority of members have only one realization, then there is a tendency to generalize the use of a predominant realization by substituting it for the others. This was the case for the French verb *trouver* 'find', which formerly had as the realization of its stem both *treuve* (*je treuve* 'I find') and *trouve* (in *nous trouvons* 'we find')[6]; the stem is now realized in the single form *trouve,* in agreement with the great majority of verbs of its morphological class: *chanter* 'sing', *parler* 'talk', and so on.

A similar phenomenon occurred in Middle English, which originally had two principal ways of forming the noun plural. When the weak class (*-n* plural: *eyen*) lost its generality, most of its members were assimilated into the other (*-s* plural: *eyes*) class. These tendencies can only be explained by admitting that the language user has an intuitive knowledge of monemes and of their syntactic classification.

To these arguments, I shall add also and above all a considerable difference in the degree of relevance of semantic phenomena compared to phonological phenomena. One can actually observe that phonological and syntactic phenomena are more highly structured—that is, they are more easily available from a mental point of view and more widespread in society than semantic ones.

It can easily be shown that a speaker generally has an intuitive knowledge of linguistic signs (e.g., *shot, satellite, orange*) and their phonic shape. But his knowledge of their semantic makeup is more hesitant and remote. If the object of linguistics is to study how speakers-hearers use their language and what its status is in their minds, then syntax (i.e., the sign level) is an integral part of this object. I will return to this later (cf. V.1).

III.3 Outstanding Syntactic Problems: Other Examples

The first syntactic problem we considered concerned determining the number of monemes contained in a sequence. Below, we shall examine two others, both concerning the setting up of moneme classes.

(a) How to select our syntactic criteria

The setting up of moneme classes is based on syntactic features or properties. Thus, verbs are subclassified in transitive and intransitive categories according to whether they take a (direct) object or not. Taking an object is one syntactic property. But verbs have numerous other properties. Should we take them all into account for the categorization of verbs? And if not, on what principle could and should the selection of classifying criteria be based?

Consider the French verbs *marcher* 'walk', *faire* 'make', *appeler* 'call', *rendre* 'render', and *voir* 'see', and the following syntactic properties:

(a) object, *(b)* object complement, and *(c)* class of object complement (noun and/or adjective). The application of the criteria to the verbs shows three hierarchical levels: *(a)*, *(b)*, and *(c)*. At each level the number of classes increases and, conversely, the number of members of each class decreases. The classes of level *(c)* all have few members (in some cases only one). See table 2.

Note that:

(i) we considered only a few syntactic properties in this classification. Among the other syntactic properties, let us cite one: the subcategory of nominal object complement, proper noun or common noun, for example:

> *Il appelle son fils Paul*
> **Il fait son fils Paul.*

(ii) Moreover, on level *(c)* we reach the lower layers of structure. Here, the acceptability of syntactic constructions is open to hesitation and indeterminacy.

(iii) Last but not least, on level (c), the criterion of classification is the distinction noun/adjective, which is not a clear-cut difference (cf. Mahmoudian et al., 1976, §22).

This example shows clearly that any consistent application of classificatory criteria leads to the setting up of moneme classes with ap-

Table 2 Classification of French verbs.

Levels	a		b	
Syntactic properties	Verbs taking object (transitive)	Verbs *not* taking object (intransitive)	Verbs taking object complement	Verbs *not* taking object complement
Class	Va1	Va2	Vb1	Vb2
Members	regarder rendre appeler faire voir	marcher	rendre appeler faire voir *	regarder

proximately one member; but this is confusing monemes and classes of monemes. A totally adequate classification must therefore be based on a selection of syntactic properties; in this case the question will be, on what grounds can we retain, as classifying criteria, certain syntactic properties and leave out some others?

The conclusion that we can draw from the above examples is that any formal, clear-cut solution will be *post hoc*. Theoretically underpinned solutions seem inevitably to be relative ones—that is, both syntactic classes and class membership are a matter of degree.

It is worth noting that the examples given are not isolated cases. A great number of other facts from different languages could be cited showing similar problems concerning classification. Let it suffice to mention the continuum sketched by Ross between moneme classes in English (cf. Ross, 1972). See also the bipolarity of the distinction between noun and adjective in French (Mahmoudian et al., 1976, pp. 366–369).

(b) One or two classes?

Let us take as an example the monemes, in French, called possessive, which are traditionally divided into two classes: the possessive adjectives *mon* 'my' (m.), *ma* 'my' (f.), *mes* 'my' (pl.), *ton* 'your' (m.), *ta* 'your' (f.), *tes* 'your' (pl.), and so on, and the possessive pronouns *mien* 'mine',

c

verbs taking object complement			Examples:	
noun class	adjective class	both noun and adjective class	* *Il rend son fils malade*	'He makes his son sick'
			Il appelle son fils Paul	'He calls his son Paul'
Vc1	Vc2	Vc3	*Il fait son fils général*	'He makes his son a general'
			Il voit son fils général	'He sees his son as a general'
faire appeler	rendre	voir	** *Il voit son fils heureux*	'He sees his son is happy'
			Il voit son fils roi de France	'He sees his son as the king of France'

**

tien 'yours', and so on. The former correspond to modifiers and the latter to dependents (as defined by Martinet, 1960, 1962). This distinction is based on the idea that the two paradigms are different from the point of view of their signifiants and their combinatory properties, and that these differences are sufficient to make two distinct classes. The resemblance of the signifiants is considered irrelevant, whether it is partial, as in *ton* 'your'/*tien* 'yours' or *notre* 'our'/*nôtre* 'ours', or complete, as in *leur* (*livre*) 'their' (book)/(*le*) *leur* 'theirs'—which could be classed as a case of syncretism (and hence belongs to morphology).

A different description of the same facts is possible: all the personal monemes *mon, ma, mes, mien(s)* 'mine' (m.,sg./pl.), *mienne(s)* 'mine' (f.,sg./pl.), and so on could be put in a single class. The differences between the signifiants, which could be described in terms of contextual conditioning, would then be considered to be irrelevant and classed as a case of morphological variation. Every member of this class can be subordinated to nouns as well as to verbs. For example, the possessive second person singular moneme subordinated to a noun has the form *ton* (*Minou joue avec ton livre* 'Kittycat is playing with your book') but the form *tien* when attached to a verb (*Minou joue avec le tien* 'Kittycat is playing with yours').

This solution, although not very common, is not in contradiction with any principles. Do we have any theoretical reason to exclude the possibility of a class of monemes which can be subordinated to both nouns and verbs? Such cases are known in French, for example, the noun class. In the sentences

> *il parlait d'un grand voyage*
> 'he spoke of a big trip' and
> *il avait le projet d'un grand voyage*
> 'he had plans for a big trip'

voyage is subordinate to (i.e., a complement of) a verb in the first, a noun in the second.

A third solution would be to group personal pronouns, possessive adjectives, and pronouns in one class. In this case, *je* 'I', *me* 'me, myself', *moi* 'me, myself', *mon, ma, mes, mien(s)*, and *mienne(s)* 'my' would be morphological variants of the first person singular moneme.

The fourth solution would consist in putting together *je, me, moi, mien(s)*, and *mienne(s)*, thus forming a class of dependent monemes distinct from the class of modifiers *mon, ma, mes,* and so forth. All these solutions are consistent with the basic principles, and I do not see any reason—besides personal taste—for one to be preferred to the others.

III.4 Semantic Analysis

The aim of semantic analysis is to determine what features (semes) make up a signifié and to what extent and under what conditions its semes vary. In a general way, we could say that all semantic analyses have the same goal but differ from each other with regard to the procedure they adopt and to the limits they set: should we go from complex to simple (e.g., from sentence to moneme) or from simple to complex (from moneme to sentence); should we give priority to the paradigmatic axis (e.g., semantic field theory) or to the syntagmatic axis (sentence analysis); should we restrict semantic analysis to the grammatical monemes, to the lexical monemes, or extend it to both; and so forth.

Generally speaking, no theoretical principle—*stricto sensu*—has been proposed to solve both problems of procedures and limits. Let us take the first one: what permits us to choose one and only one procedure for the investigation of meaning? Analytic procedures can and must be considered as complementary; one given procedure could be more adequate than another depending on the kind of significant units to be examined. For instance, the meaning of a grammatical unit—say *-ed* in *walked*—is easier to grasp in its linguistic context than in isolation, hence the appropriateness of a procedure going from sentence to moneme. Conversely, lexical monemes like *table, tree,* or *food* can be identified and described in isolation as well; here a procedure from simple to complex is also applicable.

Semantic analysis has a certain similarity to phonological analysis. Consider the French moneme *fille* 'girl, daughter'; its semantic description would show up the following relevant features: 'human', 'female', and 'nonadult'. The operation and its results remind us closely of what is done for phonemes, let us say, /t/: 'apicodental', 'oral (or nonnasal)', 'unvoiced', and 'occlusive'. This is the method *grosso modo* in the analyses proposed by Hjelmslev as early as the 1940s. And the descriptive model proposed by Katz and Fodor in the 1960s is based on more or less the same principles.

So far, so good. Now consider the realizations of the signifié of *fille* in the following contexts:

Minou est fille de Mistigri
'Minou is Mistigri's daughter'
Jacques est une fille
literally, 'Jack is a girl' ('Jack is womanish')
Marie est une vieille fille
'Mary is an old maid'.

These sentences show at least one shortcoming of such an analysis: in each one, a semantic feature is missing: 'human' in the first sentence, 'female' in the second one and 'nonadult' in the last one.

From the above counterexamples, I want to conclude that "strictly speaking the semantic features we attributed to the moneme *fille* are not relevant in the same way as the phonological features of the phoneme /t/."[7]

This conclusion is not based on the use of particularly favorable examples; the problem seems to be more general, and numerous other examples could be mentioned.

Pottier's study (Pottier, 1963, 1965) of the semantic field of 'seat' provides an illustration of the scope and limitations of such analyses. Basically, he defines the contents of the moneme French *fauteuil* 'armchair' as follows: 1. 'seat', 2. 'with a solid frame', 3. 'with a back', and 4. 'with arms'. This analysis certainly has some advantages, but it encounters limitations. The feature 'solid' is surely necessary to distinguish some lexical items from others, for example, *tabouret* 'stool' and *pouf* 'pouf'. But is it a necessary attribute of every *fauteuil*? Should we separate armchairs made of synthetic foam, or those which are inflatable?

Analogous problems have been raised in American linguistics: can we analyze the contents of *bachelor* as 'unmarried man'? Is it possible to consider the meaning of *kill* as equivalent to 'cause to become not-alive'? The discussions of Katz and Fodor's semantic analysis (1963) and also of Fillmore's (1968) pointed out obvious limitations, even if the limitations were not all of equal value.

III.5 Phonological and Semantic Analyses

For the comparison of phonological and semantic analyses, let us set aside mental and social variations. In my view, one of the most important differences between the two types of relevant features lies in the fact that while phonological features are necessary and sufficient, this is not the case for semantic features. In other words, while we can establish an equivalence between a bundle of relevant features and a phonological unit, this cannot be done for semantic entities. That is, any occurrence of the phoneme /t/ is an occurrence of the bundle of its relevant features, and conversely, any occurrence of this bundle of relevant features is an occurrence of the phoneme /t/. On the contrary, content analyses do not lead to such equivalences: in an occurrence of French *fille* (or *fauteuil,* or English *kill* or *bachelor*) some of its relevant features may be lacking; and conversely, the whole bundle of semantic features of French *fille* may be represented by another moneme or sequence of monemes in the utterance.

I can imagine two objections to my argument.

(i) One could object that some of the examples are cases of metaphorical use, and hence beyond the framework of denotational semantics.

But I would like to have clear criteria for distinguishing metaphorical as opposed to nonmetaphorical uses. This seems to be a fair requirement; otherwise the concept of metaphor may become a convenient dumping place for describers confronted with embarrassing counterexamples. Besides, an attempt to define metaphor precisely would shed new light on the diachronic process which links the literal meaning to the metaphorical one and vice versa.

(ii) Another possible objection could be based on the comparison of phonological neutralization with cases of fading out of some semantic features.

One answer would be this: for phonological neutralization, the conditioning environment can be formulated precisely. Is this also possible in the case of semantic features? Let us examine this problem in some detail. The English phonemes /p/ and /b/ have the same features except for 'voice': /b/ is voiced but /p/ is voiceless. In some dialects of English the opposition voiced/voiceless disappears if the preceding phoneme is voiceless: for example, in *it's blended* the letter *b* has the same phonic realization as the *p* in *it's splendid*. One can remark that in the clusters /s/ + /p/ or /s/ + /b/ the first phoneme (/s/ in this case) is the source of the contextual conditioning and the second (/b/ or /p/) the target, and not vice versa. Precise formulations like this cannot be proposed when semantic features are under consideration. For instance in French *Marie est une vieille fille* 'Mary is an old maid', *vieille* and *fille* have opposite features: respectively, 'adult' and 'nonadult'. In this context the moneme *fille* loses its meaning feature 'nonadult'. This is parallel to phonological neutralization and can be formulated as follows: if, in a sentence, the complement has a semantic feature opposed to one of the features of the subject, then this feature is lost.

Were this rule (to a certain extent) general, the same should happen in the other sentences. But this is not the case for *Jacques est une fille* 'Jack is a girl' ('Jack is womanish'). Here, the feature 'female' does not disappear but is realized in a nuanced manner: 'effeminate, womanish'.

On the basis of the above asymmetry, different conclusions have been drawn. The most extreme solution was that of Z.S. Harris, which aimed at the exclusion of semantics from the field of linguistics. As we said above, this solution is not based on any solid argument, be it theoretical or empirical.

As for me, I consider the difference between semantic and phonological structures as a difference of degree and not of nature. It is a well-known fact that whereas phonology operates with a limited number of units, semantics has to handle a great—perhaps unlimited—number of units. This is another aspect of the asymmetry between phonology and semantics. Both contain structural variations (fuzziness, etc.), but to a lower degree in phonology and a higher degree in semantics. In the next chapter, I shall suggest an operational procedure for measuring variation so that the hypothesis might be open to refutation.

III.6 Semantics, Syntax, and Cognition

It is a commonplace to say that the user's syntactic and cognitive (or pragmatic) knowledge helps him to grasp the meaning of utterances. Every French speaker would understand *manguier,* even if he has never seen a mango tree. I was witness to the facility with which normal persons (i.e., nonlinguists!) understood *tomatier* 'tomato tree' and *concomb(r)ier* 'cucumber tree', invented by a four-year-old child. With this example I want to illustrate the role that syntactic cues play in the process of intercomprehension.

Another example: in a sentence like *son oncle était médecin de campagne* 'His uncle was a country doctor', the syntactic construction gives the information that 'his uncle' is the one previously known (topic) and that 'country doctor' is new information (focus) carried by the sentence. In other words, syntactic cues—whether *(a)* the position of nominal syntagms with respect to the verb, *(b)* the presence of a modifier (*son*) in the first nominal syntagm and its absence in the other, or both *(a)* and *(b)*—provide us with some knowledge about a state of affairs.

This is what we would expect if language were supposed to fulfill the function of communication and if syntax were supposed to be instrumental in the construction of meaning. But this is not always the case. In certain contexts, we have to resort to our knowledge about a state of affairs in order to decide what meaning is probable and find out the syntactic function of constituents in a sequence. Consider the French syntactic pattern *quels Américains lisent encore aujourd'hui Corneille et Racine?* 'which Americans still read Corneille and Racine today?' or 'which Americans are still read by Corneille and Racine today?' In this case, the most important cues for deciphering the meaning of the sentence would come from our knowledge of the world. If we know that Corneille and Racine are not alive, then we are brought to consider *quels Américains* as subject. Were "Michel Butor et Claude Simon" substituted for "Corneille et Racine," the situation would be quite different. The knowledge that Butor and Simon are our contemporaries makes it possible that they are either the readers of Americans or are read by them.

Evidence from language acquisition and diachronic studies could be evoked, tending to show that different factors enter into action for the constitution of meaning.

On an empirical level, it would be instructive to examine what means of access a language user has to the meaning attributed by a speech community to words. In my view, these means are of two types.

(i) Linguistic means: paraphrase seems to be the most appropriate way to convey and grasp the meaning of *people's capitalism, Greek democracy, gentlemen's agreement,* and so on. Could these semantic entities possibly be subject to demonstration or ostentation?

(ii) Nonlinguistic ones: in this case, we use elements of the external world to gain access to the meanings of linguistic items.

This is the route children have to follow in order to become familiar with linguistic meaning. As an example familiar to linguists, one could cite Pike's monolingual approach, which is almost an exclusive recourse to nonlinguistic data for elicitation of linguistic meaning. If we were suddenly to find ourselves in the same situation as Gulliver, in a strange land where everything was unknown, this is the method we would also have to adopt.

If both linguistic and nonlinguistic criteria are relevant in the field of semantics, then the semantic component will have to be conceived of as a highly complex structure; that is, in order to find the meaning of a word, linguists need to set up two or three types of techniques: (i) recourse to linguistic cues (or techniques); (ii) recourse to both linguistic and nonlinguistic cues; and (iii) recourse to exclusively nonlinguistic cues.

It doesn't seem possible to establish a fixed hierarchy among these criteria. The choice of criteria and the value attributed to them depend on several factors. Let us take the example of a few words denoting 'trees': *oak, beech, teak*. How should the denotational contents of these words be defined? One answer could be that the denotation of the words is given if we list specifications for these trees such as the climate in which they grow and the size, shape and color of their parts (trunk, branches, leaves, fruit, flowers, etc.). This is the way the French word *figuier* is defined in *Le Petit Robert*.[8] During a series of courses on semantics, I presented this definition to some fifty students, all native French speakers, and only three identified it as the definition of a fig tree.

This amounts to saying that a semantic definition of these terms should be an exposition of the way in which language users know them; a precise definition of these trees with reference to the criteria of a nonlinguistic science—for example, botany—would be of almost no linguistic relevance. Depending on the user's way of knowing these trees, we will have to vary our selection of criteria. Hence there is a certain inconsistency in definitional procedures.

If one compares the definitions of *oak* and *beech* with that of *teak* in the *Concise Oxford Dictionary* one finds such an inconsistency: for the latter, the definition mentions only properties of the timber, while for the other two entries, a number of other specifications are also given.[9] This inconsistency is to be appreciated positively because it reflects the semantic intuition of the language user.

III.7 Laxity of Structure of the Signifié
The example of French *figuier* could be used for another purpose. Probably every member of the French-speaking community knows the fruit *figue*. It is likely that a considerable number of northern French have no idea of fig trees. The definition in Larousse—although quasi-tautologic—is probably the only valid definition with regard to France

as a whole! But if we want our definition to be suitable in a narrower manner, then we shall have to divide the French-speaking community and give for each subgroup an adapted definition.

The same goes for *bachelor;* the four definitions of this word are not valid for all divisions of the English-speaking community. Does the man on the street know that *bachelor* can refer to 'a young male fur seal when without a mate during the breeding time'? If not, Katz and Fodor's definition of bachelor is not adapted to everyone's semantic structure, that is, to everyone's internalized language habits (cf. Katz and Fodor, 1963).[10]

If semantic features are related to our experience of the world, and if this experience is variable, I wonder how we could ever establish a constant and finite number of relevant semantic features.

There is one asymmetry between phonology and semantics which we pointed out earlier in this chapter (cf. 11.4–6). In phonology, variations affect the peripheral areas of the system, while in semantics they occupy a much larger place.

To recapitulate, the structure of semantics is in my view considerably more complex than that of phonology or syntax. However, this complexity should not discourage our interest in semantics but rather encourage us to set up adequate descriptive techniques. The simplicity of a theory or description is not in itself a virtue. Were it so, physicists should abandon the theory of quantum mechanics and go back to the conception of the world made up of the four elements: earth, water, wind, and fire.

Such a higher degree of complexity might be defined precisely and thus be open to measurement and experimentation. My hypothesis is that, once compared, the phonological and semantic components must show considerable differences on the mental and social planes or dimensions. From this point of view, morphology and syntax seem to occupy intermediate positions, as seen in figure 1.

One of the consequences of the looseness (laxity) of semantic structure is that it is more subject to fluctuations, and therefore introspection might give more unreliable results than for the other levels of linguistic structure. This might explain the disappointment of the first structuralists, who were in search of a system of semantics as rigorous as the one they were used to from their phonological experience, a disappointment that drove them to banish—*de facto,* if not always *de jure*—semantics from the realm of linguistics.

Figure 1 Continuum of complexity.

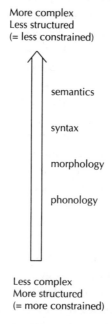

More complex
Less structured
(= less constrained)

semantics

syntax

morphology

phonology

Less complex
More structured
(= more constrained)

This diagram situates the various levels of a linguistic system on a continuum of increasing/decreasing complexity, structuration, and constraint.

The same factors should permit us to explain why in phonology we can obtain valuable results on the basis of data obtained from the describer's introspection.

It should be noted that questioning linguistic theories and/or descriptions does not mean that they are totally invalid. Constructive criticism aims necessarily at doing better, without ignoring the value of what is acquired. For example, the relativistic conception of physics began with a sound criticism of Newton's mechanics. This didn't mean that Newtonian theory was thenceforth completely devoid of value.

IV Toward an Experimentally Based Model for Linguistics

IV.0 Synopsis

My intention will be to illustrate by example the scope and limits of a model set up for experimentation. According to this model, the mental and social dimensions of language phenomena are correlated and together make up an *extrinsic* hierarchy. In addition, the dimensions of frequency in usage and integration in the system are related to each other and constitute the *intrinsic* hierarchy. The two hierarchies are correlated and allow for the establishment of a unique hierarchy whose poles are a *central* zone (hard core) and a peripheral or *marginal* zone (loose ends).

Empirical studies would seem to confirm the theses regarding the extrinsic hierarchy.

IV.1 Atomism and Globalism

The claim of autonomy for linguistics has not prevented the development of empirical research by recourse to psychic and/or social dimensions of language phenomena. Such work has mostly been subsumed under psycholinguistics or sociolinguistics. I won't discuss the legitimacy of such terms. Let it suffice to say that it is of course useful to separate psycholinguistic and sociolinguistic research from "pure" linguistics. But this means neither that these domains are cut off by a no-man's-land, nor that pure linguistics cannot have recourse to psychic or social data and techniques in its investigation. It is worth pointing out that if the term experimental linguistics is recent (cf. G. Prideaux, 1979, 1980), empirical works on language are not.

Linguistic surveys are empirical works, and depending on their degree of elaboration, they are more or less close to experimental research. They might be considered as naive forms or germs of experimentation in linguistics.

When we consider experimental research in linguistics, two diametrically opposed positions seem to emerge: atomism and globalism. In the first tendency microsystems are set up, whereas the second one aims at establishing overall patterns. Neither of these goals is objectionable in itself, but what I regret is the lack of a relation between the two. No attempt has been made—to my knowledge—to unite the two currents and relate them to pure linguistics by means of organic links. This synthesis is what I am aiming at. Atomism could be compared with the observation of objects through lenses or microscopes. The image we obtain in globalism reminds me of the photos of our globe taken by satellite. Both atomism and globalism show an aspect of reality. In my view, one or several intermediate scales needed to relate the two poles are missing.

As examples of these, consider phonological structure. We can give an overall view of the phonemes of a language, showing the units of which the system is composed and the relations that link them to each other. But by doing so we restrict ourselves to a given usage or to the most general features of the dominant usages. At the same time, we forgo circumscribing certain details such as those concerning the following problems.

—To what extent are such features widespread in the speech community?

—Under which precise contextual and/or situational conditions do users of a given social class realize or leave out such and such optional features or units?

—What happens if language users of different social classes and ages come into contact? To what degree do they understand each other? What is the adaptation process, if any—does one abandon one's own usage and adopt the other's? Do both take a step toward each other?

—and so forth.

Such problems could not be dealt with adequately in an overall view. For this purpose, we need more detailed descriptions, such as those aimed at by sociolinguistic (Labov, 1972a, 1972b) and psycholinguistic studies (Bever, 1975).

But this does not mean that an overall description is totally devoid of value. It supplies us with invaluable data and tools when we want to outline what happens if two languages—let us say English and German—come into contact (cf. Moulton, 1968, and Weinreich, 1964), or when we want to sketch the resemblances and differences between two or several languages in a typological framework (Martinet, 1962, §III). For such purposes, a detailed description is not adequate.

IV.2 Further Remarks on Experimentation

Experimentation can be based on the direct observation of data, whether it is behavioral or intuitive. The examples given above (cf. II.4–6) are instances of direct observation. Further examples: we can observe how sequences like *dark* and *dock* are pronounced; we can also ask informants if these are identical or different. This procedure is also possible on the level of significant units: we can observe how a speaker reports on an extralinguistic event or what meaning he attributes to a sentence.

Experimentation can also be indirect. My suggestion regarding the evaluation of the degree of relevance by recourse to a user's behavior and intuition could qualify as experimentation based on direct observation. The means proposed for determining the limits of classification should be viewed as indirect, owing to the fact that the boundaries should be set up according to the economy that classification could provide. Any recourse to the criterion of simplicity is also to be considered as a case of exploration rather than direct observation.

I would like to emphasize that both types of experimentation—based on direct and indirect observation—imply premises.[11] There is no God's truth in the one nor hocus-pocus in the other. In both cases, we have a set of premises allowing our hypotheses to be confronted with empirical data. The difference can be put roughly like this: whereas in direct observation the premises concern the techniques used for experimentation, indirect observation calls on other premises too. As an illustration, let us take the case of the classification of linguistic units. We can refer directly to linguistic behavior and/or intuition in order to find out how

English speakers classify words; this is what Miller does (Miller, 1969) when he tries to find out if words are classified according to taxonomic (hierarchical, in his terminology[12]) organization of their semantic features. This experiment assumes at least that speakers have an intuitive knowledge of (a) the semantic constitution of words, and (b) the hierarchy of their semantic features. These are what the researcher considers probable properties of the object and what he wants to examine in the light of empirical data.

On the other hand, this experiment takes for granted, among other things, that sorting is an appropriate technique for highlighting semantic features and their hierarchy. The appropriateness of sorting for this study is presupposed by this type of experimentation. This is its premise, and concerns only the techniques for data collection. In some cases, direct observation does not seem possible. Let us take again French verbs. How deep should we go in the subdivision of this moneme class? One solution to this problem could be that the subdivision should be continued as long as the classification provides us with economy.

This is the same as saying that it is justified to set up subclasses as long as it is economical to use syntactic classes and rules for producing and understanding moneme combinations. Beyond this limit we consider the members of each subclass as isolated entities, each having specific syntactic features (and not as members of an even smaller subclass). We shall come back to this in more detail (cf. V.3). For the moment, let it suffice to say that if we undertake experimentation in this perspective, we should have, among the premises, one that states that the *raison d'être* of syntactic classes is the economy they provide for the manipulation of language. As the premise of economy does not concern data collection, experiments based on economy should be considered as being based on indirect observation.

Incidentally, this premise implies that human behavior is ruled by economy. I think that the whole debate about the criterion of simplicity and its value in the description or explanation of language phenomena—if not *ad hoc*—has its point of departure in the principle of economy.

Experimentation is a thankless task because to resolve a restricted problem we need to deploy considerable means. Besides, the conclusions that we draw from the results are not self-evident; therefore caution is needed in generalization. For instance, if our experiment happens to yield positive results, we cannot then claim that our hypothesis is proven. If the sorting technique, for instance, results in a hierarchical organization, we cannot conclude without circumspection that the monemes of human language are ordered according to such a pattern. Strictly speaking, the eventual success of an experiment might be due to several other reasons: (i) the pattern under study is valid for English, and not for just any language; (ii) it is the case that the lexical monemes of English have such an organization (in contradistinction to grammatical ones); (iii) the pattern is valid only for a part of the English lexicon from which we have chosen our items (not for the whole lexicon); and so on.

No theoretically based argument allows us to rule out any of these explanations.

The assumptions contained in an experimental model concern—as I said above—two aspects: the data and the conditions of their observation (i.e., premise, indirect observation) on the one hand, and on the other the properties of the observables (i.e., hypothesis). Consider vowel length in the French spoken in Lausanne. We might have an idea of its relevance in certain positions, as in word final: ami 'friend, m.'/amie 'friend, f.', and we may want to find out what happens in other positions. We can advance the hypothesis that there is an opposition between /-VC/ and /-V:C/.

One aspect that the model has to specify, in order to make experimentation possible, is connected with the data, such as choice of informants, choice of words, and choice of means of access (i.e., behavior or intuition, written questionnaire or some more sophisticated way of soliciting answers, etc.). The other aspect is concerned with the properties of the data, namely the duration of these vowels and its phonological relevance. It may happen that one of the parameters is not well chosen; then the whole result will be inconclusive. These remarks are made to compensate any pessimism about experimental research that an oversimplified view might cause.

I shall now comment on a number of hypotheses (listed below) and illustrate them with examples from French, with hints on practical procedures.

IV.3   A Methodological Framework
Consider again the distinction between two kinds of assumptions: primitive premise and hypothesis. If we aim at empirically establishing the

precise value of different factors in a language, we change one and only one factor at a time. In a single model we can include variations of either observational techniques or the properties of the object. In other words, an assumption *per se* is neither a hypothesis nor a premise. It is a premise when we take it for granted in experimentation. It will be a hypothesis if it corresponds to what we want to evaluate empirically. Observational techniques can thus be questioned and evaluated. In such cases, the models cover a wider scope and provide us with a methodological framework. On the contrary, models aiming at determining the characteristics and value of a given linguistic phenomenon have a narrower scope and take as given the methodological framework. The hypotheses presented here, seven in all, are set up in order to form a methodological framework for case studies. I will first describe them in general terms before commenting on them in more detail with some illustration.

Hypothesis 1. The social variations of linguistic phenomena are not accidental but structured and present a hierarchy.

Hypothesis 2. The mental variations are also structured and form a hierarchy.

Hypothesis 3. The two hierarchies, social and mental, are correlated and form the extrinsic hierarchy.

Hypothesis 4. Linguistic phenomena can be ordered in a hierarchy according to their frequency in discourse (or on the syntagmatic axis).

Hypothesis 5. Linguistic phenomena can also be ordered according to their integration in the system (or on the paradigmatic axis).

Hypothesis 6. The dimensions of frequency and integration are linked by a constant function and together form the intrinsic hierarchy.

Hypothesis 7. The extrinsic and intrinsic hierarchies are correlated and allow for establishing a single hierarchy whose poles are the central zone (hard core) and peripheral or marginal zone (loose ends).

IV.4 Social Hierarchy

Let us recall, in general terms, the intuitive content of this hypothesis (discussed above). It is generally admitted that (i) a language makes communication between members of a speech community possible, and that (ii) language structure is not homogeneous: that is, the members of a speech community do not have exactly the same language habits. Obviously, we are in the presence of a paradox. In the case that the same linguistic utterance refers to event A for the speaker but to event B for the hearer, intercomprehension is jeopardized. As an example, let us take a sentence like *all the boys didn't arrive*. This can mean either (a) *not all the boys arrived* or (b) *all the boys failed to arrive* (Carden, 1973). If communication is possible, it is due to the fact that, despite variable phenomena, speakers and hearers possess common habits on which they rely. One way of evaluating the part that a series of data plays in a communicative act is to measure how widespread they are relative to each other. For this purpose, I may adopt the following procedure.

I can submit a set of linguistic phenomena to the intuitive judgment of a relatively homogeneous group of informants—homogeneous, that is, on a certain socio-geographico-economic level. If all the answers to a question are in agreement, then the consensus is maximal. If the effective answers are equally distributed between possible answers, the consensus is minimal (or the dissension is maximal) (cf. Hypothesis 1).

Guy Carden proceeded with a series of interviews on the meaning of *all the boys didn't arrive:* sixteen informants declared that (a) was the only possible meaning, four reported that the only reading possible was (b), and twenty considered that the sentence was ambiguous between (a) and (b) (cf. Carden, 1973, pp. 171–182). This allowed him to consider (a) the favored reading of the sentence. Obviously, the favored reading is estimated according to how widespread it is in society. I will illustrate this below with some examples from French (cf. IV.6).

It is worth noting that the setting up of a social hierarchy is the most classical of experimental methods. Martinet's survey on French phonology (1944) is based on this principle. We have solid reasons to believe that this hierarchy is not due to chance: repeated under similar conditions, the experiment gives similar results again (cf. Reichstein, 1960, and Deyhime, 1967).

IV.5 Psychic Hierarchy

The coexistence of communicative function and language variations remains paradoxical unless we admit that even the language user has a knowledge of dialectal differences within a language, that is, he knows that the same language phenomenon has a range of realizations besides the one(s) familiar to him. But this knowledge has not the same accuracy and certitude, for not all the variants are accessible with equal ease: some are sure (certain) and immediate, others remote (unfamiliar) and subject to hesitation. In other words, variants are hierarchized. This hierarchy can be empirically evaluated by following the procedure described below.

Given a group of informants, I ask them questions about phenomena of their language. My questionnaire gives them the opportunity to pronounce several judgments about the same phenomenon. If all the answers of an informant show exactly the same judgment, then his certainty is maximal. At the opposite end, if his answers are equally distributed between possible alternatives, then his certainty is minimal (or his hesitation is maximal) (cf. Hypothesis 2). For an example from French, see IV.6 below.

IV.6 Extrinsic (or External) Hierarchy

A priori, there is no reason to rule out that the social and mental hierarchies are independent dimensions. But if we conceive of communication as a cooperation between individuals within a speech community, the correlation of the two dimensions suggests itself. The efficiency of communication requires that those language phenomena which are certain (in the individual mind) are also widespread (in society). And conversely, what is uncertain in one's mind is also not widely spread in the community. This correlation can be empirically tested.

If we classify items on the basis of their statistical value in the psychic dimension on the one hand, and on the basis of their statistical value on the axis of the social dimension on the other, the two classifications yield equal values (cf. Hypothesis 3).

The extrinsic hierarchy could thus be represented by a single measure: rigor (vs. laxity).

(a) Example 1: The attribute adjective in French

Attribute constructions in French seem to offer a good subject for experimentation. Grammar manuals, which devote several paragraphs to the position of the attribute, consider it as relevant for some adjectives: *brave homme/homme brave* ('worthy man'/'courageous man'), *pauvre fille/fille pauvre* ('unfortunate girl'/'needy girl'), *rude homme/homme rude* ('uncouth man'/'tough man'),[13] and so forth, and set up a list, which differs from manual to manual.

To find out to what extent the position of the attribute adjective is relevant, we carried out a survey based on questionnaires which asked informants to judge the possibility (or impossibility) of certain syntactical constructions and the meaning they attributed to them. For example, pairs of sentences were given like:

> *c'était une élégante femme/c'était une femme élégante*
> 'that (it, she) was an elegant woman'
> *c'était un vilain homme/c'était un homme vilain*
> 'that (it, he) was a nasty/ugly/villainous man'
> *c'était une commune femme/c'était une femme commune*
> 'that (it, she) was a vulgar woman'.

The informants were asked to say for each pair of sentences whether both were possible, and, if the reply was affirmative, if they had the same meaning or two different ones. Other questionnaires distributed to the same informants gave them an opportunity to use some of these adjectives in pre- or postposition in a very precise semantic context and to judge the acceptability of sentences with those structures, as with for example, the adjective *rude*.

—Use:

> *Admirez son exploit. Il faut être un . . . homme . . . pour traverser la Manche à la nage*
> 'Admire his exploit. You have to be a . . . man . . . to swim across the Channel'.

—Acceptability judgment:

> *Il traversa la Manche à la nage, c'est vraiment un homme rude*
> 'He swam across the Channel, he's a tough man'.

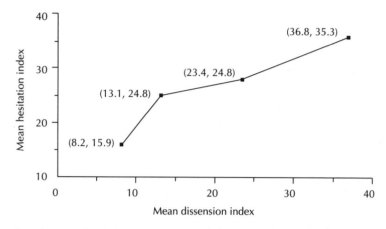

The replies were classified according to the increase of the hesitation index and divided into four equal classes. For each class, the mean of the individual hesitation index and the mean of the social dissension index were calculated. The graph shows the correspondence between the averages obtained.

Figure 2 Adjectives in French.

The informants thus had an opportunity to show their hesitation and uncertainty. A statistical analysis of the survey carried out on some three hundred French speakers proved the existence of a correlation between individual hesitation and social dissension; in other words, the more an individual hesitates, the more the speech community is divided. Inversely, the surer an individual reaction is, the more collective reactions converge, as shown by figure 2.

(b) Example 2: Pronouns in French

What rules govern the insertion of French pronouns into the verbal syntagm? The answer is easy if one limits oneself to very simple sentences like subject + verb or verb + object. For example, *je vous le donne* ('I give it to you') and *il te le donne* ('he gives it to you') are possible sequences, but *je le vous donne* and *il le te donne* are, even if not impossible, at least unusual (in common use) except in certain restricted parts of the French-speaking community like St.-Etienne. For the possible sequences there is no doubt as to the function of *vous, te,* or *le*.

However, this is not the case for more complex sequences; the possibility of certain combinations as well as the meaning of possible combinations raise a number of problems (even if the examination of the meaning is limited to its syntactic aspects, i.e., 'agent', 'goal', or 'beneficiary'). This is well illustrated by the case of sentences which contain an inflected verb followed by an infinitive. Who are the participants of the uninflected verb? Which ones is it possible to express? It is certainly possible to join an 'agent', 'goal', or 'beneficiary' to the infinitive. But is the simultaneous presence of all three possible? In other words, is a sentence like *je le la leur fais faire* possible? As to the relation between expression and contents, the sentence *on me l'a fait amener* can be given as an example. Does it mean 'I was entrusted to bring it (him, her)' or 'Someone was entrusted to bring it (him, her) to me'? These are questions that cannot be solved except in an arbitrary manner. Here again, the survey confirmed the existence of rigorously structured as well as loosely structured zones. It also revealed a clear correlation between hesitation and dissension, as well as between certainty and consensus (see figure 3).

Hypothesis 3—and perhaps the second one as well—does not seem to have been explicitly advanced by other researchers. However, socio-

Figure 3 Pronouns in French: global results showing correlation between consensus and certainty.

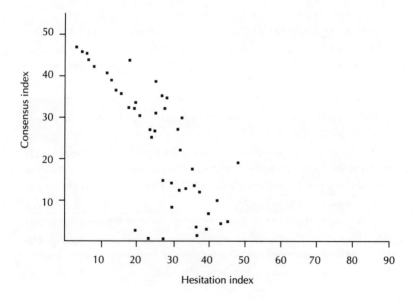

linguists have almost always been able to gain access to the mental dimension, just as psycholinguists are currently taking account of the social dimension.

This correlation seems to me rich in implications, among them the following.

   —Language phenomena have a social aspect and a mental one. Each of these conditions the other.

   —The whole debate over the question of whether linguistics is a social or a psychological discipline is vacuous.

It must be admitted that our surveys were not carried out according to an elaborate methodology. If we establish a more rigorous, sophisticated device for survey, it must be possible to work out a much more precise or more accurate measuring technique for the social or mental hierarchies, so that with few informants, considerable generalization and prediction become possible.

IV.7 Frequency

Laxity and rigor are determined with reference to the importance of linguistic phenomena for the individual and for the speech community, factors which are external to the linguistic phenomena themselves. This is why we consider this hierarchy extrinsic.

It is also possible to hierarchize linguistic phenomena in terms of internal factors which would lead to an intrinsic hierarchy. In this view, only elements and their relations (syntagmatic or paradigmatic) would be taken into account: for instance, frequency and integration. The basic idea is a twofold one: on the one hand, we think it possible to establish in this way a hierarchy that is meaningful and enlightening; on the other, we maintain that such a hierarchy has close relations with the extrinsic hierarchy and that consequently it would be possible to reduce both to one and the same hierarchy. This means that a certain number of zones (central, marginal, median, etc.) could be delimited in a nonarbitrary way in a given linguistic system.

First of all I would like to illustrate with examples the intuitive meaning of these concepts and their relevance in distinguishing different layers of linguistic structure. The interest of frequency and integration for diachronic phonology has been demonstrated by André Martinet

(1955). Attention will be drawn to monematics and in particular its synchronic aspect.

If the recurrence of monematic units and complexes in a corpus is examined, we notice that some of them crop up more frequently than others. This difference in frequency could form a criterion for hierarchization. If this study is carried out on the verb class, verbs like *être* 'to be' and *avoir* 'to have' will be found at the top of the hierarchy among the most frequent, whereas others like *résoudre* 'resolve' and *clore* 'conclude'/'close' will be found at the bottom of the scale among the rarest.

From another angle, the morphological behavior of these units can be observed in speakers' usage of them; it will be found that the morphology of the verbs *être* and *avoir* is rigorously structured, whereas that of verbs like *résoudre* is lax. Indeed, every French speaker—or nearly every—is capable of conjugating the verbs *avoir* and *être*. This is not the case for *résoudre,* as any French speaker may hesitate or make a mistake for some part of the conjugation. It should be noticed that this difference in the mastery of verbal forms is not due to the inherent complexity of the morphology of *résoudre* nor to the simplicity of that of *avoir*. If morphological complexity is measured by the number of stems (morphological variants) which each verb has, then *avoir* is far more complex, morphologically speaking, than *résoudre*.

It can thus be concluded that high frequency may have as a consequence a rigorous structure, whereas low frequency can entail a lax structure.

> On the syntagmatic axis, linguistic units are hierarchized as to their frequency of occurrence. Therefore, it is possible to classify these units on the basis of their frequency value (cf. Hypothesis 4).

IV.8 Integration
Above, I established a relation between frequency and rigorous structure. However, I would not like to be misunderstood on this point: I am simply affirming that all elements of high frequency are rigorously structured. I do not want to say that everything that is part of a rigorous structure is also of high frequency. In fact, there are verbs whose conjugation causes no problem (and which thus belong to the rigorous zones of morphological structure) but which are not of high frequency,

for example *cacaber* 'to make the noise of a partridge' and *blatérer* 'to roar', for camels, which are verbs of very low frequency, or *gabouiller,* whose frequency is nil (as I have just invented it).

What makes the usage of such verbs easier is the fact that they share their morphological properties with a large number of other verbs. The extensive recurrence of these properties makes them more accessible in the memory and thus makes their use easy. We can therefore say that in certain cases the rigor of the structure is due to the strong integration of a unit in its class.

The notion of integration supposes that an element is conceived of as being made up of a set of properties. The more widespread properties are in the class to which the element belongs, the more integrated an element is. Conversely, an element whose properties are hardly or not at all shared by other elements is poorly integrated. This definition of integration is only a reformulation of the one given by André Martinet for phonemes; it is more general in that it does not specify the phonological or monematic nature of the element and can therefore be applied, *mutatis mutandis,* to monemes. The integration of monemes can be defined on at least two distinct levels: on the morphological level, the signifiant of a moneme can be thought of as the set of morphological variants by which it is realized. The morphological integration of a moneme is even greater when the type of its morphological variations and their conditioning are shared by a great number of monemes. On the syntactic level, a moneme can be considered as the set of its combinatory features. In this case, the syntactic integration of a moneme can be defined by the extent of its combinatory features. A moneme is even better integrated when its combinatory features are valid for a large number of monemes. A moneme that is not at all integrated would be composed of combinatory features that it would be the only one to possess. We may thus suggest the following.

> On the paradigmatic axis, linguistic units are hierarchized according to their integration. The more a unit shares its structural properties with other units, the more it is integrated (cf. Hypothesis 5).

IV.9   Intrinsic Hierarchy: Relation Frequency/Integration

We have seen that high frequency of an element corresponds to a high degree of rigor in the structure. In the same way, strong integration implies that the element is endowed with a rigorous structure. This causes a problem: that of the relation between frequency and integration.

Let us first summarize the arguments that would allow us to think that such a relation exists. In synchrony, it can be affirmed that the most frequent monemes are those that are generally the least integrated. For example, verbs like *avoir* and *être* are virtually not integrated morphologically. In diachrony, it can be observed that analogic changes (whose effect is to integrate isolated or badly integrated monemes into a large morphological class) do not affect verbs of high frequency: a verb like *pouvoir* 'can', 'be able' has kept the two forms /puv/ and /pœv/ (in *pouvez* '[you/pl] can' and *peuvent* '[they] can', respectively) which resulted from the phonologization of the stressed and unstressed variants of the root vowel, whereas the two forms of the verb *trouver* 'to find', which were the result of the same process, have become one. *Trouver,* which is not so frequent, has thus become integrated in the morphological class of verbs with a single stem, but *pouvoir,* which is very frequent, has remained badly integrated morphologically.

These and many other examples tend to indicate that the notions of frequency and integration are linked to each other both synchronically and diachronically. The above examples show that, from a synchronic point of view, monemes of high frequency and weak integration belong to the rigorous structure in the same way as monemes of low frequency and strong integration. The zone of lax structure includes monemes which are not sufficiently frequent and are not well integrated.

Everything seems to indicate that for a moneme to be part of the central zone of linguistic structure (and thus of the zone of rigorous structure), it must be either of high frequency or well integrated or of medium frequency and integration. It thus seems that high frequency makes up for weak integration in the same way that strong integration makes up for low frequency. In other words, the resultant of frequency and integration must be high for an individual to master with certainty a monematic fact, and the speech community must be unanimous about it. In yet other terms, for a given degree of rigor, the resultant of frequency and integration is constant. This constant must necessarily be determined empirically.

It is in terms of the value frequency/integration that elements can be hierarchized in an intrinsic dimension, where two poles should be distinguished: generality and restriction. The pole of generality corresponds to the maximum value of the resultant frequency/integration; a minimum value of this resultant characterizes the pole of restriction. This can be formulated as follows.

> The frequency of linguistic units and their integration are linked; their relation can be expressed by a constant function. Thus, the intrinsic hierarchy could also be represented by only one measurement: generality (as opposed to restrictedness) (cf. Hypothesis 6).

IV.10   Central and Marginal Zones

The discussion of frequency, integration, and their relation has led us to talk of the relations which link the intrinsic and extrinsic hierarchies. We have said that this relation seems to be one of parallelism: the pole of generality corresponds to that of rigorous structure, restriction coinciding with laxity. This can be formulated as follows.

> The extrinsic and intrinsic hierarchies are parallel. In other words, those linguistic phenomena which are of a high level of generality are also characterized by a high degree of rigor and vice versa (cf. Hypothesis 7).

This is shown in figure 4.

Here it is a question of theses which must be submitted to empirical validation and which might be confirmed, falsified, modified, or nuanced by the results of experimental research. However, intuitively, they have a certain likelihood. It seems normal that what is general— by its frequency or integration—is also more rigorously structured; that is to say, it is more easily accessible in the intuition of the speaker, more easily produced, and more immediately understood. It can also be expected that elements of restricted scope—due to their low frequency or their weak integration—are of lax structure; usually of late acquisition, they are badly incorporated into the linguistic knowledge of the speaker, which explains his great hesitation. Because they are acquired by each individual in different contexts and situations, each person knows one aspect (for example, a variant of the signifié or one of its syntactical combinations in the case of monemes), which is why there is disagreement. Our proposal is to reduce these intuitive concepts to explicit and verifiable hypotheses so that the center and margins of a linguistic system can be objectively delimited.

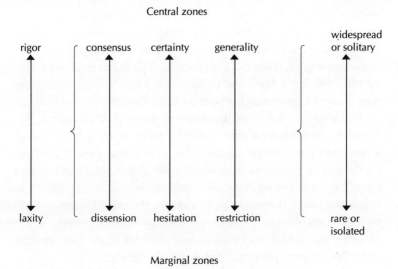

Figure 4   Structural hierarchies and their parallelism.

If the project is carried out and the underlying assumptions are well chosen, we will be able to complete current linguistic descriptions by taking account of the degree of relevance of the described phenomena. We will also be capable of setting theoretically motivated limits to our description or to our data collection.

If this hierarchy gives access to a quantitative index of the role that items play in the communication process, it is easy to imagine what it entails for applicational purposes such as language teaching, speech therapy, language pathology, language planning, and so forth.

IV.11   Perspectives
The above data on the extrinsic level were obtained by recourse to the users' intuition. *Mutatis mutandis,* the hypotheses should be equally valid if the data are collected by observing the users' behavior. Moreover, a comparison of the results obtained by different techniques could be instructive; it might show what relationship holds between the layers of structure and the observational techniques.

Consider the case of phonological surveys again. As we said above, there is no single answer to the question of what technique to use for collecting phonological data. The choice of technique depends on what we are aiming at in a survey, for not just any technique is appropriate for just any layer of structure. In a study of the vowel system of the French spoken in the canton of Vaud (Switzerland), two different techniques were used: reading of texts on the one hand and of minimal pairs on the other (cf. Schoch and de Spengler, 1980). On the whole, the data showed a correlation between the individual dimension (hesitation vs. certainty) and the social dimension (dissension vs. consensus). For instance, the opposition *mâle* 'male' vs. *malle* 'trunk' which appears among the higher ranks of hesitation has at the same time a higher rank on the axis of dissension. At the opposite end, the distinction between *était* '(he) was' and *été* 'summer' corresponds both to minimal hesitation and minimal dissension. In addition, the study brought to light discrepancies between the results obtained by different techniques. But these discrepancies are not equally distributed among the data; they are important for some phonemes but negligible for others.

It seems reasonable to assume that if we establish and apply several different methods for getting access to linguistic data, the common parts of their results must be the hard core of the system. This hypothesis has not been empirically tested.

Our research on the intrinsic hierarchy is not sufficiently advanced; as yet, it is too early to report on it in general terms.

In conclusion, I would like to emphasize that theoretical and experimental research are complementary. The bolder our theoretical reflection, the more promising our experimental perspectives. And conversely, the more precise our experimental research, the greater our chance of success in our search for insight. If I opt for experimental rather than for theoretical study, it doesn't mean that I find the latter uninteresting or unnecessary. My choice is based on my personal affinities and interest.

In this chapter, I have tried to give a general idea of experimentation and have avoided going into too much technical detail. Two problems arise from this approach: I have probably given the impression, on the one hand, that the hypotheses put forward are totally confirmed by the facts, and on the other, that no valid experimentation has been carried out in linguistics other than what has been presented here. I will attempt to rectify this in the subsequent chapters.

PART TWO

In Part One, my aim was to present a broad view of the main problems of today's linguistics. Such an attempt, however necessary, takes it for granted that some terminological problems have been resolved, and therefore that it is legitimate to consider as equivalent some concepts developed within different theoretical frameworks. Such an attempt makes reference to technical data inevitable and thus may be detrimental to a clear exposition of the problems raised and the solutions proposed by linguistic research. Therefore, extensive discussion on the conceptual equivalences that can be found behind the differing terminologies is necessary before getting to the core of the problem, that is, the theoretical debate. Actual discussions of a theoretical nature will be the core of the following chapters; I will thus present the problems and perspectives of linguistics more precisely, on the one hand, and on the other I will situate our model with respect to other experimental works in linguistics.

V. Outstanding Problems in Syntax

V.0 Synopsis

Despite divergences, current linguistic thought is based on a few principles widely admitted across theories and schools, except for extreme cases. Common principles could represent the state of the art in syntax. Beyond these, we reach the level of problems still pending. If, starting from different theoretical views, linguistic descriptions show similar difficulties, we can consider these difficulties actual limitations in our conception of language structure and try to remedy them. This chapter focuses on two important syntactic problems: class, function, and their relation on the one hand, and on the other, minimal units and their identification. In both cases, I shall first try to remove terminological obstacles in order to focus better on conceptual differences. Next, I shall ask what empirical solution we can conceive for these problems. Finally, I shall present brief remarks on other residual problems.

V.1 The State of the Art

What do we know for sure about syntax?

What justifies this question is the emphasis I put in the preceding sections on controversial theses and the divergent interpretations of them. This emphasis, however necessary for showing the value of experimental methods, might lead one to believe that nothing is known for sure about syntactic structure.

To put it roughly, one might say that, across the boundaries of schools and theories, the following principles are widely admitted.

(i) A linguistic utterance has two aspects, a content associated with an expression.

(ii) The association of content and expression produces a threefold structure for significant units:
   (a) syntax: the study of linguistic signs as wholes;
   (b) morphology: the study of the expression side of linguistic signs; and
   (c) semantics: the study of the content side of linguistic signs.

(iii) A linguistic utterance may be articulated (i.e., structured):
   (a) it may be a combination of smaller recurrent units; and
   (b) the combination of these units is rule governed (i.e., it is not free).

(iv) Syntactic analysis uses essentially combinatory properties as criteria. It is supposed to reveal the syntactic mechanisms by recourse to:
   (a) syntactic classes; and
   (b) combinatory properties (i.e., syntactic rules).

(v) Syntactic phenomena are hierarchized. They can be subclassified on the basis of bipolar distinctions such as:
   (a) syntagmatic (flectional) constructions vs. synthematic constructions (word formation e.g., composition, derivation);
   (b) grammar vs. lexicon;
   (c) units (monemes or morphemes, items) vs. relations (functions, rules); and
   (d) degrees of independence.

(vi) Linguistic operations (or components or levels) are ordered.

Some of these principles have been presented and discussed above. Let us take principle (i). When discussing the distributional thesis, we said that the total exclusion of meaning was theoretically absurd and practically fallacious (cf. I.5).

As for principle (ii), that is, the trichotomy morphology/syntax/semantics, I have already discussed the necessity of syntax (cf. III.2).

It is worth noting that there is no empirical proof showing that one can do without a syntactic component, since to our knowledge no thorough, full-fledged description of a language has been made on such a theoretical basis. If ever applied, such a theory—for instance, generative semantics—would have to have some part devoted to the sign level. Otherwise, it would fail to be an account of what a speaker-hearer does while using his language, even if by any chance, it generates, as an outdated slogan claimed, all grammatical sentences and nothing but grammatical sentences (which seems to me highly improbable).

The interest and necessity of semantics is too obvious today to warrant discussion.

As for morphology, some linguistic currents questioned whether it was a necessary level of analysis, or even a component of linguistic theory. But these linguistic currents examine in other sections of language description what are currently considered to be morphological phenomena. For instance, Hjelmslev suggests abandoning the normal distinction between morphology, syntax, and so on (cf. Hjelmslev, 1953). Elsewhere, he says that an expression like French, -*ra* in (*il*) *aimera* '(he) will like' corresponds to four elements on the content plane: 'future', 'indicative', 'third person', and 'singular'. This is precisely an example of what I subsumed under morphology (cf. Hjelmslev, 1966, p. 55).

Another example of this can be found in Chomsky's work. Reacting against the discovery procedures elaborated by distributional linguistics, Chomsky (1962, §IV) finds unnecessarily complicated, devoid of interest and *ad hoc* the procedures that aim at solving a problem like "which part of the word /tuk/ is the past tense morpheme (i.e., is it the /u/ or a replacive (ey→u), or a zero morpheme that determines a special allomorph of /teyk/, and so on)?"

Nevertheless, the transformational solution he proposes for such problems is based on the idea that there are complications on the expression level for some monemes, the identity of which on the content level is never in doubt. This is morphology in our terminology.

In both cases, morphological problems are examined but are not grouped in an autonomous section of the description. This simply implies that such problems exist but some linguists place them in one part of the language design, whereas others place them elsewhere.[14]

Hierarchy (principle (v)) is one of the concepts—if not terms—widely used to characterize the syntactic structure, on the intuitive basis that different constituents (say, monemes) do not appear under the same conditions in the complex (e.g., the sentence), and do not play an equally important role in the constitution of this complex. Constituents can thus be subcategorized according to their role.

Several dimensions are used in practice for establishing the hierarchy. Three of them—(a), (b), and (c) above—seem self-evident, perhaps due in part to the fact that terminology has no great diversity here. The distinction between flection (syntagmatic construction) and word formation (synthematic construction) is one of them. It has been proposed that this distinction should be based on the criterion of productivity (Martinet, 1960; Chomsky, 1965). Even if the purposes of these theses are not identical along the whole line, the basic idea is the same: syntactic rules are very general in one case, that is, the combination with tense, mood, and so forth is possible for every verb (e.g., *he comes, he would come, he would have come,* or French *nous donnons* 'we give', *nous donnerons* 'we will give', *nous donnerions* 'we would give'), whereas the same does not apply for affixes. There are no general rules for the derivation of action nouns from verb stems; for example, of the following four verbs, two have a derived action noun and two do not.

flight	(n)	vs.	*fly*	(v)
ride	(n)	vs.	*ride*	(v)
but				
?	(n)	vs.	*come*	(v)
?	(n)	vs.	*go*	(v)

As for (d) degree of independence, this is a dimension that is very often used but not always discussed on a theoretical level. The problem is now to determine which is the smallest string of significant units that can serve as a normal utterance in the use of language (it is again a matter of terminological choice to call such a string a sentence, a situation-independent utterance, or something else). Once this has been determined, what are its constitutive parts? Which parts are obligatory? Which are optional? Under what conditions do the optional constituents appear? And so forth. (For example, the famous rewrite rules such as S → NP + VP are answers to some of the above questions.) The constituent which can appear without other constituents as a full sentence can qualify as independent and be construed as a reference point for measuring the degree of dependence of the others.

It is immaterial whether this central constituent is called predicate or verb. What does matter, however, is to notice that it is not always the same class of monemes that fulfills the same function. This is the advantage of the terminological distinction between verb and predicate (cf. Martinet, 1960). But this distinction can be conveyed by other terms, for example, by distinguishing surface verb and deep verb as in TGG (transformational generative grammar).

Considering what has been said above, one could imagine that degree of independence is based solely on logical implication. Such logical relations, it is true, are considered for this purpose, but conjointly with semantic criteria. The duality of the criteria, both implicational and semantic, creates situations of conflict that we will discuss in the next section.

The principle that is least commonly agreed upon is (vi), the order of operations. What is meant by this term is the admission that linguistic operations follow an order: some are executed prior to others. What is the nature of this priority? Logical? Chronological? Is the order of operations a descriptive device? Or has it a mental or behavioral counterpart? These are questions that divide linguists into different camps. For instance, the order accepted by classical structuralism is phonology—morphology—syntax—semantics, while for TG (transformational grammar), syntax is the first component, followed by phonology and semantics. The existence of such an order seems to be the only feature common to all linguistic schools, including TG. At its earliest stage, transformational linguistics seemed to reject discovery procedures, but it finally established a set of new procedures with a rigid order. Long discussions have since ensued to decide whether transformation T should be applied before or after T'.

One could easily show that some of the principles are implied by a more general principle. This is the case for what I call the hierarchy of syntactic phenomena (principle (v)). It is not possible to develop, within the present framework, an extensive discussion of all the principles mentioned in this section. Yet, given that some continuing and tenacious misunderstandings subsist, I shall make a few remarks about these principles. The first remark concerns principle (iii), namely the articulation of the utterance. This implies that an utterance is made up of smaller units. The combination of these units provides the language user with a very large—perhaps infinite—number of utterances. Long dissertations have been written, starting with Chomsky's, on the creativity of language, which is presented as a revolutionary concept. Clearly unfolded, creativity means that the speaker-hearer does not stock utterances (or sentences) one by one in his memory but uses rules and items to produce his utterances (cf. Postal, 1968). If this is the case, then the difference between the principles of articulation and creativity is quite immaterial; it concerns above all the author's style and terminology.

The other remark concerns the notion of combination. In its everyday meaning, the term refers to the assembly of items. If the items are pure signifiants, then combination and distribution are the same. But the items are regarded as an association of signifié and signifiant in most European linguistic theories, especially in those currents inspired by de Saussure's conception of language. Therefore it would be a gross exaggeration to consider all linguistic theories prior to transformational grammar to be equivalent to distributional linguistics. This is what many authors did (e.g., Postal, 1968, and Ruwet, 1964) when they tried to show the originality of the transformational theory. But this confusion goes back as early as the distributional era. When Harris presented his linguistic methods he considered Sapir's work an example of distributional analysis (Harris, 1954).

The above remarks show that the common purport of linguistic theories may be obscured not only by different terminologies but also by the fact that, in their arguments, the point of departure is not the same for different currents.

Last but not least, uttering a theoretical principle does not guarantee its application by the utterer. Transformational grammar has devoted sophisticated arguments and long discussions to refuting taxonomy in linguistics. Nonetheless, transformational grammar introduced the age of New Taxonomy, as Fillmore judiciously put it (cf. Fillmore, 1972).

The common principles pointed out above are to my mind neither a compromise nor an unfounded attempt to give the appearance of unity to a discipline whose very foundations are questioned. My conviction is that if scholars of different persuasions who view language from different angles arrive at the same or very similar conclusions, then these form the common body of received knowledge of the science of language.

V.2 Unresolved Questions and their Significance

Syntactic analysis often raises the question of the possibility of more than one descriptive solution. If none of the theoretical principles on which the analysis is based allows a choice to be made between descriptive solutions, then I shall consider the case an unresolved question unless the principles support the notion that language users' habits themselves manifest such fluctuations. (I think that this is pretty close to the everyday meaning of the term.) Admitting that a phenomenon P is an exception with respect to a rule R is to admit a theoretical shortcoming: it means that the theory which allows for establishing rule R leaves out phenomenon P; thus, for P a special rule is needed. Such theoretical shortcomings can reasonably be presented in terms of rule and exception, if the applicability of the exception is considerably more limited than that of the rule. It is a matter of personal judgment whether such a difference between rule and exception is considerable (cf. Chomsky, 1965, p.231, n. 21 to chap. 4).

An exception is a counterexample that has been put aside for the time being and by implication considered irrelevant. However, putting the counterexamples aside means that the theoretical shortcomings they reveal have not been remedied.

Let us take the function called subject. What is its meaning? In a number of its occurrences, the subject expresses the actor of the action conveyed by the verb:

The man killed the animal
John loves Mary.

But not in all cases:

The man has been killed by the animal
John frightens easily.

The latter constitute counterexamples to the statement about the semantic content of the subject function.

With regard to counterexamples, two responses seem possible.

(i) One can support the theoretical principles, and, for this, one can take it for granted that counterexamples are a negligible quantity. Thus, the unresolved questions will remain unresolved because of a lack of interest in certain linguistic phenomena, in which case there is no more to say. The only question pertinent to this issue is whether linguistic studies should aim for objectivity. If the answer is in the affirmative, rule and exception can and must be defined precisely and subjected to statistical considerations. Another way of keeping to the theoretical principles is to search for *ad hoc* solutions. In this case, the theory misses its goals and cannot fulfill its supposed role.

(ii) One can, on the contrary, question the theoretical principles and try to readjust them in order to cover a larger range of data. Such a readjustment may affect the levels of analysis (the components of linguistic structure). The introduction of deep structure and the adjunction of semantic components are examples of this in generative grammar.

Readjustments may also be made on another level: the nature— formal or random—of linguistic structure and its constitutive parts. This is the case when linguists reject the discreteness of linguistic units (cf. Labov, 1973) or attribute some relevance to statistical aspects of data. The first type of readjustment is currently made in "classical" linguistics, whereas the second is the norm in sociolinguistics, psycholinguistics (cf. Rosch, 1978), experimental linguistics, and other fields.

From the above considerations, I want to conclude that whenever descriptive or theoretical principles are confronted with counterexamples, that is, limitations in their applicability, it is worth paying serious attention to these cases. Establishing residual classes—groups of exceptions—is surely an appropriate decision, if we view it tactically. But, if we want to understand the makeup of these classes and bring to light their theoretical implications, more should be done. Sound reflection is needed to reveal what regularities apply to them, for residual classes are generally based on a negative statement; the type of rules under study do not apply to such a subset.

Two examples will illustrate this. In his study on instrumental adverbs, Lakoff states that not all speakers agreed with his data; some speakers found grammatical what he judged to be ungrammatical (Lakoff, 1968, p. 23). Further discussions showed that these were not the only cases of disagreement. A sound study of such disagreement would necessarily, I am convinced, lead to the conclusion that variability is to some extent inherent in linguistic structure,—in other words, to a position close to Labov's (Labov, 1972a, 1972b) or Rosch's (Rosch and Lloyd, 1978). In this paper, Lakoff's purpose is to estimate the value of the criteria on which the boundaries of deep structure are based. By doing so, he questions the components of linguistic structure as conceived by Chomsky. No question is raised here as to the nature of these components; whether they have a clear-cut shape or whether they form continua is not at issue. Other investigations lead Lakoff later to question the nature of linguistic structure. This is what he does when he considers the boundaries of word classes or when he examines meaning criteria and their hierarchy (cf. Lakoff, 1972).

The second example is about semantic fields and their limits. In his case studies Mounin considers domestic animals on the one hand and habitation on the other. His purpose is to determine as precisely as possible the value and limitations of linguistic procedures when one tries to circumscribe these fields. By avoiding recourse to an *ad hoc* solution and refusing to play the rule/exception game, he brings to light an important property of semantic fields: the boundaries between a given semantic field and those adjacent to it are not clear-cut (cf. Mounin, 1965a, 1965b).

I have drawn the above examples from different theoretical frameworks: generative grammar and functional linguistics. In neither case were counterexamples or indeterminacies left out and put into residual classes. The authors tried to comprehend pending problems more deeply. These efforts brought to light some fundamental features concerning the syntactic or semantic structures: they are not absolute but relative (or hierarchized).

My concern in this section is parallel to that of the preceding one (V.1): if, in originating from different theoretical views, linguistic descriptions show similar difficulties, we can then consider these difficulties actual limitations on our conception of language structure and try to remedy them.

In the following sections, I will take a few examples of such unresolved problems in syntax and examine whether and to what extent experimental work can shed new light on them.

V.3 Class and Function

The notions of moneme class and syntactic function are generally admitted and currently used in linguistic analysis, whatever the terms used to name them (cf. V.1). When applying them, both create problems that to my knowledge have not been solved in a satisfactory way.

The issue I raise is threefold.

(a) Concepts and terms: are there conceptual affinities that are obscured by terminological differences?

(b) Tenets of the debate: have the difficulties concerning these con-

cepts been clearly stated? If so, to what explicit problems are we led when clarifying the debate on these unresolved questions?
(c) Empirical solutions: what empirical solutions to these problems could be envisaged?

I will focus on two problems: the relation between class and function and the limits of analysis.

(a) Concepts and terms
What criteria allow us to establish moneme classes that are relevant with respect to the functioning of syntax? Linguistic schools do not all pay equal attention to this question. In the tradition of de Saussure's teaching, European structural linguistics has always devoted theoretical discussions to this problem (cf. Hjelmslev, 1949; Martinet, 1960; and Tesnière, 1959). It considers that language units can be adequately identified on the basis of their syntagmatic and paradigmatic relations. On the moneme level, syntagmatic relations can be assimilated to combinatory properties (i.e., syntactic features or rules) and normally provide us with the criteria for establishing moneme classes.

Syntactic features are not homogeneous, and can be subdivided on the basis of the logical implications holding between the constituents of an utterance. Take as an example the following sentence:

Baby Jack finished his scotch broth and french fries.

Here, *broth* can be partially characterized by the implication relations shown in figure 5, if we examine the conditions that must be fulfilled in order to integrate the constitutive parts in the sentence as a whole.

A function is the relation of a presupposing item to its presupposed (or implied) item. Thus function is part of the syntactic features of a moneme.

On the whole, American structuralism sets up moneme classes on the basis of combinatory criteria too.[15] The main difference, in this respect, from European linguistics lies in the fact that it does not usually make theoretical issues of such problems as class and function.[16] Consider Chomsky's position in this matter: classes (termed major categories) such as noun, verb, adjective, and others are taken for granted, without any theoretical argumentation to substantiate their existence. On the contrary, details of the division into subclasses (i.e., subcategorization) and the criteria on which it should be based have been extensively discussed. It seems that combinatory features in fact provide these criteria; hence, subcategories are set up on the basis of selectional restrictions (which make up part of the combinatory features). However, the status of subclasses is ambiguous. What allows us to establish subcategories? Are they a descriptive necessity? Do they correspond to an aspect of (mental or behavioral) reality? The issue is unclear (cf. Chomsky, 1965, 1968).

In distributional linguistics, classes are deemed to be based on criteria that originate in the distribution of sound segments along the speech chain (syntagmatic axis), and as such to be free of any semantic considerations. In fact, meaning features are taken into account in distributional descriptions, though they are not cited as classificatory criteria. This explains why distributional analyses manifest results which closely resemble descriptions based on other structural theories.

This situation is not very much different for the concept of function: despite its current and widespread use, its definition is either lacking or varies from one theoretical framework to another.

In extreme cases—such as distributional descriptions—the term func-

Figure 5 Implicational relations.

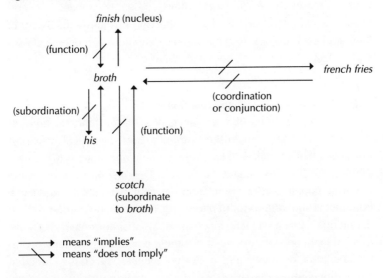

```
                  finish (nucleus)
                      ↑
   (function)   ⤢ |
                      ↓
                  broth          ────────────⤢──────────→  french fries
                      ↑            ←────────────⤢──────────
                   |  |              (coordination
(subordination) ⤢ |  |              or conjunction)
                   ↓  | ⤢
                  his     (function)
                      |
                      ↓
                  scotch
                  (subordinate
                  to broth)
```

———→ means "implies"
—⤫→ means "does not imply"

The above schema does not represent all the syntactic relations; many are left out, such as the relation between *french fries* and *finish*, or that between *-ed* and *finish*, etc.

tion is not used. However, the notion is not absent. Consider the sentence

She made him a good husband because she made him a good wife.

The two clauses, separated by *because,* are composed of segments that belong to the same classes but that do not hold the same relationship on the content plane. The difference of meaning is currently accounted for in part by assigning different functions to them. Distributionalists do not deny the difference of meaning, but try to account for it by utilizing distributional criteria (cf. Harris, 1951, 16.33 and 17.33). One has the impression that some hocus-pocus is used to avoid using the notion of function, tainted by semantics.

Except for such extreme cases, the concept and term function are current in general usage. As for the definition of function, this is either lacking or not sufficiently explicit. This amounts to saying that the concepts of class and function are necessary, and if we try to put them out through the door, they come back through the window.

(b) The tenets of the debate
One can reasonably require that, within a descriptive model, concepts should be defined clearly enough so that one can justify the extent of their application. It seems to me that the definitions of moneme classes and syntactic functions do not satisfy this requirement.

(i) Relation between class and function
For instance, admitting the relevance of syntactic function presents an advantage compared to the distributionalist theoretical positions. But saying that grammatical functions are relational notions (Chomsky, 1965, p. 68 ff.) is too vague a definition. Defining this relation as the linguistic counterpart of the relation between elements of experience (Martinet, 1960, 1964) is a step forward. The common purport of both definitions is that a syntactic function has a semantic content and refers to relational concepts. But neither of them provides us with any operational criteria for identifying, in given sequences, the class or function of the monemes.

Let us take as an example a pair of sentences such as

Jack built his house
Jack ruined his house.

According to both Martinet and Chomsky—and joining grammatical tradition—*house* has the same function in the above sentences. On what criteria is this identification based? Among phenomena taken for granted for this purpose, the class of verbal monemes tops the list. One of the reasons one generally finds it judicious to consider the functions of *house* in these sentences equivalent is that *build* and *ruin* are considered members of the same class (namely, transitive verbs). But this membership is a mere hypothesis when starting the descriptive analysis. We could also base our analysis on another hypothesis. It is possible to regard these verbs as belonging to different classes; the identity of the functions in the two sentences would then be questioned.

Consider now

He is now jogging
This is his present job.

Is the function of *now* identical to that of *present*? This question is generally not even raised; but when it is, the answer is currently negative. Both *now* and *present,* however, modify monemes—namely, *jog* and *job*—and give information about their temporal dimension. The reason an equivalence is not proposed for the functions of *now* and *present* is that their nucleus (or head) is not from the same class: *now* has a verbal nucleus, whereas *present* has a noun nucleus. What I conclude from this is that when we start to identify a function (e.g., the function of *now* or *present*), we consider that the class (verb, noun, adverb, adjective, etc.) has already been identified. The same goes for the class: when we establish the identity of classes, we consider the functions to be known. The subdivision of the verb class into transitive and intransitive is based on functional criteria: transitive verbs can have an object as a subordinate, whereas intransitive verbs cannot.

This is clearly a case of circularity; classes constitute defining criteria for functions, yet at the same time, their definitions are based on functional criteria. Functions are both identified by class criteria and used as criteria for class identification. This is too important a problem to be left aside. If much of recent discussion about how to identify functions or classes has been distorted, it is partly due to ignorance of this circularity.

This circularity entails that two or more descriptions can each be quite coherent and yet bring out divergent results. Such divergences are due to a difference in the assumptions admitted at the outset. Consider again the following pair of sentences:

> *Jack built his house*
> *Jack ruined his house.*

If in identifying functions one assumes that *build* and *ruin* belong to the same class, the function of *house* is equivalent in both sentences; conversely, if in characterizing classes the functional equivalence of *house* in the two sentences is the point of departure, this entails that *build* and *ruin* belong to the same class.

If we reconsider the point of departure, another descriptive solution appears, which is neither less nor more coherent than the former. One could assume that *house* does not have an identical function in the above sentences. This is what Fillmore does in opposing an "effectum object" (existing prior to the action) to an "affectum object" (resulting from the action; cf. Fillmore, 1968, p. 4). This assumption entails the subdivision of transitive verbs into two classes: in one are verbs like *build* that can have as their subordinate an effectum; in the other are those verbs that can be the nucleus for an affectum, for example, *ruin*.

I will not develop this discussion any further. I think that one can see that any initial decision when establishing syntactic classes for a set of monemes has repercussions on the number and the definition of syntactic functions for the same set of units. In other words, class and function are interdependent concepts.

(ii) Limits of analysis

What has been said previously about the relationship between class and function is also valid for the other syntactic properties (combinatory features); that is, syntactic features and moneme classes are interdependent.

In the above example, the classification of verbs was founded on their subordinatory properties. A stringent classification must be based on all the combinatory properties, be they function, subordination, or coordination. One can easily imagine that if all the combinatory features are taken into account, the resulting classes will each contain about one moneme. Empirical works tend to prove this (cf. Gross, 1975; Hoekstra,

1980). The implication is clear: the systematic application of classifying criteria has as its consequence the disappearance of moneme classes. Therefore, we will have either to abandon the notion of class or to envisage a procedure for the selection of relevant features.

I don't know of any linguistic current which supports the first solution. It seems obvious that leaving out the notion of class has considerable disadvantages. Let us consider some consequences of the absence of moneme classes in a syntactic structure. Each set of syntactic features (or rules) will be specific to one and only one moneme; conversely, each moneme will have its own combinatory properties. In order to learn such a syntactic structure, language users would have to memorize the monemes and for each moneme a separate list of syntactic features. The economy of language articulation would be annihilated by such a structure. This type of language would lack universality and creativity. As I said above, empirical evidence tends to prove that language users have a practical knowledge of moneme classes.

The second solution consists of sorting (or selecting) from among the numerous combinatory properties those which are relevant with respect to the syntactic functioning of a language. I think that this selection is focused on in different theoretical currents and is one of the main objects of debate about syntactic structure. Considering that not very long ago scholars—for instance, Bloomfield, Hjelmslev and Harris—stated that the combinatory features should be exhaustively examined and used for syntactic analysis, it should be noticed that recognizing (explicitly or not) the necessity of sorting between combinatory features is a step toward clarifying syntactic problems. Secondly, the sorting of syntactic criteria is implicit. For instance, Chomsky's discussion of selectional restrictions and subcategorization (cf. Chomsky, 1965, pp. 111ff.) is often based on one of these implicit principles: either moneme classes are an indispensable component of syntactic structure, or such a sorting is necessary.

To clarify the issue, I should remark that (a) the distinction between classes (N, V, A, . . .) and subcategories (human, nonhuman, animate, nonanimate, . . .) is one of degree rather than of kind. Likewise, grammatical rules and selectional restrictions are different in degree and not in nature; and (b) the two principles are interdependent; that is, if we draw a boundary between classes and subcategories, the distinction between syntactic rules and selectional restrictions ensues, and vice versa.

If we consider the problems this way, we should expect the arbitrary placing of a boundary on continua to be questioned. The debate over the legitimacy and the place of the boundary between syntactic (deep) structure and (lexical) semantic structure exemplifies this (cf. Lakoff, 1968, 1969, and Chomsky, 1972).

As for Martinet, his definitions of class and moneme are an effort to limit the scope of both function and class and thus to contribute to clarifying the conception of the problem. Here, at the outset, the problem of moneme classes is presented in a straightforward manner: as his moneme classes are, in contradistinction to Chomsky's, not universal, the describer has the task of determining the moneme classes. This classification is based (or mainly based) on the functions a group of monemes can fulfill (cf. Martinet, 1960, §4.41). Function is defined, as we saw above, as "the linguistic counterpart of the relationship between one element of experience and the whole of experience" (cf. Martinet, 1962, p. 49; see also Martinet, 1960, §4.12). This seems to be an attempt to avoid circularity. Thus function is prior to class: it is determined on the basis of the semantic content it conveys. (I think the signifié is to be taken in this framework as the linguistic counterpart of the extralinguistic experience language users have.)

One of the problems is to determine to what degree the analysis of the semantic content of functions should be refined: should we restrict the analysis of functions to a distinction like subject/object? Should we go deeper in the analysis and set up two functions such as affectum object/effectum object? There are no explicit principles to provide clear answers to such questions. The reason object should be regarded as one function seems to be because of grammatical traditions or describers' intuition.

The same goes for class: should French verbs be divided into subclasses? How refined should this subclassification be? I cannot see any theoretically founded answers to these questions. If one decides that French verbs form only one class, this decision has no theoretical foundation (cf. Mahmoudian, 1980, p. 155).

Consider the pair of sentences given by Fillmore (cf. Fillmore, 1968):

John ruined the table
John built the table.

Table is considered an affectum in the first sentence but an effectum in the second, when the question is phrased: "Is the object understood as existing antecedent to John's activities?" But why precisely this question, and not others such as: "Is the object understood as existing subsequently to John's activities?" The answer would be yes for the above sentences but 'no' for the following one:

John demolished the table.

Hence a third function. (It is no use proposing a Latin term for this function!) But it is easy to imagine that this subdivision is not finished. The objects can be further subdivided, for example according to the degree of affectedness: to what degree of ruin or demolition is a table still a table?

From the above, I would conclude that the criteria currently used for determining moneme classes and syntactic functions are, however indispensable and useful, not satisfactory; their coherent application will end in such a multiplication of classes and functions that the result will be in contradiction with the aims generally assigned to syntactic structure. A selection is needed to restrict their application. As far as I know, the selection criteria are either implicit or *ad hoc*. Moreover, class and function raise difficulties in whatever theoretical framework we choose to examine them.

(c) Toward an empirical solution

If we drop the dogma of formal structure, the problems can then be considered from a new angle. Instead of asking yes-or-no questions, we will be led to ask, to what degree.

Syntactic notions will thus be viewed as continua. As for functions, one should not ask if a given moneme m has the function f in the utterance u, but to what degree it has this function. Likewise, a good question would be, to what extent are the functions f and f' the same?

Identity and equivalence thus become a matter of degree. In the same way, syntactic notions become complex phenomena with multiple dimensions and various manifestations. For instance, the function "object" will then be conceived of as endowed with not only one but with multiple features of meaning, some of these being more typically object function than others.

It will then be possible to elaborate adequate empirical methods for evaluating the relevance of each semantic feature with respect to the degree to which it approximates to the object function.[17] For example, one could try to find out whether nouns denoting ostensible things (i.e., concrete nouns, in traditional grammar) are conceived by language users to be more or less object than nouns referring to nonostensible things (abstract nouns in traditional grammar). Alternatively, are nouns that refer to time or space as likely to be the object as others? For example, which of the objects in the following sentences is less or more typical of an object than the others?

> *He transformed an old mill into a splendid house*
> *He transformed a dictatorship into a democracy*
> *He passed an hour on the river bank*

To what extent does the kind of activity denoted by the verb and the sort of being denoted by the subject determine the perception of the object by language users? For instance, are *hours, sparrows* and *soldiers* equally conceived of as objects in the following?

> *He didn't see the soldiers pass*
> *He didn't see the sparrows pass*
> *He didn't see the hours pass*

The questions raised above are linked with the semantic aspect of object. As I said above, syntactic functions are also characterized by the logical implications the monemes contract with each other. For instance, an object O implies a verb, but a verb V does not imply an object.

$$O \rightarrow V$$
$$V \nrightarrow O$$

This general statement is true to variable degrees for different verbs. Some verbs can be used with or without an object ('eat'); whereas some others require an object ('give,' 'pour'); and some others present considerable semantic differences in constructions with or without an object ('walk'):

> *He is eating*
> *He is eating an apple*

He gave the girl a book
He poured the wine
The man is walking
The man is walking the dog.

There are other formal characteristics or features of the object, such as permutation, in

John hits Paul
Paul hits John,

or in French,

Jean bat Paul
Paul bat Jean,

where a change in the order of the constituents entails a change in the relational meanings. This is not true to the same degree in all cases. Above (III.6) I gave as a counterexample *quels Americains lisent Michel Butor et Claude Simon?* In nonformal French, a sequence like *une jolie tête avait la Martine,* literally 'a pretty head had the Martine' ('Martine was pretty') is another counterexample. In an exacting description, one cannot satisfy oneself with noticing that there are exceptions to the general rule of the relevant position of the object. One should also search for the conditions that make these exceptions possible and the proportion of these exceptions in the use of the language under study. The object function is also characterized by other formal features, such as those called in TGG passivization, pronominalization, and relativization. These are not all applicable to the object, in all its occurrences, to the same degree. For counterexamples, consider the following French constructions.[18] All the features are applicable in the first context.

1. (a) *La lame a emporté le baigneur*
   'The wave carried away the swimmer'
   (b) *Le baigneur a été emporté par la lame*
   'The swimmer was carried away by the wave'
   (c) *Le baigneur que la lame a emporté*
   'The swimmer (that) the wave carried away'
   (d) *Le baigneur, la lame l'a emporté*
   (lit.) 'The swimmer, the wave carried him away'

Passivization is not applicable in the second context.

    2. (a) *Le petit garçon a monté l'escalier*
        'The boy went up the stairs'
      (b) **L'escalier a été monté par le petit garçon*
        '*The stairs were gone up by the boy'
      (c) *L'escalier que le petit garçon a monté*
        'The stairs (that) the boy went up'
      (d) *L'escalier, le petit garçon l'a monté*
        (lit.*) 'The stairs, the boy went up them'

Besides the feature "passivization"—nonapplicable in the third context—the feature "pronominalization" is uncertain.

    3. (a) *Ce livre lui a valu le prix Nobel*
        'This book earned him the Nobel prize'
      (b) **Le prix Nobel lui a été valu par ce livre*
        *'The Nobel prize was earned him by this book'
      (c) *Le prix Nobel que lui a valu ce livre*
        'The Nobel prize (which) this book earned him'
      (d) *?'Le prix Nobel, ce livre le lui a valu'*
        ?'The Nobel prize, this book earned it for him'

There remains only one feature—namely, passivization—common to both context 1 and context 4.

    4. (a) **Tous les sujets obéiront le prince*
        'All subjects will obey the prince'
      (b) *Le prince sera obéi par tous les sujets*
        'The prince will be obeyed by all subjects'
      (c) **Le prince que les sujets obéiront*
        'The prince (that) all subjects will obey'
      (d) **Le prince, les sujets l'obéiront*
        'The prince, all subjects will obey him'[19]

Our discussion of functions focused on one single function in English or French. But a detailed study will discover similar problems in the identification of other functions in the same languages as well as in other languages (cf. among others Lazard, 1979, 1985).

As for classification problems, I have already given an example of the difficulties one faces when one tries to identify exactly the sub-classes of French transitive verbs (cf. IV.2). Another example óf this is the French infinitive: it resembles nouns in its functional properties (it can be subject, object, prepositional complement, etc.) and is close to verbs in its subordinatory properties (it can take certain modifiers— e.g., tense, negation—and complements—e.g., object—of the verbs (cf. Mahmoudian et al., 1976, pp. 395–398)). On both sides of the Atlantic, quite a number of studies have been devoted to problems of classification.[20] They show that, unless we take an *ad hoc* decision, moneme classes have no sharp boundaries; they can and must be regarded as constituting continua. In other words, a moneme class overlaps another moneme class at their fringes, but they remain quite distinct from each other at their center (cf. Ross, 1972, and Mahmoudian, 1980).

For all that experimental methods may be complicated, their main virtue is that without them research remains wholly dependent on the linguist's introspection. If the methods are successful, the linguist has the satisfaction of obtaining results that remain valid within limits set up beforehand (e.g., as to the domain, scope, community, and access techniques considered in the research).

V.4 Identification of Minimal Significant Units

One of the main problems of syntax is to find out the units that make up a sequence and the contexts in which these units appear. This section is devoted to such problems.

It is worth noting that this is not a minor taxonomic problem, as some linguists have been tempted to view it (cf. Ruwet, 1964). It has bearing on fundamental principles like articulation in Saussurean linguistics or competence and creativity in TGG. In order to examine this problem, I will focus on derivational phenomena and their status in functional linguistics and TGG. It should be noted that derivational constructions share some of their fundamental features (properties) with compounds. As an example, one could cite Chomsky's endeavor to assimilate syntactic and other moneme combinations, for which Martinet proposes "syntheme" as a generic term. The following discussion is about the syn-themes in general, though the examples are taken from the derivational domain. I will follow here roughly the same plan as in the preceding section.

(a) Concepts and terms

Are there conceptual affinities that are obscured by expository procedures and by a difference in the emphasis put on partial aspects?

Although derivational phenomena are dealt with in both theories,
the issue raised is apparently not the same. In functional syntax, the
segmentation of the speech chain into significant units is based on the
commutation test. This allows French *Professeur* 'Professor' to be separated from *travaillait* '(he or she) worked'. The first can be analyzed into
two monemes. This analysis is not possible for the second in a sentence like *c'est un bon professeur* 'he is a good professor'. From the two
potential components of *professeur, profess-* is commutable with a set
of verbal monemes like *cherch-* 'research'-, *travaill-* 'work', and so on.
On the contrary, *-eur* is not commutable either with another (affixal)
moneme or with zero (cf. Martinet, 1960, §4.40; Martinet, 1967; Martinet, 1962; and Mahmoudian, 1975). Strictly speaking, we will have
either to consider *professeur* a single moneme or to consider the commutation test invalid and ineffective for segmentation and abandon it.
But neither of these seems to be a very satisfactory solution. In TGG,
derivational phenomena are dealt with in other terms. No attention is
paid to the way in which one obtains units or sequences of units. On the
contrary, rules and items are discussed in detail as to their adequacy:
it is expected that language regularities on both expression and content
levels should be accounted for by recourse to rules and items. In derivation, rules are often very specific. Hence the dilemma: on the one hand,
the rules are not justified unless they are of some generality; on the
other, if we refuse to apply some (transformational) rules to derivational
constructions, we miss some relevant features of syntax. For instance, a
transformational rule could show that *it frightens (reddens, softens, etc.)
John* corresponds to the underlying structure 'it makes John afraid (red,
soft, etc.)'. In other words, *frighten* is, so to speak, analyzed into causative + adjective. If we adopt such an analysis, then we will have to
consider sincerity a defective predicate. Thus the syntagm *their sincerity*
has, on a certain level, an underlying structure like 'they are sincere'. In
other words, the nominal phrase *their sincerity* is equivalent to 'they are
sincere', that is, the word *sincerity* is a sequence made of *D is sincere.*
If we consider other examples, we will realize that the transformational
rules mentioned above lack generality. For example, some adjectives—

say, *grey, tender,* or *happy*—don't have a verbal counterpart as do *red, soft,* and *afraid.* We shall then subdivide the adjectives accordingly.

In some cases, the rules are much more specific. Consider the following series:

horror	*horrid*	*horrible*	*horrify*
terror	**terrid*	*terrible*	*terrify*
candor	*candid*	**candible*	**candify*

or

telegraph	*telegram*	*telephone*	*telescope*
phonograph	*?phonogram*	**phonophone*	**phonoscope.*

In such cases, it seems impossible to lay down any general rules. Therefore, in a TGG framework, one will be tempted to consider these sequences devoid of internal structure, that is, each as a minimal significant unit (cf. Chomsky, 1965, chap. 4, §2.3). The brief report above on derivational problems shows that the declared concerns are not the same: functional syntax is in search of the minimal units of which an utterance is made, whereas TGG is looking for general rules. But it should be noted that the general rules aimed at by TGG are—as we have seen above—about the internal structure of a sentence in terms of units and relations. This is to say that TGG is also concerned with minimal units.

In addition, functional syntax, while trying to find the minimal constitutive units of an utterance, has to concern itself with combinatory properties (syntactic features) that relate them to each other. (Let it be said again, the difference between syntactic features and syntactic rules are, in my view, purely terminological.) As we will see below, the generality or restrictedness of combinatory features has to be taken into account when we characterize derivational phenomena.

(b) Tenets of the debate
Have the difficulties concerning these concepts been clearly stated? If so, to what explicit problems are we led when clarifying the debate on these unresolved questions? To answer these questions, I will first discuss how the problem is examined in Saussurean linguistics. Here, any

string is conceived of as an assembly of units; each of these can appear in other contexts, and each can combine with other units to give new strings. To identify a unit, two conditions should be fulfilled: on the one hand, a given segment should be substitutable by other segments in the sequence; on the other, this substitution should be possible in other contexts. The commutation test subsumes these requirements. Let *A* be a segment, *B* its context, and *C* the sequence including *A* and *B*. *A* and *B* must both be commutable in order to prove the identity of *A* as a significant unit. It should also be noted that *A, B,* and *C* must all be significant units or sequences.

An illustration seems useful. In *I worked in the garden,* the string *I worked* can be analyzed into three monemes, each being commutable with other monemes or with zero. We can substitute *you, he, John,* and so forth for *I.* In place of *work-,* one can put *walk-, talk-,* and so on. And *-ed* can be substituted by zero. It is the same for French *Je travaillais dans le jardin* 'I worked in the garden'. The string /ʒətravajɛ/ can be segmented into three monemes, /ʒə/, /travaj/, and /ɛ/, on the basis of their possible commutations:

—/ʒə/ is commutable with /ty/*tu* 'you', /il/*il* 'he', /pɔl/*Paul,* and so on;
—/travaj/*travaill-* is commutable with /marʃ/*march-* 'walk', /ʃãt/ *chant-* 'sing', and so on;
—/ɛ/ is commutable with conditional /rɛ/-*rais* (or *-rait*), future /re/, *-rai,* /ra/-*ras* or *-ra,* and so on.

One cannot make an analogous commutation test within a string like /tɔ:k/*talk,* which bears a partial phonic similarity, but no semantic one, to another string like /wɔ:k/*walk.* In other words, here substitution helps us to identify units (as in the case of /t/ and /w/ in the context /-ɔ:k/) or sequences (as in /tejkiŋ/*taking* vs. /kiŋ/*king* or /spa:kliŋ/*sparkling* vs. /kliŋ/*cling*), but only on the plane of the signifiant, that is, phonemes or phoneme sequences.

Similarly, one cannot consider as a moneme the segment /ã/ of French /pimã/*piment* 'chili' despite its phonic similarity with the segment /ã/ of /ʃarmã/*charmant* 'delightful', /dezɔlã/*désolant* 'distressing', and so forth.

The above examples show clearly the interest of the commutation test. But its efficiency is limited in certain contexts, for example, in derivational constructions, as seen above. And this limitation is rich in implications for the determination of significant units.

The debate is obscured owing to the fact that the problem is stated too intuitively in a way that immunizes the principles from critical evaluation.

For instance, the identification of monemes is based on the commutation test (Martinet, 1985, §3.1). Empirically, one can object that *sincerity* and French *professeur* should each be considered as one moneme and not as a syntheme. Theoretically, it can be required that when a descriptive device is proposed, its field of application should be explicitly mentioned. In this case, if we base moneme identification on the commutation test, we will have to state precisely the conditions under which the test identifies synthemes rather than monemes.

The criterion for identifying synthemes seems to lie in the fact that they have, with regard to other monemes, the same syntactic behavior as a single moneme. Here again, the conception of syntheme is subject to criticism. Empirically, one can observe that a syntheme is by definition a sequence of monemes; its constitutive parts may contract syntactic relations with monemes outside (the syntheme), as is the case in *pre- and postoperative care,* French *a- ou immoral* 'amoral or immoral', or German *ein- und ausgehen* 'to go in and out'. Here, the coordination holds between prefixes and not between the syntheme as a whole and another moneme or sequence of monemes. The same holds for subordination: for instance, in German *Langstreckenläufer* 'long-distance runner', the component *lang* 'long' is a subordinate of another component (*Strecke*) and not of *Streckenläufer* as a whole.

Theoretically, from this definition of syntheme ensue different problems for description. When we carry out the syntactic analysis within the functional framework, the significant units (monemes and synthemes) are not available at the outset. The description is supposed to provide us with them. But the identification of synthemes implies that monemes have been previously identified. The problem is that the moneme is both the object we want to identify and a means of identification. Moreover, if identification is based on syntactic properties, then monemes and synthemes would be confused. Let it be said again that the commutation test has a certain relevance but is restricted in its application; this rules out any extreme choice either of abandoning the commutation test or of applying it too rigidly.

The partial relevance and limitation of the commutation test is, in my view, a hint that syntactic structure is too complex to be accounted for by a single analytic procedure. One should examine the dilemma seriously and search for new ways of analyzing synthemes.

Empirically, we can observe that the feature common to all synthemes as opposed to syntagms is the generality of the latter and the restrictedness of the former. As an example, I will take a few nouns and consider two bundles of combinatory features: modifiers on the one hand and derivational affixes on the other. The comparison seems suggestive.

The sporadic character of derivational combination is by no means an exception. Georges Mounin in his semantic study on domestic ani-

Table 3   The combination of verbs with modifiers and suffixes in French.

	infin- itive	past parti- ciple	pres- ent parti- ciple	pres- ent	simple past	imper- fect	future	pres- ent	imper- fect	present condi- tional	imper- ative
enseigner	+	+	+	+	+	+	+	+	+	+	+
aérer	+	+	+	+	+	+	+	+	+	+	+
blesser	+	+	+	+	+	+	+	+	+	+	+
espérer	+	+	+	+	+	+	+	+	+	+	+
glisser	+	+	+	+	+	+	+	+	+	+	+
balayer	+	+	+	+	+	+	+	+	+	+	+
habiter	+	+	+	+	+	+	+	+	+	+	+
boiter	+	+	+	+	+	+	+	+	+	+	+
apaiser	+	+	+	+	+	+	+	+	+	+	+
tirer	+	+	+	+	+	+	+	+	+	+	+

(a) + means that the combination is possible. (b) An empty box means that the combination is impossible or doubtful. (c) The information concerning the suffixes is taken from a dictionary (cf. *Le Petit Robert*, 1966). I have not made a survey as to what extent these combinations are acceptable or comprehensible. (d) Suffix combinations have been examined with regard to the syntactic class of the resulting syntheme as follows: V + *-ement* > N , V + *-age* > N, V + *-tion* > N, V + *-ure* > N, V + *-ance* > N. (e) To simplify the discussion, I was led to make some *ad hoc*

mals set up a table of terms obtained by derivation from animal names (Mounin, 1965a). All the columns and lines show up gaps in the pattern.

The strict regularity of the combination *V + modifier* and the sporadic combination of *V + suffix* is clearly shown in this table. This is what I mean by the opposition generality/restrictedness. And the problem seems to be the following: given the totally different behavior of these combinations, how can we best account for them, in accordance with the users' intuition and behavior?

-ement	-age	-ation	-ure	-ance	-ade	-eur	-able	-eux	-ant	-ailler
+										
	+	+					+			
			+					+		
			+							
+	+				+	+			+	
	+		+			+				
		+					+			
+								+		
+									+	
	+				+	+				+

decisions: for instance, I have taken no account of the adjectival uses of *enseignant* (e.g., *corps enseignant, personnel enseignant,* etc.) which are not general. If we take account of this, then *-ant* would get the productivity index 4. But this has no bearing on the issue raised. My concern here is to illustrate the way—that is, one of the ways—productivity can be measured, and not to give an accurate productivity measurement of the items considered.

(c) Toward empirical solutions

What empirical solutions to these problems could be envisaged?

In order to answer this question, I would like to pose a preliminary question: why didn't the research mentioned above succeed in adequately describing derivational phenomena? In my view, three factors are fundamental here. The first is the formal framework within which one is bound to divide the combinations into two discrete classes, syntagms and synthemes. And when one admits that between the two some intermediate phenomena are to be found,[21] these are considered mere nonsignificant exceptions. In other words, the theoretical framework resists the introduction of continua and gradients. This seems to be the reason Chomsky fails to suggest a choice between descriptive solutions. On the one hand he proposes applying transformational rules only to productive derivational processes, but on the other he states: "Perhaps one must regard the gap as accidental, at least in some such cases, and incorporate in the grammar overly general rules that allow for nonoccurring as well as actual cases" (Chomsky, 1965, p. 187).

Here Chomsky seems to be accommodating himself to the empirical inadequacy of the description so as to avoid the complexity of the grammar ensuing from specific rules. I won't insist on the obvious inconveniences of this solution, namely that the grammar will generate a great number of phantom derivates.

The second factor is that these studies have been carried out exclusively from an intrinsic point of view, so that the only criterion for the adequacy of the description is the describer's introspection.

And last but not least, derivational constructions are taken for granted and not identified by an appropriate analysis. If derivational constructions are productive (i.e., subject to general regularities), then why should they be separated from other moneme sequences? Respect for a grammatical tradition is surely not a sufficient reason. But if the analyst has intuitive reasons for saying that derivational constructions, at least in most cases, constitute a distinct category, this intuition should be made explicit and stated as a hypothesis so that a confrontation with empirical facts is possible and its adequacy appreciated.

For measuring the generality (the productivity) of a syntactic rule (the property), one can take as a criterion the size of the inventories to which a rule is applicable. The larger the inventory, the more extensive and, by implication, the more general the rule.

In the above table, one can see that the suffix *-aill(er)* is applicable to only one verb stem (*tir[er]*), whereas *-ement* is applicable to four verb stems. On this basis, these suffixes can be presented in order of decreasing productivity as follows.

Suffix	Productivity index
-ement, -age, -eur	4
-ant	3
-ation, -ure, -ade	2
-ance, -eux, -aill(er), -able	1

If one compares conjugational and derivational processes, the disparity is obvious. All the modifiers can be combined with all the verbal stems —that is, each modifier has an equal productivity index of ten.

It goes without saying that the inventories I examined here are by no means representative of verbs, modifiers, and suffixes. Larger inventories will show gaps in verb + modifier combinations: for instance, French *frire* 'to fry' is not combinable with the indicative imperfect. A sound examination of affixes will bring out some items more productive than those of the table above. For example, the prefix *re-* is very extensively combinable with verbs in French: *reglisser* 'to slip again', *rebalayer* 'to sweep again', and so on. However, there are verbs which do not usually enter into such a combination; for example, *aller* 'to go' (*raller*). Therefore, it is necessary to undertake a relatively thorough description. If the hypothesis of generality is correct, a complete description will demonstrate that lacunae are accidental in conjugations, but that, on the contrary, derivations present important gaps. Incidentally, such a conclusion, if empirically confirmed, means that the traditional distinction between word formation and flection, though expressed in intuitive terms, is justified.

When one examines combinatory phenomena from this point of view, one arrives at the conclusion that in some areas syntagms and synthemes have pretty similar (syntactic) properties. But in my view this is not by itself a problem; if the data are spread along a continuum, our task as linguists is to admit it and not force them into a dichotomy (like productive vs. nonproductive processes) or a trichotomy (like: productive/quasi-productive/nonproductive phenomena). Such classes can and must be either conceived of as hypothetical or obtained as the output of empirical research. At any rate, they remain subject to caution as long as their relevance for language behavior and intuition is not proved.

What is the significance of such a ranking? If one admits that the object of linguistic study is the intuition and behavior of the speaker-hearer, then this ranking should help us to understand them. Otherwise, however explicitly defined and strictly applied, the ranking may be based on nonrelevant features. Its significance cannot conceivably be admitted unless we admit at the same time that linguistic structure is multilayered and that the higher the level (or rank) of the language phenomena, the more precise the knowledge and the handling of these by the language users. This entails that, at the highest level, the users know of what parts a syntheme is made up and what the signifié of each constituent and of the whole is, whereas at the lowest level, the internal structure of synthemes is not usually perceived by the users and they are not aware of the signifié either of the constitutive parts or of the whole.

I know of no experimental research in this perspective. Yet scattered observations tend to support the hypothesis of the multilayered structure of synthemes with regard to linguistic intuition and behavior.

For instance, in French *accusation,* the suffix *-ation* and its signifié are easily grasped. But how about *accuse*? Normal hearers-speakers don't seem to be aware of its complex makeup: *ac + cuse.* One must have a certain knowledge of etymology or a certain curiosity to compare it with *excuse* and *recuse;* otherwise *accuse* is perceived as a simple moneme. The identification of French *-ig-* (in *exiger* 'require', *rédiger* 'to edit', *transiger* 'to compromise') and *-act-* (in *rédacteur* 'editor', *rédaction* 'edition') is still more far-fetched.

We have discussed here and there the idea that theoretical research and empirical research are the introduction and conclusion of each other. The identification of minimal significant units is a good example reminding us of the debate about articulation and commutation.

First, it should be noted that commutation is a logical entailment of language articulation; hence, it is not necessary to make of it a defining character of language as Hjelmslev does (cf. Hjelmslev, 1968b). If linguistic utterances are articulated into parts, these must be removable and replaceable to show the articulated structure; and this is commutation, as defined and practiced by European structural linguistics. Articulation cannot conceivably exist in a language without commutation. If commutation is presupposed by articulation, then a presentation of the commutation test and its relevance must begin with a discussion of the raison d'être and the limits of articulation.

I said above that if language is conceived of as a communication tool endowed with semiotic omnipotence (universality) and economy, it can only have an articulated (creative) structure. Therefore articulation is justified as long as it provides language with economy. If an articulated structure happens to involve an effort equal or superior to that of a global (non-articulated) structure, then the articulation tends to disappear, as it loses its *raison d'être*. As language evolution is not instantaneous, every synchronic state of language contains groups of phenomena situated somewhere between the two poles of articulated and global structures. Synthemes can be conceived of as intermediate phenomena of this sort, somewhere between the extremes. In this conception, precise models can be elaborated allowing a confrontation between hypothesis and data.

We must dwell a little longer on this aspect of the problem. We saw above that syntax—conceived of as the combination of monemes—is subject to certain restrictions. But these restrictions vary considerably from case to case. Degrees of generality/restriction can be deemed to be relevant. In order to verify this relevance one should make explicit hypotheses, such as: the more general a rule, the more evident its status in language behavior and intuition.

From this hypothesis it follows that if we establish on the one hand a hierarchy for a bundle of combinatory features based on their generality, and on the other a hierarchy based on their certainty in behavior and intuition, the two hierarchies should be correlated.

Let us take two groups of monemes:

Pronouns	Prefixes
je 'I'	*pré-* 'pre-'
tu 'you'	*re-* 're-'
il 'he'	*dé-* 'de-/dis-'
nous 'we'	*sur-* 'over-'

Both pronouns and prefixes are combinable with verbs, but not with the same generality. Take a few verbs like *faire* 'do, make', *nager* 'swim', *coudre* 'sew', and *dire* 'say, tell'. We can rank the pronouns and suffixes on the basis of their generality indices.

Monemes	Combinatory features	Generality	Rank
je,tu,	combinable with all four verbs		
il,nous		4	1
re-	combinable with all the four verbs: *refaire, recoudre, redire, renager*	4	1
dé-	combinable with three verbs: *défaire, découdre, dédire*	3	2
sur-	combinable with two verbs: *surfaire, surnager*	2	3
pré-	combinable with one verb: *prédire*	1	4

It is obvious that ranking must be based on combination with all the verbs (and not only a few, as in this illustration). If our hypothesis is correct and if our practical procedure for the calculation of the generality index is appropriate, then such a ranking must correlate with the ranking based on the observation of language behavior and the intuition. The higher the rank of the prefix, the higher the speaker-hearer's certainty in the use and understanding of its derivates, that is, the hierarchy based on generality allows us to predict to what extent the users are conscious of the internal structure of derivates. This provides us with an empirical method for determining what constructs are perceived by users as sequences made up of more than one significative unit.

It seems reasonable to put the lower limit for derivational processes at the point where all the language users (or almost all) think that a construct is made up of only one significative unit.

In this case, the ranking of combinatory rules is not gratuitous but constitutes a step in a sequence of operations aiming at clarifying the status of the derivation. If we adopt this view, then some facts construed as problematic will be quite normal. For instance: that rules are more or less general is an inherent property of language structure.

It is perhaps useful to point out some problems that arise from the ranking of derivational constructions. The distinction between two different affixes and two occurrences of the same affix is not always easy.

At one end, it is clear that *dé-* is the same moneme in *défaire* 'undo' (cf. *faire* 'do') and *découdre* 'unpick' (cf. *coudre* 'sew'). At the other end, it is clear that *démanger* 'to itch' is not made of the same prefix *dé-* and the verb *manger* 'eat' (semantic and syntactic arguments could be evoked for this). But in between, there are cases where it is difficult to decide: is *dé-* of *dédire* 'to gainsay' or *déchanter* 'to come down a peg or two' the same as that of *défaire* and *découdre*?

Above, generality has been examined out of context. If we examine it in the context of the sentence, we will obtain a more refined measurement of the generality index. We will find that the combination of verbs and modifiers also presents asymmetries. As an example, one could take the verbal syntagm *nous fassions* 'we do' (subjunct.) in a sentence like *elle attend que nous fassions ses bagages* 'she is waiting for us to pack her bags'. In colloquial French, the only possible commutation of modifiers is between present (*fassions*) and past (*ayons fait*), the subjunctive being obligatory here; that is, due to the context the whole paradigm of verb modifiers is reduced to two elements.

Likewise, a syntheme placed in the context of a sentence is subject to constraints: its combinatory features are submitted to new restrictions. In the same sentence, the prefix paradigm is reduced to two items: *dé-* (*défassions*) '(we) undo' (subjunct.) and *re-* (*refassions*) '(we) do again' (subjunct.).

So far, the contextual restrictions seem parallel for modifiers and prefixes. But a considerable difference separates the two processes. The rule restricting the modifier paradigm is valid whatever the verb or the object. The paradigm of modifiers remains almost the same even if we replace *faire* 'do' with *prendre* 'take', *porter* 'carry', and so on.

elle attend que nous	*fassions*	*ses bagages*
	ayons fait	
	prenions	
	ayons pris	
	portions	
	ayons porté	
	etc.	

It is the same for the object; whatever the lexical item that fills this function, the modifier paradigm does not change.

> *elle attend que nous* *fassions* *ses bagages*
> *ayons fait* *devoirs* 'do her home-
>   work'
> *prix* 'fix her prices'

It is quite different for prefixes; their paradigm varies according to the verb that is used to replace *faire*. Out of context, *prendre* can be combined with two of the four prefixes considered above: *re-* (*reprendre* 'take again') and *sur-* (*surprendre* 'to surprise').[22] Here only *re-* is possible.

> *elle attend que nous* *prenions* *ses bagages*
> *reprenions*

Similarly, out of context, *faire* can combine with three of the four prefixes; but in this context, only two can appear: *re-* (*refaire* 'do again') and *dé-* (*défaire* 'undo').

> *elle attend que nous* *fassions* *ses bagages*
> *refassions*
> *défassions*

The prefix paradigm also varies according to the noun used in the function "object." If we replace *bagages* with *prix,* the prefixes possible then will be *sur-* (*surfaire* 'overcharge') and *re-* (*refaire* 'do again').

> *elle attend que nous* *fassions* *ses prix*
> *refassions*
> *surfassions*

It appears that the influence of context on the modifier paradigm is general and valid for all members of the verb class, whereas the prefix paradigms vary in a given context with respect to verbal monemes; that is, the prefix paradigms are considerably more open to the influences of lexicosemantic factors. The examples above have been given in order to show the problems one faces when one tries to measure the generality of combinatory features; complex statistical tools and elaborate models are needed to make an appropriate generality measurement.

Other models can be set up for determining the lower limit of moneme sequences. I will now give an outline of a model, based on economy, for indirect experimentation.

It is known that the existence of classes and combinatory rules has as its advantage economy in the manipulating of language. But a rule is economical only if it can be applied to a group of elements. The greater the number of elements, the more economical the rule.

The invariability of paradigms (i.e., integration of rules) increases the economy of the system: if two rules R_1 and R_2 concern exactly the same group A, they are more economical than two rules R_3 and R_4 that each relate to a subgroup of A; for example, R_3 applies to elements A_1 and A_2 but not to A_3, whereas R_4 applies to elements A_2 and A_3 but not to A_1. If the number of exceptions increases and the number of elements in the group decreases, it entails a lowering in the economy provided by rules. Under certain conditions, the global manipulation of the combination of elements can also be economical, indeed more economical than the manipulation of the same combinations in terms of classes and rules (cf. Prieto, 1966).

An example[23] will illustrate this better. For the manipulation of complexes and elements, one can resort to two different procedures.

(i) A global procedure, which consists in treating each complex as a new unit.

(ii) articulation, that is to say, the analysis of complexes into elements, the setting up of classes of elements and combinatory rules (with their restrictions and exceptions).

Let us consider the binary combinations that can be obtained from three classes having

—class A comprising a_1, a_2, a_3;
—class B comprising b_1, b_2, b_3; and
—class C comprising c_1, c_2, c_3.

The question that should be asked is to what extent one or each of the two procedures (i) and (ii) is economical. It is supposed that the manipulation of a classifying or a combinatory rule involves the same effort as the manipulation of a combination (sequence).

(iii) Suppose that each element in a class can combine with each element in another class. This gives twenty-seven binary combinations. These combinations can be obtained from six rules, three of which list the elements contained in each group, the three others specifying that every a is combinable with every b, every a is combinable with every c, and every b is combinable with every c. (We suppose that the order of elements in the combination is not relevant and that every element has an independent existence outside the sequences considered here.)

Here we can see the economy that manipulation by the articulation of sequences presents: 6/27.

(iv) Now suppose that, other things being equal, the combination has the following exceptions:
$-a_3$ cannot be combined with any b;
$-a_2$ cannot be combined with any c;
$-b_1$ cannot be combined with any c.

With this, the number of rules increases to nine, whereas the number of combinations is reduced to eighteen. Here again, articulation offers an obvious economy: 9/18. But this is lower than in (iii).

(v) Finally, suppose that the following exceptions are added to the above nine rules:
$-a_2$ cannot be combined with b_1 or b_2;
$-a_1$ cannot be combined with c_2 or c_3; and
$-b_3$ cannot be combined with c_1 or c_3.

The combinations have been reduced to twelve, whereas the number of rules has reached twelve. It seems that under these conditions, for the manipulation (acquisition, memorization) of combinations, the global procedure is just as economical as recourse to articulation (i.e., classes and rules).

Cases where the global procedure would be more economical than the articulatory procedure can be easily imagined.

If we elaborate an appropriate method for measuring the economy of articulated structure, we can set a boundary between moneme and syntheme where the articulated structure ceases to be economical. Such a boundary is based on intrinsic criteria. We have to confront it with extrinsic data in order to evaluate its relevance: it is expected that where the economy provided by articulation drops abruptly, the consciousness and the handling of internal structures of sequences show an analogous decrease of certainty. It is at this point that the boundary moneme/sequence should be set.

As for the appropriate measuring method, I think that the only way of working it out is by trial and error.

I conclude this section with a retrospective look at this issue.

The idea of distinguishing two types of moneme sequences is ancient. In their practice, traditional grammarians separated word formation and flection, though a principled description of these was missing. The division of the task between grammar and lexicon is significant in this respect: flectional processes are the task of the grammarian, whereas derivational phenomena are part of the lexicographers' task. This division hints at an awareness—at least on a practical level—of a quantitative difference between these types. Moreover, for flectional constructions, the gaps were singled out by listing a few items (e.g., defective verbs), but for derivates, every individual construction is listed in the dictionary.

This means that, for example, verbs and modifiers can combine if not otherwise indicated. But the combination verbs + affixes is subject to much more restriction so that it is more economical to learn and handle each derivate individually.

More recently, Bloomfield drew attention to this disparity: he characterized inflection in contrast to word formation by its rigid parallelism (generality, in our terms). A sharp distinction was made between the two types both in traditional grammar and in Bloomfield's work. This can be construed as a contradiction: word formation and inflection are defined and distinguished formally on the one hand, while on the other quantitative criteria are evoked to separate them. One could criticize these theses for their formal/random contradiction. But it seems to me more interesting to try to find out whether this contradiction is not the manifestation, within a complex structure, of conflicting factors, factors that were not sufficiently known to allow a synthesis. If so, a contradiction might reveal a structure considerably more complex than we imagine at a given point in the development of a science.

V.5 Other Residual Problems in Syntax

The exhaustivity aimed at in the discussion above entails limitations with respect to both theories and problems. On the one hand the theories considered have been limited to functional linguistics and transformational generative grammar. While examining other theories such as tagmemics (Pike, 1967), stratificational grammar (Lamb, 1966; Lockwood, 1972) or systemic linguistics (Berry, 1975), I have arrived at similar results: once the problems due to the choice of terminology and expository procedures have been cleared up, these theories show the same concern for class, function, and unit, and the tenets of the debate about these are much the same. This cannot be discussed in detail within the present framework. On the other hand, the problems raised have been restricted to the identification of classes, functions, and minimal units.

In this section, I will broaden the scope with a brief discussion on the logical and semantic aspects of syntactic functions.

A syntactic function is generally defined on a double basis: logical implication and semantic properties. For instance, the subject is defined in functional syntax both as an obligatory dependant of a predicate and as a term that has a certain semantic relation with the predicate; that is, it refers to the agent of the action expressed by a verbal predicate, or perhaps also to the topic of a comment expressed by a copulative syntagm.

The first criterion is of an implicational nature and can be represented by $a \rightarrow b$ and $b \nrightarrow a$. The second is obviously semantic and is implied by the definition of the syntactic function as the linguistic counterpart of the relation between an element of experience with the experience as a whole. The two criteria seem to me necessary. If one drops the semantic criterion, then one is not able to distinguish the function of French *Jean* and *voilà* 'here is' in the following sentences:

> *Voilà le printemps*
> 'Here is spring'
> *Jean partirait cet après-midi pour Londres*
> 'John would leave for London this afternoon'.

Conversely, if we leave out logical implication, then we are led to attributing the same syntactic structure to almost any language. What differentiates French and Cambodian syntax is the fact that whereas in French the expression of the agent is obligatory, in Cambodian it can be left out (cf. Martini, 1968).

Likewise, the implicational aspect of the function is necessary to show clearly the differences between Russian and English syntactic structure (cf. Jakobson, 1959).

The same goes for TGG where the subject is conceived of as an obligatory constitutive part of the sentence by virtue of the axiom $P \rightarrow NP +$

VP, where NP is subject. On the other hand the subject is conceived of as agent.

This twofold definition is not operational unless implicational and semantic criteria are in concord. But this concord is not general, that is, the parallelism implication/semantics can be ruptured. Hence the problems that arise in determining the syntactic function of units in certain contexts.

On a theoretical level, we have no argument for excluding a conflict between the semantic and implicational properties of a syntactic function, and empirically, numerous examples could be cited from different languages showing such conflicting cases. Let us take the subject function in French. In a context like

Les enfants chantaient dans le jardin un air populaire
'The children were singing a popular song in the garden'

the subject is easily identified owing to the fact that implicational and semantic properties are on a par. But this is not always the case. In

J'entendais les enfants chanter dans le jardin un air populaire
'I heard the children singing a popular song in the garden'

the subject *les enfants* 'the children' has only its semantic feature "agent" to the exclusion of its implicational properties. Here it is not an obligatory constituent of the sentence; it can be omitted as can the other expansions *dans le jardin* 'in the garden' and *un air populaire* 'a popular song':

J'entendais chanter dans le jardin un air populaire;
J'entendais les enfants chanter dans le jardin;
J'entendais les enfants chanter un air populaire;
J'entendais chanter;
and so on.

In other contexts, the subject function may have its implicational character but lose its semantic feature. This is the case in utterances like *il pleut* 'it is raining', *il fait beau* 'the weather is fine', *il passe trop de voitures sous votre fenêtre* 'too many cars pass under your window', *il y a encore quelques contestataires à l'Université* 'there are still some protesters at the university'. Here, *il* is an obligatory constituent of the sentence, but it cannot be construed as agent in any definite sense. These examples give obvious cases of a rupture in the parallelism between implicational and semantic criteria. The description here is either problematic or *ad hoc*. Long discussions have been devoted to this problem (see, for instance, Li, 1976). Many linguists approach it as if the question were ill-formed and search for syntactic models that are supposed to solve analogous problems or avoid such false problems.

In order to resolve such descriptive problems, one should examine the relationship of implicational and semantic criteria which define syntactic functions and establish a hierarchy among them. One could, by hypothesis, attribute primacy to implicational criteria over semantic ones. Conversely, one could attribute a higher relevance to semantic features than to implicational ones. For both hypotheses, counterexamples can be given.

The examples given above to support the necessity of using semantic criteria for defining the subject can be considered counterexamples to the absolute primacy of implicational criteria over semantic ones. Similarly, the examples given to show the necessity of implicational features can be used as counterexamples to the absolute primacy of semantic features over implicational ones. I see no advantage in multiplying the examples unless we wish to examine the problem seriously from a statistical point of view. Instead, I will concentrate on the problems raised should one give primacy to the semantic features of syntactic functions.

The primacy of semantic features for identifying a syntactic function is not always clearly declared, yet many descriptive solutions are implicitly based on such a primacy. For instance, some linguists admit that *John,* in *John frightens easily,* is not subject but object, and that the subject in this sentence pattern is not expressed (cf. Chomsky, 1965, p. 221, n. 35); this amounts to recognizing the primacy of semantic features (in this case, the feature agent) for the identification of the function (here, subject). Similarly, the distinction made in traditional grammar between a real (or logical) subject and an apparent subject is based on the same admission—that what is important for the identity of the subject is the semantic feature of "agentivity," which allows French *voitures* to be considered as the real subject and *il* as an immaterial formal accident in *il passe trop de voitures sous sa fenêtre.* Such an implicit admission also allows verbs like French *pleuvoir* 'to rain', *neiger* 'to snow', and so on to be set apart and considered impersonal verbs, because their use in a sentence does not require the expression of a person as agent. Incidentally, the confusion of person with agent in traditional terminology is very significant, as we will see below.

The conception of phenomena does not change whatever the terminology used; real subject/apparent subject in traditional grammar, discontinuous signifiant in functional syntax, and subject raising in transformational grammar all refer to the same phenomenon. They are all descriptive devices used to show the prevalence of semantic features over formal ones.

This prevalence is likely to be justified in some cases, and the fact that for certain problems different theoretical frameworks lead to analogous results is a hint that this primacy may have a defensible basis.

But the primacy of semantic features is open to criticism for at least one reason: its indeterminacy on a descriptive level. If the identification of agent—as opposed to instrument, for instance—is easy in some cases, like *Jean a fabriqué sa flûte d'un morceau de roseau* 'John made his flute out of a piece of reed', it is not always obvious to which semantic aspects a syntactic function corresponds. Does the notion "agent" correspond to that of "human person"? This presumed correspondence is likely to be the principle on which the confusion of agent and person in traditional grammar is based. But strictly speaking, this would exclude from the subject function all nonhuman beings. Consequently, *Fido* could not qualify as agent (hence not as subject) in *Fido comprend une vingtaine de mots* 'Fido understands twenty or so words' nor in *Fido a détecté de la drogue dans l'une des valises* 'Fido detected drugs in one of the suitcases'. The inconvenience of such a solution is quite clear. It is the same in *l'ordinateur a calculé le coefficient de sécurité* 'the computer calculated the safety coefficient' or *le robot a effectué l'assemblage de toutes les pièces* 'the robot assembled all the pieces'. If computer and robot are considered instruments because they cannot decide what they do, consistency would require that those human agents who are not responsible for the decision should be analogously considered. Thus, there is no agent expression in *ce sont des femmes qui assurent l'assemblage des montres à quartz dans ces usines* 'women carry out the assembly of quartz watches in these factories'. In fact, it is highly improbable that the laborers on an assembly line take part in the decision. Without going into details, I want to remark that the subject cannot be conceived of as a simple concept; it is a complex phenomenon. It has on the one hand a set of implicational properties, and on the other, semantic properties. As each of these sets is complex, it is quite predictable that there will be indeterminacy as to the subject function of a moneme in certain contexts. It is possible that the indeterminacy comes from the shortcomings of our descriptive models, but the possibility that indeterminacies are inherent in language structure should not be excluded. In this case, users' behavior and intuition could help us to decide where indeterminacies appear and to what semantic or implicational factors they are due.

In this chapter, we have discussed the syntactic status of object and subject. The problems raised in this discussion are by no means limited to these two functions. It can be expected that the double aspect of other functional notions, in a thorough examination, will raise similar problems. This is the case for the predicate in functional syntax or, in TGG, for the near-equivalent notion of verb.

To conclude, I would like to emphasize that the double criterion for the definition of syntactic functions has consequences that should be clearly discussed. I think that logical and semantic criteria may be in conflict in certain cases and may therefore raise problems. These problems cannot be solved unless we determine precisely the conditions under which one criterion prevails over the other. This calls for explicit hypotheses and experimental research.

The complexity of the phenomena could easily be illustrated with examples from many other domains, such as the identity of the adjective class in French and its boundaries with the noun class on the one hand and with the adverb class on the other. The same goes for the subclasses of adverbs in French. I cannot tackle these problems here, but it seems to me that in all these cases perspectives of experimental solutions suggest themselves.

VI More about Semantics: Feasibility and Perspectives

VI.0 Synopsis

In spite of the diversity of viewpoints with respect to the structure of the signifié, there are points in common that can be taken as basic principles. There are also specific problems for which different solutions— let us call them models—have been proposed. I would like to emphasize that different models can coexist quite well within the framework of a general theory, given the complexity of a global system made up of subsystems governed by regularities that are of variable extent (depending on the class of units, the sections of the community, etc.). Finally, the dynamics and evolution of the signifié systems can be explained— at least in part—by the coexistence of mutually conflicting subsystems.

I will first give an overall view of lexical and grammatical semantics and compare them. My purpose is to show that the notions of *features, fields,* and *context* are all used in semantics and that, despite their interest, they present difficulties and limitations that should be clearly discussed in order to advance semantic studies. I support the thesis that the three notions are interdependent in lexicon and in grammar. But, owing to the specific character of grammatical units, the hierarchy necessary to account for the respective relevance of each of these concepts is different from that of lexical units.

I will finish the chapter with a discussion of a theoretical issue in order to highlight current semantic problems.

VI.1 The Semantic Jungle

The great diversity one encounters in studies on the signifié is very discouraging for the student or researcher. Even specialists often have the impression that different points of view are—if not diametrically opposed—at least irreducible to a global theory of the signifié and its structure.

First, there is the great diversity in terminology. Take, for instance, the designations that different research trends have given themselves: structural semantics, generative semantics, interpretative semantics, psychological semantics, componential semantics, instructional semantics, denotational semantics, noology, axiology, pragmatics, and many others are common labels in the specialized literature.

The theoretical principles these currents share are obscured not only by terminological differences but also by the fact that when any research work is presented, its originality is often emphasized to the detriment of points it has in common with other conceptions and studies of semantic phenomena. Access is made difficult by the diversity with respect to the central points of interest. A researcher might examine the signifié in a certain perspective (perception, for example) taking into account some part of the system (the subject and object functions) of a specific language (English) and collect his data according to a precise technique (survey), and so on. The results of this type of research are doubtless of interest for our understanding of the signifié system; but by wanting to generalize them in order to cover human language in its totality, one may fall into the trap of hasty extrapolation. Restricting oneself to microscopic studies has its own flaws, but in the other direction, one fails to come to grips with the global system formed by the elements of the signifié in the language under study.

My intention here is not to undertake a thorough analysis of works on semantics to illustrate this flaw, nor to acclaim the exceptions. I wish only to point out first the basic principles common to different theories of the signifié; next, to insist on the complementarity of descriptive models; and finally, to explain the dynamics and evolution of the signifié systems.

VI.2 The Object of the Study of the Signifié

Since the calming down of the antisemantic fervor of the 1930s through the 1950s, all linguistic currents have become interested in the issue of problems of meaning. The fact that an increasing number of linguists now direct their energy—at least part of it—to this issue shows that meaning is no longer considered a disorganized mass of ill-assorted items or as a group of facts in areas that are out of bounds to linguists.

The properties of the organization of meaning are generally described by means of the concepts of relevant feature (called also semantic feature or component), semantic field, and context. Below I will present these concepts and illustrate them with examples to show their necessity as well as their limitations.

(a) Relevant features

How can we account for the meaning of French *courir* 'to run' without resorting to such notions as 'way of moving', 'speed', and 'human activity'? Defining it in this way reduces its signifié to relevant features: the feature that characterizes *courir* as opposed to *marcher* 'to walk' is 'speed'; what distinguishes *courir* from another human function *crier* 'to shout', for example, is 'moving', and so on.

If the describer does not analyze a signifié into its features, he is restricted to stating that *courir* is globally different from *marcher, crier* 'to shout', *s'élancer* 'to spring', *bondir* 'to leap', and so on. Emphasizing this type of opposition, however indispensable it might be, gives only a partial account of semantic reality. Linguists who were satisfied with this were doubtless guided by a tactical choice;[24] this limitation seemed judicious at a certain point in their research. Yet the speaker-hearer who uses these elements is conscious not only of the difference between *marcher* and other terms but also of its positive properties which make an analysis in terms of features possible. This is so widely accepted that it can be stated as a principle.

> (i) Semantic phenomena can be reduced to their ultimate elements—that is, semantic relevant features; their combination produces the meaning of significant units or sequences of units.[25]

(b) Semantic fields

It is generally admitted that relevant features are revealed when one signifié is opposed to others. The problem is that, unlike distinctive units, linguistic signs are unlimited in number, and it is materially impossible to oppose them all in order to sift out the relevant features and set up classes (like orders and series) as is done for phonemes. Besides, it is very unlikely that the user makes such a comparison to understand a signifié. These comparisons are useful only within a restricted framework where the units under study have one or more semantic properties in common. From this comes the idea of semantic fields. In fact, opposing *courir* and *crier* is not very instructive: we are led to the conclusion that each term refers to a different event. At best, what we might find to be a characteristic common to both is that they designate any activity of men or animals. Opposing *marcher, bondir, aller* 'to go', *fuir* 'to run away', and so on reveals their relevant properties from a semantic point of view. This thesis can be stated as follows:

> (ii) Semantic fields: In order to circumscribe these relevant features precisely, the describer situates the unit to be described within a group of units that refer to the same field of experience (called semantic or notional field). This grouping makes it possible to reveal the way in which a particular language separates and organizes extralinguistic facts.

(c) The context

The French term *courir* can appear in various contexts, for example,

> *les gens courent à ce spectacle*
> 'This show is drawing the crowds' or
> *ce cheval ne court plus tellement vite*
> 'This horse doesn't run very fast any more'.

If our semantic analysis of *courir* is accurate, it must also account for these occurrences. In each of these cases, the relevant features attributed to *courir* must be modified. In *courir à ce spectacle,* the event reported is not exactly 'quick movement', as *courir* refers more to the eagerness of the people to go to the show.

Depending on the way we formulate the relevant feature 'speed' or specify the conditions of its realization, the semantic description of *courir* can be made in such a way as to cover the two variants: 'speed' and 'eagerness'.

Another example: the *Petit Robert* notes in its definition of *courir* that the body is supported on one leg or the other. This characterizes *courir* as an activity specific to man (or at least to bipeds). If this moneme is used to refer to a quadruped, it is understood that the weight is balanced alternatively not between two legs, but between four paws, hooves, and so on. The contribution of the context, recognized by almost all semantic currents, can be formulated in the following terms.

(iii) Context: the features brought out in this way do not have a unique and invariable expression in all the environments in which they appear; their realizations vary under the intluence of elements that are adjacent in the chain. In the same way, the situation in which a linguistic exchange takes place may exert an influence on the realization of relevant features.

We know quite well that not all semantic trends—in the presentation of their theoretical bases—admit all these theses and that a number of linguists challenge them. But we will see later (cf. VI.11–14) that these notions (relevant features, fields, context, and experience) are present everywhere, either disguised by the terminology used or in an otherwise implicit fashion.

VI.3 Limits of the Analysis
If we adhere to principles (i), (ii), and (iii), the analysis of the signifié comes up against limitations, but examining them could be instructive with respect to the nature of the object and suggestive as regards the method that should be applied.

(a) Relevant features
Relevant features are, as I believe I have shown, necessary for any semantic description; but they also create problems. Let us look again at the description in the *Petit Robert* which includes the features 'locomotion', 'speed', and 'with the legs'. Respecting this definition strictly leads to recognizing the incompatibility of *courir* with moving by car or by means of a nonhuman agent. This is the procedure that describers like Katz and Fodor followed when they considered some utterances anomalous. If we follow them, we should find a contradiction in the following utterances:

Ce cheval ne court plus tellement vite
'This horse doesn't run very fast any more'

> *Je prends ma voiture et je cours chez vous*
> 'I'll grab the car and run over to your place'.

The drawbacks of such a position are obvious: among others, instead of looking for the speaker's logic and conforming to it, the description creates its own logic and molds the structure of the language accordingly. It is better to recognize the instability of these semantic features (in this case 'with the legs') that are supposed to be relevant.

It is the same for other features of the moneme *courir*. If it is true that *courir* means 'to go quickly',[26] it would be contradictory to say *aller vite sans courir* 'to go quickly without running', although such uses seem quite normal in French.[27] That such uses are possible is due to the fact that, besides the instability of semantic features, *courir* is distinguished from *marcher* or *aller* by the feature 'speed' and also by other features such as the position of the arms, the movement of the legs, the bearing of the body, and so on. From this, moving on one's legs can be quick without necessarily being *courir*.

The last feature, locomotion, also disappears in certain uses of the term such as:

> *par les temps qui courent*
> 'nowadays', or
> *'L'intérêt de cette rente court à partir de tel jour'*
> 'The interest on this annuity accrues from a certain day onwards'.

From these remarks, I want to conclude that relevant semantic features—obligatory notions in any study of the signifié—have limits to their relevance that are difficult to grasp, and that semantic research, if it wants to progress, must take this into consideration.

(b) Semantic fields

Relevant features that appear as a result of confronting a signifié with others are on the whole dependent on what the describer chooses as the framework of comparison (or commutation). This framework, though, is not self-evident and can vary according to one's standpoint. The features contained in the definition of *courir* are not exempt from this; they result from the initial choice—indispensable but *a priori* arbitrary—which consists in regarding *courir* as basically a function of man or of

certain animals. In making this choice, many uses of the term that are
outside this framework are disregarded, such as:

> *Le chemin courait le long de la berge*
> 'The path ran alongside the bank', or
> *Le bateau courait au large*
> 'The boat stood out to sea'.

Many other examples could be given in which *courir* is used in relation with inanimate objects: *bruit* 'noise', *temps* 'time', *vent* 'wind', *eau*
'water', *nouvelle* 'news', and so on.

If the framework were conceived so as to cover these uses of the term,
the semantic features retained as relevant would be quite different. Insofar as time can run, the describer must compare *s'écouler* 'to pass',
couler 'to flow', *passer* 'to pass', and so on—in fact, all the verbs that
allow the moneme *temps* as subject. In the same way—and by virtue of
their possible combination with *bateau*—*faire route* 'to travel', *cingler*
'to sail (before the wind)', *filer* 'to make off', *voguer* 'to sail', and so on,
must be confronted with *courir* so that their common or differentiating
features can be elucidated.

By respecting this requirement, we are led to establish that *courir*
does not belong to just one semantic field but is simultaneously part of
several fields, each of which bestows semantic features.[28] The fact that
significative units belong to several semantic fields has been known for
quite some time,[29] so I will not go into greater detail. However, I would
like to insist on one point: delimiting a semantic field and determining the relevant features of the units of which it is composed are two
aspects of one and the same operation. Each semantic field is defined
by recourse to one or several relevant (or supposedly relevant) features.
Conversely, each semantic feature acquires its relevance in and by the
framework formed by the semantic field. The circularity is quite obvious. The problem is to discern whether and by what means one can
break out of this circle and the unmanageable effects that result from it.

(c) The context

It is obvious that the elements in contact in the chain are not impervi-
ous to one another's influence. Yet the context and its influence on the
units must still be explicitly formulated to allow for the confrontation of

hypothesis and empirical data (collected by means of a survey, corpus, or other techniques).

First, the context is a semantic context: what causes the realization of a signifié to be attracted toward a certain zone or to be repelled is its contact with other signifiés in the chain. As any signifié can be analyzed into features, the contextual attractions and propulsions can and must be formulated in terms of these features.

Next, the influence of the context is not a magical effect but is subject to regularities which a theory of the signifié must specify.

It is by trying to satisfy these requirements that the notions of relevant features and contextual variants have been of so much use in phonology. For example, in the preliminaries to a phonological analysis, one states that if /k/ is the only phoneme in the palatovelar zone, its realizations vary according to the vowel that follows: they are attracted to the front with a front vowel (/i/, for example), toward the back with a back vowel (like /u/), or toward the median zone with a central vowel (such as /a/).

In order to make the notion of contextual variant an explanatory concept which allows the functioning of the signifié to be understood, the vagueness of this notion must be removed in an analogous way. Is this possible, and if so, how? This is the fundamental problem created by the context. We attempted to follow this type of explicit approach (cf. VI.2[c]) for the semantic variants of the moneme *courir,* which could be presented as follows.[30]

Monemes	Relevant semantic features
courir 'run'	. . .
	'locomotion (animal)'
	'quick'
	'using one's (lower) limbs'
	. . .
enfant 'child'	. . .
	'biped'
	. . .
chien 'dog'	. . .
	'quadruped'
	. . .

This type of scheme is supposed to make explicit the contexts in which a certain variant (for example, "alternating weight of body on legs") is realized when the activity *courir* is attributed to an agent.

I will not insist here on the role of the situation in setting up a meaning, as the problems that it raises are more or less the same as those for the context. Instead of marking by linguistic means that the activity *courir* is attributed to a child, I could indicate it by extralinguistic facts (ostension, for example); the feature 'biped' is equally present in either case and has the same influence on its neighboring features.

VI.4 Interdependence of the Concepts: Features, Fields, and Context

In what precedes I have shown the indissoluble ties that link the concepts of relevant features, semantic fields, and contextual influences. Their interdependence is such, it seems to me, that they can and must be considered three facets of one and the same problem.[31] In fact, any decision taken with respect to one has consequences for the others. I have already shown this for the relation between relevant features and semantic fields. It is the same for the relation between relevant features and contextual variants.

Let us look at the following sentences:

> *l'enfant court*
> 'the child is running'
> *le petit chien court*
> 'the little dog is running'
> *je prends la voiture et je cours chez vous*
> 'I'll grab the car and run over to your place'

If *courir* is made up of two semantic features, 'movement' and 'speed', there is nothing surprising in its combining with an agent using two legs, four legs, or even four wheels.

However, when this signifié is considered to have the feature 'using limbs' as well, the combination of *courir* with *voiture* needs some comment. The way that the feature 'by means of limbs' becomes the feature 'by means of a vehicle' should be specified, whatever the descriptive solution adopted: neutralization, contextual variation, or something else.

Finally, by admitting that *courir* = 'movement' + 'speed' + 'by means of legs', the describer will have to propose a solution to the problem created by the combination 'run' + 'means: four legs' and the problem of the combination 'run' + 'means: vehicle'.

I have dwelt so long on these details in the description of the signifié because they have far-reaching consequences: the fact that the character of these concepts is not very explicit means that the descriptive solution does not follow in an obvious way from declared principles—which is the reason for the *ad hoc* nature of many semantic descriptions (cf. VI.11 below). It is also the reason for the contradictory arguments that two linguists, following their intuition or their favorable or negative predispositions, may present in the name of the same principles either to support or challenge a description.

If we want the study of the signifié to avoid this pitfall, our hypotheses about one aspect of the signifié (its constitutive features, for example) must be made clear and all inferences drawn for the others—in this case, semantic fields and contextual variations. This is what I will try to do in what follows.

VI.5   The Complexity of Semantic Phenomena and the Relevance Continuum

The position I have adopted with respect to the basic concepts of semantic structure—for example, the necessity of resorting to the concepts of fields and the difficulty in delimiting them—may seem paradoxical. This is due to the complexity of linguistic structures in general and semantic structure in particular: a fact may be relevant under some conditions but not under others. The adequacy of the descriptive model for the phenomena being described requires that this complexity be reflected in the picture that we give of semantic phenomena. I believe that the complexity of the structure has two consequences: the continuum of relevance and the relativity of the structure. I will dwell for a while on the first consequence. If we admit that the definitions in dictionaries in everyday use are of some value—and they certainly are—then we should examine the causes of this paradoxical situation: on the one hand, the definitions either have gaps, are contradictory, or both, and on the other, they are relatively valid. This is because the semantic features that make up the signifié of a moneme do not have exactly the same value but are hierarchized.

If a meaning feature is relevant in so far as it is part (or member) of the signifié of the moneme, this membership itself is a matter of degree; it can and must therefore be evaluated accurately. Reducing this hierarchy of meaning phenomena to a binary opposition is obviously an oversimplification. First of all, the facts that characterize the contents of a sign in an almost constant way (i.e., independently of the context, situation, sections of the language community, etc.) are confused with the facts that do so only incidentally. Also, the description is bound to make a choice between relevant and irrelevant, reducing the difference between the two extremes.

Thus the moneme *courir* can denote 'sporting competition' or 'speed trial' in certain contexts such as *ce cheval* (or *ce jockey*) *ne court plus* 'this horse (or this jockey) no longer competes'. But the feature 'competition' does not have the same value as the features 'movement', 'speed', or 'by means of legs'; it occupies a lower position in the hierarchy of features.[32]

Consider the next sentence:[33]

[wi: kɑ̃ti kɑ̃ti kɔmɑ̃sɛ a kuʁiʁ apʁɛ nu, bɑ: ʒɛm:ø təl diʁ æ̃, ɔ̃navɛ dɛ ʒɑ̃b]

oui quand i'(s) quand i'(s) commençai(en)t à courir après nous bah j'aime mieux te le dire hein, on avait des jambes
'yes when he(they) when he(they) started to run after us uh I tell you uh we scooted'.

A priori, nothing indicates that the feature 'competition' should be excluded or realized. However, its presence and absence are not equally probable. This sentence, in its phonic form, was presented to three groups of fifteen, twenty, and thirty-five students, and they were asked to give a paraphrase of its meaning. Without exception, the replies actualized the meaning 'pursue' for *courir*. Surveys showed afterwards that the meaning 'competition' was also possible. I have mentioned this empirical fact as an argument in favor of relativizing the structure of the signifié: by conceiving of the features of meaning as hierarchized we have the best chance of describing and explaining the behavior and intuition of the language user. These considerations can be formulated as follows.

(iv) Meaning phenomena cannot be subject to a binary selection which opposes relevant and nonrelevant but are part of a multiple graded hierarchy based on their independence of contextual, situational, mental, and social factors.

VI.6 Relativity of the Structure of the Signifié

The describer faces a more difficult task if he conceives of the structure as nonabsolute. In an absolute structure based on binary oppositions, a semantic feature is or is not retained as a characteristic of a signifié, depending on the judgment made of its relevance. It is quite different for a nonabsolute structure based on a continuum of relevance. Where should the boundary be placed between what results from the structure and what is external to it? To what degree of relevance must the features of meaning be included in a signifié? The solution to the problem depends on the purpose of the description: depending on the goal set for it—for example, the type of linguistic exchanges it should account for, the communicative situation, the sociogeographic origins of the interlocutors, the object of the communication, and so on—the description should retain or exclude a given feature.

The presence of each semantic feature adds accuracy but also implies a restriction of the signifié which limits its use. When *courir* is defined as 'to go quickly', we would expect that it would be possible to *run by plane* or *run by train* (without it implying 'sporting competition' or 'speed trial'). Yet these constructions are neither readily used nor accepted. As soon as one adds to the defining features of *courir* the role of legs, the description makes the abnormality or even impossibility of *courir en avion* or *courir en train* predictable. This addition, while solving one problem, creates another: how is a combination like *je prends la voiture et je cours chez vous* possible?

Any descriptive solution that is theoretically founded supposes a non–*ad hoc* reply to the problem raised by the choice of relevant features. Under the circumstances, the question can be asked: 'Must the definition of *courir* include a feature that specifies the role of legs in the movement?' An affirmative reply implies that one adopts a definition close to that in the *Petit Robert*. In the case of a negative reply, we would be opting for a definition close to that in the *Petit Larousse*. Each of these definitions has its advantages and disadvantages. The underspecified definition in the *Petit Larousse* has the advantage of predicting the possibility of utterances such as *à dix mois déjà, il courait partout à quatre pattes* 'already at ten months he was running everywhere on all fours', just as it gives us to understand that *courir* could refer to the movement of quadrupeds (a point in which the other definition is inadequate). The overspecified definition in the *Petit Robert* is interesting because by regarding *courir* as a particular form of locomotion, it excludes combinations like *courir en avion*.

The dilemma is to include in the definition of a signifié only the features of meaning that neither go too far by overdetermination (excess of precision) nor fall short due to underdetermination (lack of precision). A solution is possible only if one takes into account the use that the speaker-hearer makes of monemes and his intuition about this usage. This means that the description cannot retain the same meaning features as pertinent for all the varieties of a language. It must stop at the level of an approximate analysis when the object of the description is conversation intended to assure the needs of everyday life, whereas it must attain much more refined levels of analysis when it is treating uses that are made up of subtle nuances (poetic texts, puns, etc.). I'll summarize as follows.

> (v) The structure of the signifié is a nonabsolute structure whose boundaries cannot be determined without resorting to approximation.

VI.7   A Draft for a Detailed Analysis of the Signifié

I will now try to outline the semantic description of the moneme *courir,* accepting that the information provided by the *Petit Robert* is exact (i.e., that it conforms to what a rigorous survey would have given). Let us also accept that the presentation of the definition corresponds to the order of the features in the hierarchy. In this case, the semantic features listed in table 4 should be attributed to the contents of *courir*.

Each of the features mentioned in the table has a certain relevance; that is to say, each is functional in certain contexts. None of them has any absolute relevance, as I have already shown (cf. VI.3 and VI.6). Thus there is no reason inherent in the structure to make the boundary of the relevance pass on one point or the other—between twelve and thirteen, for example—rather than on another (as between eight and nine). The only reasons that justify a delimitation are external: the status of the facts concerned in the behavior and intuition of users, their frequency of use, their integration in the system, and so on. If there is one part of the

Table 4 *Courir* 'to run': semantic features and fields. (Based on the definition in the *Petit Robert*.)

No.	Semantic feature	Semantic field	Example	Remarks
1	movement	*aller* 'to go', *marcher* 'to walk'		features 1–11 are valid when the subject is animate
2	by jumps	*course* '(at a) run', *filer* 'to cut and run'		
3	by successive jumps	*galoper* 'to gallop', *trotter* 'to trot'		
4	means: legs	*bondir* 'to leap', *s'élancer* 'to spring'		features 1–5 are a block forming the 'normal meaning'
5	quickly	*calter* ' ', *se crapater* ' ', *cavaler* 'to run away', foncer 'to rush', pédaler 'to pedal', tracer 'to run out', trisser ' ', jouer des flûtes 'to show a clean pair of heels', prendre ses jambes à son cou 'to take one's heels', etc.*		
6	competition	*disputer une épreuve* 'to compete'		
7	eagerness	*se dépêcher* 'to hurry', *s'empresser* 'to show eagerness'		
8	violent hurry, haste	*se presser* 'to crowd', *se précipiter* 'to dash'		
9	to reach, attain		*je prends ma voiture et j'y cours* 'I'll take the car and pop over'	
10	to flock to, to be attracted		*les gens courent à ce spectacle* 'people are flocking to this show'	
11	to try without attaining		*tu peux toujours courir* 'you've got another think coming'	
12	to be widespread, to spread	*circuler* 'to circulate', *se propager* 'to spread'	*le bruit court que...* 'it is rumoured that...'	features 12–15 are valid only if the subject is inanimate
13	to pass	*suivre son cours* 'to run its course', *se passer* 'to elapse', *continuer* 'to continue' *passer* 'to pass'	*par les temps qui courent...* 'nowadays...' *le mois qui court* 'this month'	
14	to evolve	*se développer* 'to develop'	*laisser courir (une affaire)* 'to let business develop'	
15	to stretch	*se prolonger* 'to continue, to extend'	*le chemin court le long de la berge* 'the path follows the bank'	

language community that does not know or hardly uses the phenomena at levels nine to fifteen, a description supposed to reflect this use must be stopped at level eight. However, all the features listed up to level thirteen must—if they are all mastered by another part of the community—be retained when one comes to describing the linguistic usage of this group. Such a hierarchized description allows not only the use of different parts of the community to be accounted for but also what happens when speakers from different social classes or geographic regions are in contact. The structure of the signifié thus becomes the image of a process whose conflicting tendencies and dynamics are brought to light clearly by the description.

VI.8 Hierarchy of Fields and Concepts

What are the implications of this conception of relevant semantic features and relevance for semantic fields and contextual variations? It appears that when the analysis of a moneme into features is stopped at a certain level, concurrently, the adherence of a moneme is limited to certain semantic fields. In other words, a given level of approximation excludes at the same time certain features and semantic fields. For example, if the analysis is stopped at feature twelve (inclusive), the features *s'écouler* 'to pass', *évoluer* 'to evolve', and *s'étendre* 'to stretch' are disregarded; at the same time, this choice excludes all the monemes belonging to the same field as *s'écouler* (*suivre son cours* 'to run its course'), *évoluer* (*se développer* 'to develop'), and *s'étendre* (*se prolonger* 'to extend').

This exclusion does not mean that we deny their existence or relevance, however weak it might be; it simply means that at this level, these facts are either not taken into account or are not subject to regularities of a certain generality. Let us consider feature thirteen: its exclusion from the description of a usage implies that in this use, *courir* is not used for temporal sequence. This is the same as saying that constructions of the type temporal nouns + *courir* are not known in this use and that if there are some—like *par les temps qui courent*—they are very limited and are thus fixed (i.e., learnt and used as intangible wholes).

As for the context, it is also made up of semantic features which are not insensitive to the influence of co-occurring elements. Any context is both the source and target of influences; contextual variations are thus types of interactions. The description of the signifié cannot be restricted to an isolated element or a single field; to make contextual variations an explicit and controllable concept, it must be extended to co-occurring monemes and their fields. In this way, the variations to which a moneme is subject or that it causes when it collocates with another can be presented. That is to say, the adequacy of the description of the signifié in terms of relevant features can be evaluated by resorting to its ability to predict the rules—at least the most general ones—of contextual variations. This requires that a single scale be set up to measure the hierarchy of semantic features that can be attributed to different units. One can easily imagine the difficulties that one meets on this path.

Meanwhile, one is reduced to working on detailed problems which are rich in information if one keeps the global perspective in sight.

VI.9 Function and Structure

In order to illustrate the hierarchy, we used defining features taken from a dictionary, making it clear that this borrowing is not the equivalent of a theoretical confirmation. A good dictionary entry can only be—in the present state of things—a summary of semantic features, the contexts in which they appear, and the fields to which they belong. The lexicographer certainly attempts some kind of selection, but whatever his competence, this selection cannot take into account how socially widespread the facts listed are or their status in the intuition of the users.

Yet the reality of the phenomena of a language results from their social and mental status. This is a consequence of the communicative function, which is recognized as the main function of language. If communication implies the transmission of information, any fact endowed with communicative relevance necessarily has a social character. If the information that is transmitted must be done so intentionally for it to be a communicative act, this implies that relevant facts have a mental character. The hierarchy is supposed to reflect the more or less solid foundation of the facts of language—and moreover of semantic facts in the psyche of the user, as well as their greater or lesser extent across the collectivity.

If a hierarchy of features—for example, the one presented in V.7 [34]— is set up, it makes it possible to predict the behavior of the user when he is confronted with semantic phenomena. Semantic features high up on the scale should correspond to the most "normal" uses in which users recognize, without difficulty, the possibility of combinations and their corresponding meanings. At the other extreme, the recognition of combinations and their meanings gives rise to hesitation and dissension.[35] Thus reflection on semantics opens the way to experimentation. Because after all, a proposed structure is a linguist's hypothesis; it must be submitted to verification. This is the path that phonology followed.

The interest of experimental research does not lie solely in the fact that it allows the adequacy of the hypotheses with respect to the data to be evaluated. It can also shed new light on the object of the study. If we wish to carry out a scientific study of the signifié, one of the problems is how to get access to the facts, as nothing justifies our being satisfied with the data in dictionaries; the observation of the speaker-hearer's behavior and intuition is indispensable. But what type of data should be observed? Spontaneous linguistic material (like a corpus), or productions created for the needs of the study (as in a survey)? When one resorts to a survey, should the starting point be the form (signifiant) in order to arrive at the meaning (signifié) or vice versa? When an informant is asked to state precisely the meaning of a linguistic form, should the investigator (e.g., interviewer) orient him by offering a choice (a directing questionnaire) or not? Should the meaning be presented by recourse to the referent (ostension, staging, etc.) or by linguistic means (paraphrase)? These problems are far from being solved; some of the "isms" and "ologies" are characterized by their choice in techniques for accessing data.[36]

It seems to me that the various techniques are not mutually exclusive, first because they are not all applicable with equal ease to all domains (how can 'mental cruelty' or 'weightlessness' be indicated by ostension?) and then due to their complementarity: as the user is by turns speaker and hearer, it is also relevant to go—in a survey—from meaning to form (which the speaker does) and from form to meaning (as does the hearer). Strictly speaking, a comprehensive survey must make use of all techniques, or at least those whose application to the domain under study does not cause any major practical problems.

To illustrate the complementarity of techniques, let us look at an example we have used elsewhere:

[wi: kãti kãti kɔmãsɛ a kuʁiʁ apʁɛ nu, ba: ʒɛm:ø təl diʁ æ̃, õnavɛ dɛ ʒãb]

During a survey—see § V.5—almost all the people consulted attributed the following semantic features to *i'(s) commençai(en)t à courir après nous* 'he (they) started to run after us': subject: 'human' and 'singular'; *courir après* 'with the aim of catching up with us'. Questioned, the same people acknowledged that the subject of *courir* could also be an animal, that 'plural' was also possible, and that the meaning 'competition' could not be excluded. If the regularity of such reactions was to be confirmed by other observations, that would mean, among other things, that the primacy of the "proper meaning" of *courir* over the meaning 'competition' is a linguistic reality revealed by the behavior of the speaker-hearer. In a more general way, if the distinction between proper meaning and metaphorical meaning is founded, if it corresponds to something in the intuitions and behavior of the user, then it is by resorting to analogous procedures that this can be brought out and the various aspects of it clarified.

VI.10   Grammatical Semantics
Above, the problems of semantic analysis have been illustrated by an example drawn from lexical monemes. *A priori,* it is not obvious that the grammatical domain shows similar problems and calls for similar solutions. The following examples are given in order to demonstrate the similarities and differences between the lexical and grammatical domains.

It should be noted that lexical semantics and grammatical semantics have developed independently. Generally, each has been conceived of as having its specific characteristics that the other presumably does not share. Moreover, lexical and grammatical semantics were not of equal interest to the different linguistic currents.[37] Therefore, any attempt to compare these domains needs a clarification of the debate and an interpretation of the terminology.

In the following sections, I will first give an overall view of grammatical semantics and compare it with lexical semantics. I will finish the chapter with a discussion of a theoretical issue in order to highlight current semantic problems.

My purpose is to show that the notions of feature, field, and context are all used in grammatical semantics as well, and despite their interest, they present inconveniences and limitations that should be clearly discussed in order to advance semantic studies. I support the view that the three notions are interdependent in grammar just as they are in the lexicon. But, owing to the specific character of grammatical units, the hierarchy necessary to account for the respective relevance of each of these concepts is different from that of lexical units.

VI.11 Relevant Semantic Features in Grammar

The first problem to address concerns the status of relevant semantic features within grammar. It is astonishing that in many linguistic currents no sound discussion has been devoted to this problem; yet, reading between the lines, semantic features are present in the debates and controversies on grammatical structure and description, especially when discussing the limit between syntax and semantics.

Generally—but not exclusively—syntax is considered an independent part of language structure,[38] and its description is supposed not to be based on semantic data. Therefore, no question is put as to the status of semantic features. However, one can observe that the more refined the grammatical analysis, the closer we get to semantic phenomena. At a certain level of refinement, the analyst is inevitably led to asking questions about grammatical units and their variants; here the problem has an undoubtedly semantic aspect. Jakobson's study of the Russian case system (Jakobson, 1936 and 1984) is a typical example of this: the issue raised is to determine how many different units the Russian case system contains. Jakobson examines the different meanings of a case and tries to reduce them to a common semantic feature that he considers to be its general meaning (*Gesamtbedeutung*).[39] For instance, the meanings manifested by different uses of the instrumental—for example, 'condition' (*Bedingung*), 'restriction' (*Einschränkung*), and 'role' (*Betätigung*)—are subsumed under the general meaning of 'peripheral status' (*Randstellung*).[40] Whatever the foundations of such an operation, the identification of a case as a linguistic sign is based on semantic considerations: each case is attributed a global meaning that can presumably be realized differently, depending on the context. As one can see, the global meaning corresponds to what we have called a relevant semantic feature, and its realizations could be assimilated to its semantic variants. Thus, 'peripheral position' is the relevant feature (sememe[41]) of the Russian instrumental, and 'condition', 'limitation', and 'activity' are its variants (allosemes). This example shows how a syntactic description slips gradually toward a semantic analysis and incorporates it, at least in part. This observation seems valid for many schools and researchers in linguistics: all those who carry out a syntactic analysis before finishing a semantic one find themselves at the top of this slippery slope and inevitably have to deal with the semantic properties of the units under study.

The reason for this lies in the relation between syntax and semantics: if syntax operates with significant units, then it cannot be purely formal (i.e., dealing with signifiant only); both signifiant and signifié are integral parts of the object of syntax. In clear cases, no semantic discussion is needed: everyone would admit without argument that *racoon, sodium,* and *judge* are three distinct monemes. But the absence of argument does not mean that semantic considerations are absent from syntax. The presence of semantic factors in syntax is evident in those parts of the syntactic system where the distinction between significative units (monemes or functions) is delicate.

Let us take the French syntagm *donnerions* '(we) would give'. Apart from the lexeme *donn-* 'give' and the 'first person plural', how many other monemes are there in this sequence? On the level of the signifiant, we could consider that -*r*- represents the 'future' (cf. *donnerons* '[we] will give') and -*i*- the 'imperfect' (cf. *donnions* '[we] were giving'). This segmentation is not valid unless we can show that the signifié of *donnerions* is the sum of the signifié of the 'future' + the signifié of the 'imperfect'.

Another example: how can we characterize French *belle-fille* 'daughter-in-law/stepdaughter' as a syntheme and distinguish it from the syntagm *belle fille* 'beautiful girl'? As Martinet says (1960, §4.35.), the semantic unity of the former is the most characteristic property of a syntheme. But, given the difficulties in observing this, he proposes basing the distinction syntheme/syntagm on syntactic criteria. Here, Martinet chooses to rely on syntax because the semantic phenomena are construed to be beyond our observation. (Incidentally, if the myth of the inaccessibility of semantics falls, there is no reason then to raise, by hook or by crook, morphosyntactic phenomena to the only distinction criterion.) Likewise, Chomsky calls upon semantic criteria to reveal the difference in the syntactic relations between the constituents of the following two pairs of sentences.

I expected a specialist to examine John
I expected John to be examined by a specialist
I persuaded a specialist to examine John
I persuaded John to be examined by a specialist

He argues that in the first pair, the sentences are "cognitively synony-mous," whereas in the second, this is not the case (cf. Chomsky, 1965, p. 22). Here the semantic criteria are given overtly. Often, complex transformation devices are used to show such differences. Thus, trans-formational arguments are presented to show the differences in the syn-tactic relations in the famous sentences *John is easy to please* and *John is eager to please.* Nonetheless, the distinction criterion is of a semantic nature, though the dogma of the independence of syntax forbids any mention of semantic factors.

That analysts generally slide from syntax to semantics does not neces-sarily imply a criticism. I have invoked this observation to demonstrate that even if a linguistic description does not include a special chapter on meaning, semantic considerations are not necessarily absent. Because in a refined description of syntactic structures utilization of meaning criteria is indispensable, we should search there for the actual seman-tic analysis of grammatical monemes. From the following examples, we can see that such a description consists of assigning one or several semantic features to a significant unit and of enumerating or circum-scribing their variants. Let us take again Jakobson's study of Russian cases. He considers that the instrumental of 'stipulation' can express:

—"the source of the action [*Handlungsquelle*]," for example, *ubit vragami* 'slaughtered by the enemy',
—"the driving motive [*Triebkraft*]," for example, *uvlec'sja sportom* 'to be carried away by sport',
—"the implement [*Werkzeug*]," for example, *zat' serpom* 'to reap with a sickle',
—"the mode [*Modus*]" for example, *idti vojnoj* 'to go to war',
—"the space through which the motion occurred [*Bewegungs-raum*]," for example, *idti lesom* 'to go through the forest', and
—"the time of the action [*Zeit der Handlung*]," for example, *putese-stvovat' noc'ju* 'to travel at night' (Jakobson, 1984, p.79).

Another example can be found in Martinet's article on ergative construction; he assigns the same syntactic function to the roles played in Basque by *haurra* 'the child' and *untzia* 'the vase' in sentences like

> *haurra*   *gizonar-i*   *mintzatu-da*
> '(lit.) the child   the man-to   has talked'
>   'the child has talked to the man'

and

> *aita-k*   *untzia*   *aurdiki-du*
> '(lit.) the father-by   the vase   has thrown'
>   'the father has thrown the vase'.

As can be noted in these sentences, neither *untzia* 'vase' nor *haurra* 'child' has a function marker (inflectional suffix, in Basque). The identification of these as the same significant unit is not based on the mere resemblance of their signifiants; it supposes that the two meanings ('actor' and 'goal') have a close enough semantic kinship to be variants of the same unit. This semantic vicinity can be illustrated with nominal syntagms from many other languages: for instance, *enemy* can be either actor or goal of *the fear*, whereas *reaction* can only be the goal:

> *fear of the enemy*
> *fear of his reaction.*

Following Martinet's suggestion, we could translate using nominal constructions that correspond to these sentences:

> *haurra gizonar-i mintzatu-da*
> 'the talking of the child to the man' and
> *aita-k untzia aurdiki-du*
> 'the throwing of the vase by the father';

the functional identity of 'child' and of 'vase' becomes clearer as a result.

In some cases, the semantic aspect of the syntactic description aims at proving the semantic unity of a significant unit. This is the case in most currents of transformational grammar. As an example, one could cite Chomsky's endeavor to assimilate syntactic ('subject') and semantic ('agent') phenomena. From a methodological point of view, the procedure adopted by Jakobson, Martinet, and Chomsky is the same: at a certain level of analysis, the describer judges it necessary to complete the syntactic description with recourse to semantic considerations.

Note that for the same problems two diametrically opposed solutions can be adopted: Chomsky believes that there are two different syntactic functions in *fear of the enemy* (confused only in the surface structure), whereas Martinet takes for granted the unity of syntactic function. These differing standpoints show the bearing of semantic theory on syntactic description.

Explicit theses on the semantic features of grammatical units are more recent and less widespread. In American linguistics, all the nonstandard theories derived from TGG are concerned with the semantic aspects of syntactic structures. Their point of departure is a series of meanings, say 'agent', 'patient' and so on (in case of grammar, for example). The description should show the way these are rendered in the surface structure. For instance, 'agent' and 'patient' may receive the same expression in given conditions (e.g., ergative construction). I will not dwell further on this matter.

As for European linguistics, my first example will be the approach proposed by Luis J. Prieto (cf. Prieto, 1964). For him, the signifié of a linguistic sign is all that it can convey independent of circumstances: linguistic context and extralinguistic situation. The procedure he proposes consists of placing the same sign in the whole range of possible circumstances. Once the varying aspects of the meaning have been put aside, what remains is the semantic purport of the sign—its signifié. Prieto's effort is oriented toward the separation of the constitutive features of the signifié on the one hand, and, on the other, the contribution of context and situation. He does not go into detail, and there is to my knowledge no application of his theory to a sufficiently extensive corpus. The examples given in his 130-page booklet are elementary and cannot be construed as illustrative of the efficiency of his method.

As the next example, I cite Martinet's *axiology* (the study of the values of signifiés) applied to French (cf. Martinet et al., 1979).[42] In this work the study of meaning follows on a syntactic description; once identified and classified, the significant units are submitted to an axiological examination. Theoretically it should be based on the opposition between the monemes within a language; it is supposed to reveal the extent to which different monemes participate in the constitution of the meaning of an utterance (Martinet et al., §1.33). Practically, this amounts to giving for each moneme its value on the level of the signifié and possibly its salient variants. For instance, the instrumental function is characterized as the one implying the use of an object or a person. Thus in *il écrit avec ta plume* 'he is writing with your pen', *avec* is the expression of the instrumental. This function can also be expressed by *de* (as in *l'arbre rafraîchissait de son ombre la petite place* 'the tree made the little square cool by its shade'). In certain contexts, this function can be expressed equally by *en* or *par* : *il paye en petites coupures* or *il paye par petites coupures* 'he pays in/by small denominations'.

One should remark that, beside its instrumental value, *avec* has other values; it can be the expression of modal function (*il répond avec calme* 'he answers calmly') as well as of comitative function: *Il voyage avec ses valises* 'He travels with his suitcases' and *Il est sorti avec ses amis* 'He went out with his friends'. In the same way, *par* can express several other functions, such as 'agentive', 'distributive', and 'translative'. Certain functions such as 'subject' and 'object' are said to have no proper axiological value, their value depending on that of the verb and the lexemes appearing in these functions. Many other works could be mentioned in this respect, for instance, Ebeling, 1978.

We have just established that a syntactical description generally calls on semantic criteria. Such a recourse is not in itself open to criticism, given the connections between syntax and semantics. On the other hand, it is the *ad hoc* nature of the semantic elements referred to in the field of syntax which is to be criticized. Indeed, the syntactical description in the three examples we have just seen takes for granted the following implicit principles:

(i) The element 'instrumental' can be realized through the following variants: 'stipulation', 'restriction', and 'role' (Jakobson).

(ii) 'Stipulation' can be realized through the following variants: 'source of the action', 'motive', 'implement', 'mode', 'the space through which the motion occurred', and 'the time of the action' (Jakobson).

(iii) 'Actor' and 'goal' can be semantic variants of one and the same grammatical signifié (Martinet).

(iv) 'Actor' (John pleasing someone) and 'beneficiary' (something or someone pleasing John) cannot be semantic variants of one and the same grammatical signifié (Chomsky).

For a recourse to semantic phenomena to be theoretically justified, certain conditions must be fulfilled:[43] among others, such a recourse must be based on general explicit principles—independent from the structure of any particular language—presenting:

(i) the inventory of the semantic elements,
(ii) the semantic relationship of these elements,
(iii) the possible semantic realizations of a signifié, and
(iv) the conditions of realization for a semantic feature as variant of a signifié.

I am convinced that such principles will be of invaluable use if explicitly stated and even if provisional. Even if they do not make it possible to unify the semantic analysis of differing languages, these principles will at least stand a chance of advancing the areas in which a theoretically based study of language phenomena becomes problematic, as opposed to the domains in which this kind of study is successful. This will be a good occasion to reexamine the classical problem of what experience phenomena (semantic substance) can be structured and to what degree.[44]

VI.12   Semantic Fields in Grammar?
The concept of semantic (or notional) fields has been introduced and used exclusively with respect to the lexicon. Is it completely devoid of interest in grammar?

To answer this question, I think one should recall the *raison d'être* of this concept. Notional fields present interest for semantic studies from two points of view: (i) closure: a significant unit is integrated in a group, within which its semantic features can be extracted by the oppositions it holds with the other units. Such a characterization is not possible unless the group is closed (or limited); and (ii) the basis of comparison: the group in which a unit is integrated has some semantic features common to all of its members. This constitutes a basis for comparing the units and extracting their specific features.

The groups of grammatical monemes—be they called classes, categories or something else—generally used for semantic descriptions fulfill both conditions. It is generally admitted (often explicitly) that grammatical units constitute closed inventories (that is, they are limited or finite in number). Thus, lexical and grammatical monemes share the first characteristic: the group closure. As for the second, there is obviously no point in comparing units which do not possess common properties.

If it is possible to discover all or part of the semantic features of the grammatical units within a class, it is because they share certain semantic properties; their common feature is not only their membership in the same class.

Empirically, numerous examples would show that such common features are actually taken into account. Let us take the noun modifiers in French. Martinet groups these on the basis of their semantic features into two classes: definites (*le* 'the', *ce* 'this', and *mon* 'my') and indefinites (*un* 'a, one', *chaque* 'every, each', *tout* 'each, every', *aucun* 'any', *plusieurs* 'many', *nul* 'any, no', and *tel* 'such').

As for syntactic functions, Martinet uses in this work a closed series of items; but unlike modifiers, these do not seem to have any common basis on the semantic level (cf. Martinet et al., §4.26.c). For instance, he considers that there is no semantic value common to the different functions that he classes together under indirect functions. As for generative grammar, the notional field does not seem to be used explicitly or implicitly (at least in the standard theory, extended or not) for the study of grammatical semantics. In other currents, such as case grammar and generative semantics, the concepts of semantic field occupies a prominent place: the totality of syntactic functions is reduced to a limited number of items (six in Fillmore, 1968), and a semantic value is attributed to each case. Thus both conditions—closure and the basis of comparison—are respected.

VI.13 Context in Grammar

One of the most general features of studies on grammatical semantics is the admission that context has a role to play in the constitution and the conveying of meaning. Descriptive devices and analytic procedures are more or less based on the relevance of the context: the commutation test aims at ruling out all the semantic effects that the context has on the proper meaning of the unit(s) under study. A distributional analysis— whether it is mainly oriented toward the signifiant, as in Harris's work (cf. Harris, 1954), or toward the signifié, as suggested by Jakobson (cf. Jakobson, 1959; also Bendix, 1966)—has its foundation in the idea that the context provides sufficient information to describe the meaning (at least in its linguistic aspect).

Semantic context is also used in syntactic analysis. For instance, the distinction between an accusative construction and an ergative construction is based on the assumption that there are verbs expressing an action for which two participants—an agent and a patient—can be envisaged. (According to whether the one or the other is marked, the construction is called ergative or accusative.) These assumptions are of a semantic nature.

In transformational grammar, too, the context is used: the transformational operation itself is a recourse to context in order to bring out those semantic differences that the surface structure does not show. The use of semantic context in generative semantics is self-evident.

On a theoretical level, sound positions on the significance and limits of the context are rare. However, Prieto's work in this respect deserves to be discussed (cf. Prieto, 1964).

At the outset, Prieto observes that the goal of a communicative act is to convey a concrete meaning. If A says to B: *you've bought the book; may I have a look at it?*, what he wants to see is this particular book and not just any book. Here the linguistic context helps to actualize a given individual from among the class of objects named books. That the speaker wishes to look at this book *hic et nunc* may be understood from the extralinguistic situation—for instance, if A is there at the moment B buys the book. In this case, an utterance like *may I have a look at it?* would suffice to actualize the same concrete meaning. It is easy to imagine other circumstances—for instance, if B has bought several books—where A would have to specify in more detail (by mentioning the size, color, author, etc.) to establish the same concrete meaning. As one can see from the above example, the relevant circumstances are the set of facts that the hearer knows at the moment of the speech act but independent of this, hence, the circumstances cannot be confused with physical events. Here we arrive at a crucial point: the information received by a hearer is partly conveyed by the utterance and partly by the actual circumstances of the speech act. Languages, in contrast to other semiotic systems, have this salient property: they allow the speaker to express, by means of language units, certain parts of the information which is to be conveyed and thus leave the hearer to find other parts of the information by reference to the circumstances of the speech act. The first type of information is the signifié inherent to the linguistic sign(s) used; the latter is not.

Prieto's endeavor is to propose explicit procedures for distinguishing between the information contained in linguistic signs and that inferred by the knowledge of the circumstances of the speech act. The procedures can be summarized as follows: from among the circumstances, some have an effect on the actualization of the speaker's intended meaning, others do not. In order to bring out the relevant semantic features of an utterance, one should realize it in all possible circumstances and retain the bundle of semantic features common to all these realizations. By virtue of its independence from the factors outside the utterance, it has to be considered the meaning inherent to the utterance; this will be the signifié of that sign. If we follow this procedure in our example, we will find that the word *book* might refer to objects of different sizes, colors, covers, and so on; but none of these features is part of the meaning inherent to it.[45]

VI.14 Problems Raised by Grammatical Semantics

Above, I tried to show that syntactic descriptions comprise—explicitly or implicitly—partial semantic analyses, and that the aim of such analyses is to split global meanings into their constitutive parts (their relevant semantic features). The determination of relevant semantic features is made by means of clues provided by the semantic context, and at the same time by comparing a limited number of significant units generally endowed with a common semantic basis.

Thus, we find the three concepts (feature, field and context) currently used in lexical semantics. I think that—as I have shown above, cf. VI.4 —these concepts are interdependent. Besides, their application shows limitations that should be examined seriously in order to appreciate their adequacy. Moreover, this critical survey might point the way to setting up a more appropriate model of analysis for meaning phenomena. It might also provide hints as to the differences between lexicon and grammar from a semantic point of view.

Before entering into this discussion, I would like to emphasize one of the drawbacks that can occur when partial semantic analyses are integrated in syntax: its *ad hoc* character. I take it for granted that reliance on some semantic evidence is necessary when we tackle syntax. Such semantic data must either be very elementary, hence self-evident, or conceived of as provisional and evaluated on the basis of the results that can be obtained. But this is not the way semantic clues are generally used in syntactic analyses: they are construed as being decisive for the resolution of syntactic problems.

As an example, let us consider Jakobson's procedure of dividing the meanings of the Russian instrumental into three types and grouping each realization (or variant) under one type. I do not intend to discuss the extent to which such an analysis might be efficient or adequate. I simply want to say that there is no theoretical foundation that allows such a structure to be established for the Russian case system, because although the general Saussurean principles admit the Jakobsonian solution, they allow quite a range of others too. In the name of the same principles, one could equally well separate the meanings that Jakobson groups together. Jakobson's description seems to be an attempt to show that if a form is phonologically distinct from others then it has necessarily a distinct semantic counterpart and that if two forms are phonologically alike, then this is correlate with the counterpart of a meaning affinity. However, this could remain valid if homonymy and synonymy were to be ruled out of language structure.

Once this is admitted, it is possible to consider certain resemblances of form as morphological accidents and reduce to a single syntactic phenomenon the constructions in which the same relations are expressed by different cases. (Incidentally, this is what Martinet does in his *Grammaire fonctionnelle du français* when he conceives of *avec* as the expression of several different syntactic functions.) This would allow—following Peškovskij, 1934—the instrumental and agentive in Russian *svyrjat' kamnjami* [I] and *svyrjat' kamni* [A] '(to) throw stones' to be conceived as "stylistic homonyms". Seen from this point of view, Peškovskij's solution is as defensible as Jakobson's. This for the descriptive aspect. As for the factual aspect (is there a semantic opposition between the two?), I think that the only way to settle the question is to observe the extent to which this meaning difference corresponds to the language user's behavior and intuition. This is the only way to avoid confusing objective data with the describer's subjectivity.

A comparison within the framework of implicit grammatical semantics of Martinet's study on the 'subject' in Basque with Jakobson's on Russian cases brings up a significant difference in their analytic procedures. Martinet starts by studying the relationships between two function meanings 'agent' and 'patient'. He evokes evidence showing that these two notions are related from the point of view of their substance, because in many languages they are confused in certain construction types (especially in noun phrases). From this observation, he argues, under given conditions 'agent' and 'patient' may be contextual (semantic) real-izations of the same (syntactic) function. Here, the semantic kinship is shown and argued prior to and independently of its use as a criterion for syntactic identification. Therefore, Martinet's argumentation is not ad hoc, unlike Jakobson's.

To return to the issue raised here, three points are of interest: (a) the limitations of current semantic analyses of grammatical items; (b) the requirements of greater adequacy in grammatical semantics; and (c) the differences between grammatical and lexical items from a seman-tic point of view.

(a) Limitations of grammatical semantics

Although I do not wish to reexamine here the limitations common to lexical and grammatical semantics, I would like to insist on the fact that one of the main difficulties of current semantic descriptions of grammar lies in the fact that the relevant features supposed to form the meaning of the moneme under study are either not sufficiently specific or too specific. If they are not specific enough, the relevant semantic features will not provide us with a definition which excludes semantic entities other than the one under consideration. On the contrary, if they are too specific, the relevant semantic features will fail to account for all the occurrences of the unit under consideration. A case study does not seem necessary to illustrate this; the very question focused around the goal of grammatical semantics—global meaning or principal meaning—is a sufficient illustration.

Let it suffice to recall a previous example: if "subject" is only de-fined as a determiner of the predicate (or more precisely, as its first or its closest determiner), then French *voilà* in *voilà Paul* 'Here is Paul', 'this is Paul', or 'there is Paul' might be construed as subject, as well as *Jean* in *Jean construit une maison* 'John builds a house'. Hence this definition is too general. On the contrary, if we include 'agent' as a semantic feature common to all the occurrences of the 'subject', then the label 'subject' is not applicable to *voilà*. At the same time, introducing the feature 'agent' makes the notion of subject inapplicable to *Pierre* in French *Pierre est triste* 'Peter is sad'. Such a definition is too specific.

Here, the problem is analogous to the one we examined for the lexi-con; it concerns the choice of a relevant semantic feature. Or, if one prefers, it concerns the degree of specificity of semantic features. This choice is dependent on the way we group the units together. Should we find it desirable to group under a single syntactic function the semantic relations that hold for *Jean* and *vent* 'wind' (in *le vent chasse les nuages* 'The wind drives the clouds') in their respective utterances, the feature "agent" would be adequately conceived of as relevant. On the contrary, the same feature would not show enough specificity if we wanted to separate the function of *Jean* from that of *vent* 'wind'. The feature 'agent' would be too specific, if ever we wished to put together *voilà, vent* and *Jean* with regard to their function.

This decision in its turn has implications for, or is a consequence of, the choice made on the level of contextual conditioning. If we conceive of the mechanism of contextual influence in such a way that the variation between the 'agentivity' (of *Jean*) and the thematicity (of *Pierre*) can be fitted into our descriptive model, then the choice of the semantic feature 'agent' is justified—contingent, of course, on precaution with or adjustment of terminology. Otherwise, this choice is either over- or underspecific.

So far, grammatical semantics reveals similarities to lexical semantics. However, the two domains do not possess exactly the same characteristics. I quote below a few examples which illustrate the difficulties that arise specifically in grammatical semantics.

The structuralist ideal was to find one signifiant and one signifié for each linguistic sign. This leads to an abstract meaning whose concrete manifestations appear in the occurrences of the sign. Given the difficulties in subsuming all the semantic variants under a single signifié, certain linguists have suggested focusing on the principal meaning. This solution entails the admittance that a linguistic sign may have more than one signifié; under contextual pressure, one of the signifiés would be realized. This thesis has been explicitly stated by Prieto (cf. Prieto, 1964). He suggests that the characteristics which make up a signifié may be substitutive features depending on the circumstances of the communicative act: the signifié of French /so/*sceau, seau, saut,* and *sot* may have as its realization the concrete meaning 'seal', 'bucket', 'jump', or 'fool'. (Notice that the principle of substitutive features, although exemplified by lexical items, is presented by Prieto as general, hence valid for grammatical items as well.) As different signifiés do not necessarily have the same generality in the language, one could consider assigning *a priority* to the most important of them: the principal signifié. In this approach, one could leave out certain far-fetched or rare features that enter into the composition of the signifié.

I would like to stress some consequences of this conception: (i) the thesis of principal meaning is based on the hierarchy of semantic phenomena; and (ii) it admits that between different semantic variants there is not necessarily any affinity or kinship of substance—that is, two realizations of the same signifié could in fact have no common semantic basis. An illustration of this thesis can be found in Martinet's work on French grammar (Martinet, 1979), although the thesis is not explicitly stated. He does not take into account those uses or meanings of functional monemes that are stereotyped. For instance, he observes that for the instrumental function, French *de* and *à* are not used except in set expressions (*figements*; see Martinet, 1979, §4.32.f). For each function (i.e., semantic value) he lists a series of expressions; and, conversely, we find for a single expression (i.e., functional moneme) a number of semantic values. Thus, French *avec* 'with' might correspond to:

–instrumental: *il taille la haie avec une faucille* 'he cuts the hedge with a sickle'
–comitative: *il est parti avec sa famille* 'he has gone away with his family'
–modal: *il a répondu avec calme* 'he replied calmly',
–and so on.

Conversely, the instrumental might be expressed by, besides *avec*:

–*par: il l'a eu par l'intrigue* 'he got it by wheeling and dealing'
–*en: il arrive en avion* 'he is arriving by plane',
–and so on.

These examples show both the hierarchy and the lack of common basis for the semantic values of grammatical items. I think that this procedure represents a step forward in comparison with the search for a meaning; for in the latter global procedure, the signifié is so abstract that no real mechanism can be set up for semantic processes. No more than a dose of ingenuity is needed to group different semantic variants under a highly abstract feature: it seems quite arbitrary to gather, as Jakobson does, 'condition', 'restriction' and 'activity' under the heading of 'marginality'.

However, the same principle is not applied all through this particular work by Martinet. As for the semantic description of 'subject' or 'object', he believes that these "have no proper value" (Martinet, 1979, §4.25c; see also §4.9b and §4.19d). Such an approach to the signifiés of functions is in contradiction with a fundamental principle of Saussurean linguistics, namely the definition of the linguistic sign: how can we conceive of a sign without a signifié? But my concern here is more practical. On a descriptive level, this attitude toward the signifié of grammatical items is an obstacle to outlining a clear exposition of semantic processes. It is difficult to imagine how an item without any proper signifié can obtain one in context.

Moreover, what prevents us from conceiving of the 'subject' and 'object' as having several potential meanings without a common basis? Obviously, the search for a common semantic core for the 'subject' (or 'object') prevents Martinet from postulating a series of discontinuous meanings (meanings without a common basis). It seems possible to construe the 'subject' (or 'object')—whatever its realization, be it position as in *Mary loves John* or a specific pronoun form as in *he loves her,* or both—as an expression of different values such as 'agent', 'patient', and so on. Then, the pressure of the context could explain the fact that it has the value of 'agent' in *John reads well* but the value of 'patient' in *this book reads well*. Context and contextual conditioning thus cease to be mythical beings endowed with supernatural power.

So much for the problems created by relevant semantic features and semantic context. Let us turn now to semantic fields. As the term and the concept are reserved for the lexical domain, it is probably better to talk about groups or classes of grammatical monemes.

The first problem here is the criteria used for the grouping of items: will they be gathered together on the basis of formal (i.e., expression) or semantic (i.e., content) criteria? An example would help to state the problem more clearly. Martinet proposes two criteria for grouping monemes in one syntactic class: the same combinatory properties and mutual exclusion. In addition, he considers such classes adequate frameworks for the description of the signifié value of monemes (Martinet, 1979). This proposal seems to satisfy one of the requirements of the semantic field principle, namely that the number of units to be compared should be limited. But does it fulfill the second one, a common semantic basis? Let us take an example: *le* 'the', *chaque* 'every', *tout* 'all', and *aucun* 'no', 'any' are mutually exclusive: if one appears in a noun phrase, the others are excluded: *le livre* 'the book', *chaque livre* 'every book', and *aucun livre* 'no book' are possible constructions; but not *le chaque livre* or *l'aucun livre,* and so on. Thus, *le, chaque,* and *aucun* belong to the same class. What is the relevance of this class membership for the semantic description of these units? Martinet's answer to this question is that within the class we should compare the signifiés of the units to bring out the features that distinguish them from each other.

Such a procedure is certainly efficient when one compares *chaque* 'each' and *tout* 'every'; but what is the interest of comparing *chaque* with *le* 'the', *mon* 'my', *ce* 'this', and so on unless it is to show that their signifiés are globally different? Such a conclusion is too obvious to need procedures which if really applied would be far too fastidious. A comparison with units outside the syntactic class of noun modifiers— such as *partie d'un tout considérée à part* 'part of a whole considered apart'—is much more helpful for describing the content of *chaque*. Martinet sees this possibility but does not go into it in depth; he finds it helpful for the language user to group the French functional moneme *si* 'if' with sequences (like *dans l'hypothèse où* 'in the case that' or *dans l'invraisemblable hypothèse où* 'in the unlikely case that') that do not belong to the same class but have common bases on the level of the signifié. These are not isolated cases; similar examples could be found and cited in large numbers. Such cases point to an inadequacy: either the principle or its application is to be questioned. If the principle is not valid, then moneme classes are not an adequate framework for semantic analysis. It is unlikely that a different application of the principle could give more adequate or encouraging results for the study of the signifié. The reason for this inadequacy must be searched for in the very conception of moneme classes. As I said above, a complete syntactic description is based on criteria that are both logical and semantic. As these aspects are not always parallel, the describer often has to make a choice, giving priority to one of them. The way Martinet defines and classifies modifiers (determinant) is almost purely logical: a determinant d is the term which implies the nucleus N but is not implied by it; this relation can be represented as $d{\rightarrow}N$ and $N{\not\rightarrow}d$. Within their class, modifiers are linked to each other by mutual exclusion, which corresponds to logical disjunction (i.e., either/or but not both). As modifiers are classified on the basis of their logical relations, there is no reason they should share their semantic features or possess a common basis on the level of the signifié. It seems obvious that, thus conceived, moneme classes are not an appropriate framework for an exhaustive analysis of the signifié, although they are necessary at the start of the semantic study. In other words, when we start a description of the signifié, it is indispensable to know to which class the monemes we are studying belong. Let us take French /ver/; this can be a functional moneme *vers* 'toward', an adjective *vert* 'green', or a noun *verre* 'glass', among others. It is surely necessary to know that the unit we are studying is a functional moneme and not an adjective or a noun. This information leads us to a set of units with which it shares some of its syntactic properties. But as yet, no evidence has been put forward to support the idea that such sets constitute an adequate framework for semantic analysis. Prieto is surely right when he says that a semantic analysis based on the logical relations between signifiés will only show that two or several signifiés are distinct and not what this distinction consists of (cf. Prieto, 1964). It is obviously possible to define and classify modifiers on a semantic basis; then the class enables us to circumscribe the signifié of the units more accurately.

(b) Requirements for the greater adequacy of the semantic description of grammatical units

Above, I criticized certain descriptions of the signifié of grammatical units for their inadequacy with respect to the empirical data. This criticism should not be taken as if, on the basis of my personal intuition, I were challenging a descriptive model; my purpose was to point out that, strictly speaking, these descriptions are hypotheses, and that other hypotheses are available for solving the same problems. In order to choose the most adequate ones, the only decisive arguments can be provided by user's intuition and behavior, which, as I said above—cf. VI.9.— present a complex structure. That is, the user masters different aspects of the signifié more or less well; besides, the same semantic phenomenon occurs under different appearances, and the user has a more or less accurate knowledge of it depending on the angle from which he views it. This implies that observation techniques are not of equal efficiency for different signifiés or for different aspects of them. Consequently, the problem will be to examine which paths we can follow to gain access to semantic phenomena. In other words, what techniques can we use for the observation of the signifié? To answer this question, one has to take it for granted that such an observation is possible; on this admittance depends the feasibility of semantics, and it is implied by certain generally accepted principles such as the communicative function or language learning. If we don't accept a simplistic conception of language as innate, we are led to acknowledge that children construct linguistic meaning by matching language units with extralinguistic experience. In other words, a constructivist conception of language acquisition is based on the implicit admittance that children discover semantic structure by observation. Similarly, the communicative function supposes that it is possible to reflect with a linguistic utterance some state of affairs and *vice versa*—that it is possible to grasp this state of affairs from an utterance that is received. Hence, when we try to observe meaning phenomena—and more generally, many other linguistic phenomena, too—we submit to the language user's linguistic expressions, on the one hand, and on the other, facts from experience, and we ask him to judge the correspondence of the two sets of data. In order to investigate the means of access to meaning, we should examine what relations exist between the experience (i.e., the referent or nonlinguistic reality) and linguistic phenomena. More precisely, how are cognitive phenomena and language phenomena linked? These relations, considered from the point of view of language acquisition, seem to be as follows.

> (i) One can apprehend linguistic elements through their referents. One way of answering the question "What does the word *mahogany* mean?" is to show the thing it refers to.
>
> (ii) A linguistic unit can be apprehended by means of other linguistic units, or paraphrase—If a young speaker doesn't know the meaning of a word—*oval,* for example—one can help him to acquire it by a paraphrase like 'something that has the shape of an egg'. Most dictionary definitions illustrate this procedure.

These two relations were discussed above (cf. III.6) when I examined the ways of accessing the meanings of words. So far, a language element has been regarded as the target and the experience conveyed by it as a means. But a language user is by turns speaker and hearer; hence, we shall envisage the cases where what is aimed at is the experience:

(iii) the experience can be grasped by means of linguistic elements. All the uses of language for communicative purposes are of this type.

(iv) one can get to know (nonlinguistic) reality by means of reality. One can enable the constitution of a machine to be grasped by exhibiting it during the different phases of its assembly.

Given that our concern is the knowledge of linguistic phenomena, (iv) is of no relevance for the issue, except for showing that cognitive activity (thought, or whatever we may call it) can be independent of language.

Comparing (i) and (iii), we realize that in both, we use the same data; the difference lies in the route one follows. In (i) the fact of experience is taken for evidence we use to attain the goal, which is the linguistic unit. This corresponds to the speaker's activity. Conversely, in (iii) the linguistic element is given at the outset, and we aim for the fact of experience. This is what the hearer does during a speech act.

When using paraphrase, we can also adopt two opposite routes: use paraphrase to reveal a linguistic unit, as in (ii), or use the linguistic element to bring to the fore a paraphrase. That is, when a word—e.g., *oval*—slips from the memory of a speaker, he can ask for help by using a circumlocution: "What is the word for a thing that has the shape of an egg?"

When one looks for information about the content of a linguistic unit, one can either restrict oneself to asking a bare question (e.g., "What do you call a thing that has the shape of an egg?") or one can give some hints about what one is looking for as well: it is possible to add to the question "Is it 'oval' or something like that?"

The informal discussion above has been presented in order to demonstrate with simple and plausible examples the means language users employ to resolve semantic problems. It seems obvious that the linguist can also use these possibilities to acquire more objective knowledge about semantic phenomena and their structure. The views I have been supporting can be stated more formally:

—we can observe the signifié by using either a referent or a paraphrase;

—in this type of observation, we can go from the signifiant and look for its signifié (i.e., from F[orm] to M[eaning], $F \rightarrow M$) or we can present the signifié and try to find its signifiant $(M \rightarrow F)$;

—when searching for the signifié, we can leave the informant to orient himself (nondirective question, *ND*); or we can provide him with information about the signifié and ask him to judge it (directive question, *D*).

In all this, I take it for granted that the observation is aimed at the intuition and behavior of the individual and society, and that the signifiant can be represented by its phonic or graphic form, as is currently done.

The three dimensions proposed above provide us with a framework for the construction of different questionnaires. It cannot be taken for granted that access to a given meaning will be equally possible and equally easy through each of the procedures. One of the factors making semantic structure particularly difficult to describe precisely is that not all the relations are relevant in all cases and to the same degree; thus they cannot be used with the same interest for the description of different signifiés. If we take an example from the semantic field of feelings, it is certainly easy to make it clear to what the word *pain* or the syntagm *rancid taste* refer, through experience of them; it is not the same for *weightlessness,* as this is generally beyond the experience of most people. The elucidation of meaning in the latter case can only be based on metalinguistic procedures (paraphrase as it is generally understood, and not with its technical meaning, as in some linguistic currents—cf., for example, Hiz, 1961, and Harris, 1969). This is not specific for the lexicon. In grammar as well, some signifiés are more easily accessible than others by the same technique. One can compare two functional monemes, say French *de* 'of' and *contre* 'against'. Can we paraphrase the meaning of both of them with the same ease?

One of the advantages of the framework given above is that it shows how access to different meanings can be possible, easy, and so on. If this set of techniques for surveys is efficient, it should allow the determination of the different categories of linguistic meanings and the establishment of a hierarchy between them. There is a simple idea at the basis of this: the better a signifié is known and handled by the language users, the higher its rank in the linguistic hierarchy.

(c) Grammar versus lexicon: from a semantic point of view
What is the kind of knowledge we are seeking about the semantic phenomena? This knowledge can be compared with what a connoisseur

knows about, let us say, wine. Knowing wines is not the mere knowledge that the content of a given bottle is wine or not. A connoisseur is the one who can distinguish different varieties of wine, who can tell for instance a Bordeau from a Bourgogne. In the same way, knowing the semantic intuition of French speakers implies that one can tell in what respect this intuition differs for given units like *de* 'of' and *chien* 'dog'. More generally, the semantic description should supply us with information as to the way in which the categories—for example, grammatical and lexical ones—of semantic phenomena have different status in the user's mind and behavior. The better we know these differences, the finer we can subcategorize the semantic phenomena, and the more precisely we can account for the mechanism of communication acts (i.e., conveying the meaning), for their success or failure. The matrix presented in table 5 is an attempt to construct a tool for uncovering such differences.

Before continuing with this issue, I shall make a few remarks in order to state the problem more clearly.

—As a terminological short cut, I use *word* for a linguistic element of any length and *thing* for external reality, whatever its nature.

—I consider here the language user's ability to use things to highlight the word's meaning, or use words to highlight the meaning, or use words to highlight the thing.

—The questions we ask the informants may make use of contextual elements to a greater or lesser degree.

In other words, when we search for the meaning of a word, we can ask the user to tell us what the meaning is of a moneme (e.g., *orange*) or of a phrase (*an orange; orange shade*) or a sentence (*Bill peeled an orange; Joan prefers the orange shade*), and so on. I think that the answers to any of these questions reveal certain aspects of semantic phenomena— I take it for granted that some word meanings can be apprehended by the use of things.

The question is to find out whether this is valid to the same degree for grammar as for lexicon. Can the describer use things with the same efficiency to uncover the meaning of both grammatical and lexical units? This seems possible in certain cases, for example when the linguistic material we submit to the user's judgment is a series of sentences or at least phrases.

Let us take examples from French: the grammatical moneme *avec* 'with' and the lexical one *fleur* 'flower'. Both have semantic indeterminacies. *Avec* may be instrumental or comitative depending on the context. In certain contexts, however, both meanings are possible: *les hommes arrivent avec leurs chevaux* 'the men arrive with their horses' or *les sorcières arrivent avec leurs balais* 'the witches arrive with their brooms'. Potentially, in these contexts, *avec* means either 'instrumental' or 'comitative': men and witches can move on foot and have with them their horses or brooms; they may also use these for their locomotion.

As for French *fleur,* its meaning can be, among others, the 'reproductive organ in plant' or the 'plant' itself. Contexts may help to remove the ambiguity of *fleur;* thus, it means 'reproductive organ' in

> *Jean portait toujours une fleur à la boutonnière*
> 'John always wore a flower in his button hole',

but 'plant' in

> *Jean cultive des fleurs sur son balcon*
> 'John grows flowers on his balcony'.

Yet both meanings are possible in contexts like

> *Jean offre une fleur à Marie*
> 'John offers a flower to Mary'. (Notice that what John offers Mary may be a whole plant or just its flower.)

Are these meanings of *avec* and *fleur* equally probable, or are there factors that statistically determine their respective occurrences? It is not *a priori* sure that they occur in all circumstances with comparable ease. Observations are necessary to highlight this problem.

One possible experiment is to ask the informant to match these sentences with real events. (In practice, given the difficulties produced by recourse to real events, it is preferable to use substitutes, such as movies, figurines, photographs, or drawings, to represent the events.) The informant can be shown a setting and asked to describe it.

So far, the use either of things or of their substitutes is possible both for grammar and lexicon. This is not the case if the linguistic items we examine are not sentences but monemes. Here, we can find discrepancies between the two domains. In grammar, it seems impossible to relate things to words, for example, with *-ed, the,* or *-ing,* whereas this is quite feasible for certain (though not all) lexical monemes. In the above example, we can isolate *fleur* 'flower' from the sentence and ask the informant to give its nonlinguistic counterpart (i.e., its referent). Is the same applicable for *avec* 'with'?

From these observations, I may draw the conclusion that grammatical monemes do not have ostensible referents; one cannot show them by pointing to, picturing, or drawing. In contradistinction, the lexical domain comprises monemes with ostensible referents, although it is not composed of such monemes exclusively.

In addition to their referential difference, grammar and lexicon can be contrasted with regard to metalinguistic aspects. The question is then:

—Can a language speaker utilize words to clarify what a word means?

—Are there considerable differences from this point of view between grammar and lexicon?

—Does the use of metalinguistic means on the contrary prove equally efficient for the two types of significant units?

Here again, we cannot attribute to the grammar as a whole semantic properties opposing it to the lexicon. For in both, paraphrase (a metalinguistic device) can be used to make explicit the word's meaning. French speakers are able to express the meaning of a lexical unit like *chien* 'dog' as well as that of a grammatical unit like *avec* 'with'. Empirical research shows that in both cases different variants emerge from the informant's responses, and a hierarchy emerges from among the variants. But this is not necessarily true for all grammatical units. It is highly probable that metalinguistic devices cannot be operational in gaining access to the meaning of bound monemes.[46]

From this observation, the following conclusion suggests itself: certain grammatical monemes have a number of semantic realizations without any hierarchy. This does not seem to be the case in the lexicon. It should be noted that the semantic description must not be confused with a description of a referent from the specialist's point of view. Therefore one should not expect the informant to give for the word *electronics* the same definition as the physicist would give. As a layman, our informant might attribute to this word some semantic features like 'automation', 'precision', 'electrical', and so on.

How can we explain the specific property of *de*? One possible solution to this problem is to say that these grammatical monemes have no signifié of their own, and the context gives them their meanings (see, for instance, Martinet, 1979). But numerous facts remain unexplained by this thesis: if the context *un chef—l'armée* 'a head—the army' possesses the power of giving meaning to a meaningless sequence of phonemes, why can't it do this for nonexistent words like *gu* or *mipe,* as it does for *de* or *pour*? I won't linger on this issue here; I have presented other arguments with similar force above.

Another possible explanation could be that such a grammatical moneme has a number of semantic virtualities with the same rank in the structural hierarchy so that they are equally available in the user's memory; hence the survey presents any one of the potential meanings.

The contrast between grammar and lexicon with respect to referent or circumlocution seems rich in implications and allows one to explain the origin of some theses in semantic studies. For a long time, most linguists, especially those within the structuralist tradition, focused on grammatical semantics and took the grammar as the most, if not the only, interesting area of language phenomena.[47] Therefore they were tempted to generalize the semantic properties uncovered for grammatical units and regard them as common to all the significant units. Some dogmas, widespread across linguistic schools, can be explained by such generalizations. Consider the following theses.

—The only framework valid for semantic studies is the sentence.
—A word has no meaning out of context.
—Referents cannot be used to reveal the meaning of linguistic elements.

None of these is completely false; they are valid for certain grammatical monemes. But it is ill-advised to generalize them to cover the whole grammar and lexicon. This generalization seems to proceed from the principle that language structure is homogeneous and that structural properties are best grasped by the observation of the grammatical domain.

Two conclusions offer themselves for closing this section.

(i) The resistance offered by semantic phenomena to any simple structuration is a proof that their regularities are of a complex nature and comprise general rules with exceptions and exceptions to exceptions, and so on.

(ii) The difficulties encountered in the application of empirical devices for observation of semantic data should be examined seriously; in each case, one should try to find out what properties of the semantic phenomena are the ultimate causes of such difficulties.

These remarks, I feel, point the way toward a better understanding of meaning.

VII Some Issues and Perspectives in Linguistic Experiment

VII.0 Synopsis

This chapter opens with a discussion on the necessity of experimentation and points out the complementarity of experimental and theoretical approaches. As the empirical domain, semantics is chosen for illustration, and a framework is outlined in order to deal with meaning phenomena. An attempt is made to shed new light on some classical yet controversial theses in semantics, such as the user's awareness of meaning, semantic heterogeneity and its aspects, semantic awareness versus phonological awareness, and ways of knowing language, that is, conscious knowledge versus operational knowledge.

VII.1 Preliminary Remarks

In the preceding chapters I discussed experimentation in general terms and promised a more detailed discussion of several problems. I shall come back to these below. The problems will be examined from a theoretical point of view and illustrated by reference to empirical facts. The experimental arguments are drawn from our recent research. This choice does not in any way indicate that I consider previous empirical works to be devoid of scientific value. My choice is motivated by two considerations. First, converging results obtained by various research projects carried out independently provide additional arguments that show the correctness of the theoretical principles they are based upon. Second, a sound discussion needs a relatively extensive exposition of empirical research; my choice avoids duplicating reports on experiments already published.

Before discussing these problems in detail, I would like to make a few remarks about experimentation.

Experimentation has not always received a good press. Stereotypical ideas about experiments, their objects, and methods are widespread; some of these ideas are almost caricatures of experimental methods. For some linguists, experimentation is useless work, created and practiced by anguished people who need to substantiate with empirical arguments something that is evident for any rational person. My only answer to such an objection is that there is no equivalence between common sense and scientific knowledge in any definite sense. On the one hand, what seems evident to the man in the street may prove false for science; as a trivial example, one could cite again the immediate perception of a moving sun and fixed earth. On the other hand, scientific research aims at knowledge that is far beyond the evidence, even if the layman's common sense is part of the object of a science like linguistics.

For instance, the way a language user knows the sound features he uses in his speech is surely a part of the object the linguist is supposed to study; this, however, does not imply that the linguist's knowledge and the user's intuition should be confused. The fact that the user is normally unaware of the distinctive features of his phonological system is not a proof of their nonexistence.

For others, opposition to experimental work seems to be a way of finding moral comfort, at least in certain cases. Doubtlessly it is reassuring to rely on well-established principles and continue one's linguistic reflection using introspection or fortuitous observations of the language usages of others. By doing so, the linguist is likely to restrict considerably the scope and interest of his research. Moreover, he runs the risk of stagnation in a rigid classicism.

Conservatism is another reason certain researchers strongly dislike experiment; they seem to be afraid that questioning classical principles may jeopardize what has been acquired through past research. Such apprehension seems justified when one considers the uncompromising affirmations of certain linguists who pretended to show the complete invalidity of a theoretical concept by exposing some of its inadequacies.[48] For instance, a number of linguists thought that the concept of the phoneme had been consigned to linguistic history's wastepaper basket forever (cf. Fillmore, 1968, p. 88). They seemed to ignore the fact that most scientific discoveries do not invalidate prior results but incorporate them within a more comprehensive theory. Any inadequacy is necessarily a sign of a limitation to the theory under consideration, but this does not mean that it is totally devoid of interest. Genuine scientific reflection strives to find the reason such a theory is born and the extent of its validity; it also proposes a more general theoretical framework of which this theory can be a special case. This is the relation that exists between quantum mechanics and Newtonian theory.

Yet, when defending current theoretical principles, exaggerated criticism cannot be cited to justify exaggeration within these principles, as this might produce the same effect as conservatism or the search for moral comfort. This is what often happens when the requirements for experimentation are too stringent.

Last but not least, one of the hindrances to experimental work originates in the way its relation to theory is conceived. In some theoretical views, this relation is that of the slave to the master: the theorist accomplishes the noble tasks of thinking and constructing the conceptual framework and leaves to the experimenter the menial job of confronting the concepts with the data. From this perspective, a theory remains independent of empirical facts.[49] The experimenter is not supposed to evaluate the theoretical foundations; failure in experimental work can thus be imputed to the empirical stage of research only. This gives little chance of mutual enrichment between theory and experimentation.

VII.2 Scientific Experiments: Conditions and Objectivity

If linguistics wishes to be considered the science of language, it must follow, in the definition of its methods and object, procedures that are requirements of any scientific research. What are these requirements? Here we will first look at the sciences with a long tradition in this respect.

The physicist Louis Michel wrote: "For fifty years new domains in physics have changed its character. The history of our material universe has become the object of science. Cosmology has set fascinating problems; it introduces the notion of 'horizons' in the universe. These prevent us from making observations in some of its parts. . . . For me, these inaccessible areas are also objects of science . . . but of a different nature." It follows from this that "the method is quite different but does not remove the primordial role of the activity of experimenting."

When research does not permit the physicist to "deduce consequences that are experimentally testable," he concludes that his ambitions are based—at least in part—on his implicit belief (cf. Hamburger, 1986, p. 61).

Two complementary aspects of research, both of which could be called extreme, can be seen here: on the one hand, science sets itself ambitious objectives, and on the other it takes support from limited and local phenomena to evaluate its general theses. These two aspects are indissolubly linked by experimental activity, and it is from the two-way traffic between them and from their confrontation that significant results for the progress of knowledge are obtained.

This intimate link between theory and experimentation escapes most linguists. Some linguists are on the defensive when faced with problems of experimentation. In a talk to a group of linguists about an experiment to reveal the status of certain syntactic phenomena in the psyche of the language user, one objection raised was: "There is no experimentation in linguistics; it is the act of those who make rats run around in mazes." At the other extreme, other linguists are so attracted by the experiments that the depth of their theoretical reflections suffers a great deal as a result.[50]

In what follows, we are mainly interested in two problems: the place of experimentation in linguistic research and the extent to which experimental activity guarantees objectivity in research. First, a detour is necessary to delimit the concept of experimentation.

(a) What is not a linguistic experiment?

The prestige of the experimental method made it so attractive that some researchers wanted to apply it immediately to linguistics. For want of sufficient preparation, these attempts were more a parody than well-understood experimentation. Stuffing reports of linguistic research with numbers, filling them with mathematical (or pseudo-mathematical) formulae, and making extensive use of curves and diagrams does not make them experimental studies.

Striking examples can be found in Basil Bernstein's work (Bernstein, 1971). He established that children from a middle-class background hesitated significantly more than children of other social classes. From this he concluded that children from a relatively well-off environment have a richer language.

There is hardly any need to stress that this particular conclusion does not follow from the observations. Other conclusions could be drawn just as easily. Nothing prevents us *a priori* from regarding these hesitations as either indications of linguistic insecurity or as social signs or markers allowing identification of the social class to which a language user belongs. It is doubtless the higher opinion Bernstein has of the language of the middle classes (or its "logical organization," "conceptual development," etc.) that leads him to his conclusions.

As René Thom said: "Every experiment is the answer to a question, and if the question is idiotic, there is little chance of the answer being less so" (cf. Thom, 1986, p. 17). By the way, what was the question? Was it:

—Can the elaborated and restricted codes be observed?
—Is measuring the number and length of hesitations a good way of observing this?
—Is there a strong necessary and sufficient link between the elaborated code and hesitations?
—Or something else yet?

As the question was not really precise, the answer cannot be convincing.

(b) The conditions and consequences of experimentation

A formal definition of experimentation must be given, so as to specify its structure. Three points seem to be necessary:[51] (i) a system must be delimited and examined according to a protocol of preparation; (ii) this system must be perturbed by controlled factors; and (iii) the answers from the system must be recorded by means of an instrument whose utility and relevance are specified in the protocol of preparation. These three points are relatively independent; they can be observed at work separately or combined in the composition of the scientific work.

According to this definition,[52] experimentation has three stages. But scientific work that respects just one of these requirements is far from being devoid of interest. For example, interesting work can be done by respecting only requirement number (iii); this would be observation. If both (i) and (iii) are respected, then this would be exploration; and so on.

Transposed to linguistic research, this amounts to saying that some works based on corpuses are of the observational type, as they use stages (i) and (iii). Some surveys by Labov, however, are of the experimentational type because by asking certain questions—for example, "have you ever been in danger of death?"—he manages to perturb the linguistic behavior a subject normally adopts under survey conditions.

This formal conception of experimentation is without any doubt useful. For example, with respect to Bernstein's experiment one can ask how it transgresses the canons of experimentation. Labov's criticism (Labov, 1972b, §5) seems to concern point (ii) in that the perturbing factors were not controlled. In fact, the behavior of working-class schoolchildren was perturbed due to the presence of researchers from a different social class, unlike the situation of middle-class children, who were questioned by researchers of the same social class. The criticism I have just made of Bernstein's work concerns point (i): the delimitation of the object lacked rigor.

But it should not be forgotten that this formal conception of experimentation also has its limits. First, the processes in a scientific experiment are not distinct. For example, is the linguist who works with a corpus exploring, observing, or experimenting? Insofar as he can segment the corpus or class the segments in different ways, doesn't he perturb the object? Or yet again, is the commutation test a perturbing factor? These are all questions to which the answer is not *a priori* obvious.

Then, between the stages outlined, there is neither a logical nor a chronological order. Experimental research does not always proceed by exhaustive exploration; seeing that manipulating the object can help in the progress of knowledge without being an experiment in the formal sense of the term, experimental research can reveal new ideas about the object (such as Claude Bernard's groping experiment, which some have called "suggestive pottering about"). It can also be based on hypotheses that have little interest, yet which even so lead to significant results that were not expected at the outset ("productive errors") (Hamburger, 1986, p. 13).

Finally, even the terminological game is not safe from connotations, whether positive or negative. If experimentation has a positive connotation, then to say of some disciplines—like astronomy or historical linguistics—that they are not experimental sciences is like saying that they are not scientific (or not very scientific). These are statements that have nothing to back them up. This is reminiscent of the recent past when for some people qualifying linguistic research as observational was enough to classify it among prescientific trials (and thus oppose it to prestigious, so-called explanatory research).[53]

To the question "what is experimentation?" there is no unanimous reply, even from the ranks of sciences that have a long tradition of experimenting. However, two requirements are generally accepted. First, an experimental activity is necessarily a replicable activity; no convincing conclusions can be drawn from an isolated, nonreplicable phenomenon. Second, a scientific experiment is necessarily linked to hypotheses that precede or follow it. The two aspects of objective repetition and subjective hypotheses are indissolubly linked in experimental activity.

(c) The technical problems of experimentation

In order to examine the technical questions, let us come back to the three-point definition, even though it may seem a little too formal. Note that there are choices to be made: one choice involves the object—what one wants or ought to study; another is about the ways and means of observing this object. It is the last choice I shall call technical.

The solution adopted for technical problems is neither innocent nor without consequences. If, during my semantic research, the linguistic material I submit to the intuitive judgment of informants is made up of sentences, the results obtained will be of one type. Markedly different results will be obtained if I opt for the technical solution of questioning the language user about the meaning of isolated words.

Thus, one of the most widespread theses in linguistics—and not only in structural linguistics—concerns the role and importance of context in apprehending meaning. This results, to my mind, from a technical choice. As long as only the meaning obtained from within a sentence is considered to be valid, there is a great temptation to attribute certain semantic realizations of monemes and words to the influence of context, especially if the different meanings are too distant (like *chien* 'dog' and *chien* 'charm'—*elle a du chien* 'she has charm') to make it obvious that it is a question of trifling differences in the realization of one and the same signifié. The choice of a different technique—soliciting, for example, the intuition of the language user about the meaning of isolated elements—could lead to other theses about meaning and context.[54]

Furthermore, much criticism directed against experimental research in linguistics is on the technical level. Thus, when a survey is carried out using questionnaires, the value to be attributed to the answers collected should be questioned. How do we know the answer a language user gives to our questions corresponds to the way he handles the elements of his language? Does the language user not choose his answer in terms of his social status, or the expectations of the researcher?

Let us admit that the discrepancy is real—and it is, to some extent—between the intuition of the speaker and his linguistic behavior. Such an affirmation does not lead to a single and incontestable conclusion; it can also be concluded, among other things, that the techniques used are inadequate for the observations of the chosen phenomena, or that access to the observation of the data is not possible.

The first conclusion invites one to look for suitable techniques; it is thus on the level of models of experiment. The second conclusion, which concerns theoretical or even epistemological principles, has more general implications. Just as the first deserves attention, the second is indefensible. It amounts to denying the feasibility of gaining objective knowledge of language and admitting that the mental experiment (*Gedankenexperiment*) is the only way of gaining access to knowledge of language. I do not mean that the mental experiment—is it not the same thing as introspection?—is null and void; but I am of the opinion that in most cases any reliable data it provides remain within the limits that are known to us today. Beyond that, the risk is that it may give results that vary randomly, depending on the researcher and the conditions under which the reflection was made.

Let us come back to the technical objection. The question is often asked in absolute terms: "Is a particular technique adequate for the observation of linguistic phenomena or not?" It seems to me that the problem should be relativized, and that one should determine more closely what one wants to observe and describe by means of a given technique.

This relativity is justified by the fact that the language user does not always use the elements of his language in a unique way; he can use the same linguistic sign with more or less approximation or precision. Thus, *le caïd a tué le flic* 'the gang leader killed the cop' can mean that he did it by means of his own strength, a weapon, a trick, or through a third person. The same word *tuer* 'kill' can exclude some of the semantic virtualities in a more explicit context that, for example, takes into account the services of a paid killer. Of the two uses, the first includes a

rather rough approximation, whereas the second attains a more elaborate level in the accuracy of meaning. The technique that is adequate for
the description of the first use is not necessarily adapted to the second,
and vice versa. By using too coarse a tool, the risk is that the description
will be impoverished and that some things with which the user wanted
to load his message will escape; the use of too fine a technique risks
crediting the speaker with significant intentions that he did not have:
the speaker who says *Le caïd a tué le flic* might not have, or might not
have wanted, to provide information about details such as the direct or
indirect intervention of the gang leader.

Let us consider a dialogue in French like the following.

> *A: Tiens! Tu t'es coupé les cheveux. Moi aussi.*
> 'Hey! You've cut your hair. Me too.'
> *B: Non. Tu t'es coupé les cheveux. Moi, je me les suis fait couper.*[55]
> 'No. You've cut your hair. Me, I have had mine cut.'

To describe the meanings produced by the two occurrences of *tu t'es
coupé les cheveux,* two different scales must be used, and different techniques are needed. *B* uses this syntagm, contrasting it with the causative,
whereas *A* uses it in nondifferentiated context.

Generally, the better a technique accounts for fine nuances, the more
it is valued. A fine instrument like an ordinance survey map certainly
helps a walker to find his way more easily, yet it is quite useless for showing the meteorological situation of a continent, for this a less detailed
map, like a satellite photograph, is more suitable.

In phonology, the fineness of the tool is not always a virtue either.
Thus, certain fine survey techniques, like Labov's, allow the social status
of certain elements to be recorded quite accurately; but they are useless
when describing the system used by distant groups of one community
in their linguistic exchanges. That is to say, insofar as the object of a
study—in this case a language—is a complex structure composed of
many strata, diverse techniques are necessary to describe and explain
the functioning of each of these strata. Sometimes only the combined
use of several techniques permits us to understand phenomena that
would otherwise escape us. In this way, the observation of a discrepancy between linguistic behavior and intuition enabled Labov to display
the phenomenon of hypercorrection.

We have just discussed some of the technical objections directed at experimental research. We have tried to show that experimentation is an obligatory procedure when objectivity is aimed at in the knowledge of language; that technical problems are not insoluble; and that the conditions of experimentation and the very relativity of the structure and use of language impose certain restrictions on the objectivity of our knowledge of linguistic phenomena.

However, it should be recognized that some of the reticence shown with respect to some experimental research work arises from the excesses of out-and-out experimenters. The rejection in this case appears to be a normal reaction to excessive questioning of introspective research work.[56] The layered structure of a language implies the existence of very solid strata that are virtually impermeable to variations and fluctuations. In this type of strata, as the intuition of one user corroborates that of another, introspection might be sufficient as a way of obtaining data. Surveys have been made on the opposition /p/–/b/ in initial position in words in French. The results correspond to the reply that any French-speaking phonologist would give when delving into his intuition.

(d) Experimentation *stricto sensu*

To conclude this section, let me return to the initial problem of experimentation.

We saw that in the "exact" sciences, there is no unanimity about either the definition of experimentation or its role in research. However, there is some consensus: the experimental method corresponds more to a state of mind. The researcher continually keeps in mind the possible distortion that inevitably results from the vision he has of the object; this distortion presents in a clear-cut way the scope and limits of research. It is only in this way that mathematicians can be understood when they consider that experimentation has its place in mathematics. But alongside this broad conception of scientific experimentation, I think it is advisable to delimit a more restricted field in which to place experimentation in the strict sense of the term.

It seems obvious to me that in spite of the resemblance, a pure and simple linguistic observation is not to be confused with an experiment *stricto sensu,* that is, one carried out according to the requirements formulated in points (i)–(iii) above. It is true that the means used for observation carry the risk of distorting somewhat the behavior of the object (for example, there is a risk that the language user will produce less spontaneous utterances in front of a microphone). This is valid to the extent that any experimental study of the survey type must have recourse to specific techniques (both in data collection and in the interpretation of results) to deal with the distortions caused by the methods used. That is to say, the data collected in this way are not conceived of from the outset as exempt from variations and heterogeneity due to the choice of technique, whereas one might have expected that a homogeneous system would be obtained by the corpus method.

From this, drawing a distinction between experimentation *stricto sensu* and other types of research (like observation and exploration) is possible, although not always easy. And it is in this sense that I will continue to use the terms experiment and experimentation.

Can one hope, one day, to escape from the subjectivity that is inherent in any scientific knowledge? A negative reply could be given to this question, such as the one given by the biologist Jean Hamburger (Hamburger, 1986, p. 6), or a more optimistic one like that given by the physicist Bernard d'Espagnat (Espagnat, 1986, pp. 107–109). The fact remains that those who undertake research do so with the conviction that the margins of subjectivity can still be reduced.

VII.3   Linguistic Experimentation: Its Scope, Achievements, and Perspectives

Above, we discussed the prerequisites and implications of experimentation in scientific research as a whole. This issue is relevant to the humanities, and more specifically to linguistics, because research should satisfy the same general requirements. Besides, linguistic research has additional requirements owing to the specific characteristics of its object; thus, a general framework can be established for experimental studies in linguistics.

(a) Observational techniques

I will not attempt to set up such a general framework here, however interesting and promising it might be, because the task is too enormous. My purpose is (i) to outline briefly such a framework and discuss the relevance of the various dimensions of its constitution; (ii) to examine the empirical adequacy of certain semantic theses; and (iii) to look at the implications of such semantic studies for other parts of linguistic structure.

(i) A framework for semantic experiments

In discussing the means of gaining access to meaning (VI.14.ii), I pointed out the relations existing between linguistic elements (words) and extra-linguistic experiences (things) as follows: One can give the meaning of a word by the use of things. This ensues from the communicative function of language, since communication implies linking linguistic elements with elements of experience we have from the external world. The user is also able to give us information about the meaning of a word by using other words; this is an entailment of the semiotic omnipotence (or universality) of language. Were these principles, communication and omnipotence, absolute, either of the above techniques should be usable for a linguistic element, whatever it is, and provide us with identical descriptions for a given unit or sequence. Were this the case, far-reaching conclusions would result: for instance, quite a range of controversies concerning the adequacy of either referent or paraphrase in semantic studies would prove totally vacuous. Were it not, then we should question the validity—or at least the equivalence—of the above techniques for data collection and/or the underlying principles. Moreover, we should look for the reasons why one technique gives more convincing results than the other. One of these reasons could be the heterogeneity of semantic facts; this entails that semantic elements can be divided into types according to the techniques that can be applied to them.

It appears to me that such a framework has a twofold interest. Firstly, it allows for a classification of semantic phenomena; and secondly, it can be construed as a framework for the typology and comparison of semantic studies. This sort of comparison might reveal the extent to which certain results of semantic studies have been influenced by the analyst's choice of object or techniques, that is, by what amounts to the analyst's preconceptions.

Up to now, the discussion concerning categories of meaning and types of survey techniques has been linked to the relative relevance of *paraphrase* (or, more generally, *circumlocution*) or *referent* in semantic studies; let us call this dimension *mode* (of access). Two other dimensions are relevant in this respect: the user's *role* and the observer's *interference*.

Given that any language user can assume in turn the role of hearer or speaker of linguistic messages, the describer can take as a hypothesis that uttering and receiving are symmetrical acts. In this case, semantic facts should show the same structural properties independently of the role of the user whose linguistic usage is described. However, the linguist can also adopt the other extreme position and consider uttering and understanding linguistic messages to be totally different acts. In this case, a semantic study does not have to find any parts—features or units—common to both the hearer's and the speaker's meaning. None of these extreme positions is totally supported by any linguistic theory; the theses are generally more nuanced. The asymmetry of linguistic acts is currently admitted, but its bearing and relevance are evaluated differently and illustrated by selected examples.

As for the describer's interference, the problem is ascertaining whether there is any linguistic raw material that is pure—that is, data completely unaffected by the devices the describer uses to observe them—and if so, to know how we can gain access to them. A classical solution to this problem is based on the admission that language phenomena are subject to distortion under observational conditions. Therefore, it would be impossible to obtain linguistic data that are completely untouched by the observer's hands. Hence, the interference by the linguist must be reduced to a minimum. Only then will we have a chance of collecting relatively valid data. The conception of the corpus in classical structuralism as the only reliable collection of data is based on such a thesis. On the basis of this assumption, one should expect the results obtained by different observational devices to be completely different.

Given the lacunae in corpuses and the fragmentary data they provide, to restrict data collection to a corpus is to pay too highly for the relative objectivity or spontaneity it is supposed to provide. The describer can also assume that the observer's intervention causes little or no distortion. If this were true, then the results obtained from a corpus or a survey should be similar. Here again, the main difference concerns the amount of distortion due to observational devices.

A matrix for the collection of data. These problems have been discussed *in extenso* from a theoretical point of view. My concern is an empirical examination of these theses. Each has implications on a descriptive level and allows us to predict some properties of the structure we obtain by the use of given observational techniques. To what extent are these predictions effectively realized? To answer this question, I propose the definition of a fixed collection of data with respect to each of the above dimensions; we will thus be able to determine the effects of a given device—for example, the presence or absence of the observer's interference—on the semantic data and their structure. If we make a binary distinction for each dimension, we will find a matrix of eight entries: (1) mode of access: use of referent (*Ref*) or paraphrase (*Par*); (2) user's role: speaker, who starts from the meaning and has the form as goal ($M{\rightarrow}F$), and hearer, who goes from the form to the meaning ($F{\rightarrow}M$); (3) interference (or directivity): directive (*D*): linguistic elements are given some characteristcs and the informant is asked to judge this characterization; nondirective (*ND*): linguistic elements are submitted to the user, who is supposed to characterize them.

It is worth noting that the above matrix is somewhat simplified. For instance, the binary division is arbitrary; for each dimension, intermediate entries could be inserted which might prove useful. Thus, questionnaires may be more or less directive. Moreover, not all the data collection techniques are taken into account: for instance, the corpus is not included in this matrix (since it did not prove particularly helpful in gathering useful data). However, comparisons should permit new light to be shed on the relevance and limits of the corpus.

(ii) Some semantic theses and their empirical adequacy
Consider the matrix; the example illustrating it has been chosen so that the whole range of the proposed devices is applicable. For instance, one may have noticed that the linguistic element (or item) under study is a sentence. Were it just a moneme—like French *avec*—would it be possible to use the referent in order to make its meaning explicit? Moreover, the item is not just any sentence. If our example were a sentence such as *all his hopes vanished,* would the referent mode be usable?

To answer these questions and others put in previous chapters, I will first report on some empirical research. I will then try to use the results of these in order to propose solutions to the problems.

Gabriella Oberlé (1988) carried out a survey on the meaning of some syntactic functions. Her objective was twofold: on the one hand, to find

Table 5 Study of the meaning: illustration of proposed techniques.

Procedures	Stimuli	Reactions
ND F > S Par.	A sentence is given such as: John is arriving with his horse (or the witch with her broom, etc.)	A paraphrase of the meaning of the given sentence is requested
D F > S Par.	A sentence is given: John is arriving with his horse	The informant is asked to choose the paraphrase which corresponds to it: (i) John is arriving accompanied by his horse (ii) John is arriving mounted on his horse (iii) John is arriving accompanied by or mounted on his horse
ND S > F Par.	Two sentences are given such as: (a) John is arriving, and he is riding his horse (b) John is arriving, and he is accompanied by his horse	A paraphrase of both (a) and (b) is requested
D S > F Par.	Two sentences are given such as: (a) John is arriving, and he is riding his horse (b) John is arriving, and he is accompanied by his horse	The sentence John is arriving with his horse is given and the informant is asked if it means (a); the same procedure is then used for (b)
ND F > S Ref.	A phrase is given such as: John is arriving with his horse	The informant is asked to put it in the situation it represents, either with objects or by drawing it
D S > F Ref.	A scenario is presented (with figures, a film, a drawing, etc.): (a) A man on a horse (b) A man on foot accompanied by a horse	The informant is asked which sentences correspond to it: (i) John is arriving with his horse (ii) John is arriving accompanied by his horse (iii) John is arriving mounted on his horse
ND S > F Ref.	A scenario is presented of: (a) A man on a horse (b) A man on foot accompanied by a horse	The informant is asked to describe scenario (a) and then scenario (b)
D F>S Ref.	A sentence is given: John is arriving with his horse	The informant is presented scenario (a)—a man on a horse — and asked if it corresponds to the sentence. Then, same procedure for scenario (b)—a man on foot accompanied by a horse.

ND: nondirective; D: directive; F > S: from formal stimulus to semantic reaction; S > F: from semantic stimulus to formal reaction; Par.: meaning explained by paraphrase; Ref.: recourse to referent to explain the meaning.

This particular questionnaire was designed for French *avec*, and cannot be transposed to English *with*, given that the syntactico-semantic constraints are not the same. The English translation is to be regarded as an aid to the reader unfamiliar with French. For a precise evaluation of the matrix, see the original with French example, as given in table 6.

(a)

(b)

(c)

Figure 6 French *avec* : 'instrumental' vs. 'comitative'.

out how tight or loose the interrelations of the meanings 'instrumental' and 'comitative' were in two contexts, and on the other, to examine what this difference, if any, implied for the distinction between syntax and semantics. I am citing this work for its first aspect, which is pertinent with respect to the present issue. The questionnaire was built on the bases suggested in the above matrix;[57] French *avec* was the first example studied. Drawings were used as a substitute for things. There were seventeen informants. Consider the following questions and respective answers relating to figure 6.

Question 3 (*Ref, F→S, D*) Which of the pictures represents the meaning of the following sentence?

> *Les hommes arrivent avec leurs chevaux*
> 'The men are arriving with their horses'

Answers: (a) 8, (b) 9, (c) 9

Question 4 (Par, F→S, D) What does the following sentence mean?

The men are arriving with their horses

Answers: (a) The men are arriving on their horses, 3; (b) The men are arriving accompanied by their horses, 5; (c) The men are arriving either accompanied by their horses or mounted on their horses, 12

As one can see from the reactions, the sentence has an inherent variability: it can denote for the horse an 'instrumental' relation or a 'comitative' one or either of them. But these interpretations are not equally valid. Question 4 provokes considerably more (c) answers than question 3. Given the fact that these questions are otherwise equivalent, this difference must be imputed to the difference of mode (i.e., referent in question 3 and paraphrase in question 4). In other words, recourse to paraphrase confirms the user in his belief that in this sentence, *avec* may mean both 'instrumental' and 'comitative'.[58]

Singy carried out a survey on the semantic values of the French verbal syntagm 'indicative imperfect' (cf. Singy, 1988). The survey aimed at discovering—besides the interrelations syntax/semantics—the extent to which this syntagm can refer to an actual or a hypothetical event. The questionnaire[59] was based on the above matrix. Twenty informants were questioned, and drawings were used instead of things. The results reveal discrepancies between the informants' responses due to the difference of role. Compare the following questions:

Question 1 (*Ref, ND, F→S*)[60] Can you put the following sentence into a scene by means of a drawing?

Il faisait beau, je sortais
'The weather was nice, I was going (or went) out.'

Question 2 (*Ref, ND, S→F*) The following drawings represent a situation that happened yesterday when I said, "the weather is nice, I am going out." How can the situation represented by the pictures be narrated?

Twenty informants out of twenty responded to question 1 with drawings showing an actual event. However, the responses to question 2 were not so unanimous: sixteen informants used the imperfect only to denote a real event; two informants used it for both real and hypothetical events; and two gave no answer, either for (a) or for (b) in figure 7, of the type *il faisait beau, je sortais*.

Given the fact that the only difference between these questions is one of role, the discrepancies can reasonably be interpreted as a result of role difference. In other words, the user, in the role of hearer, is tempted to recognize the imperfect as the expression of a real event, whereas while speaking he can use the same item to refer to a real event, a hypothetical event, or both.

The same survey provides us with data that show discrepancies due to differences in the surveyor's interference:

Q.4	Q.7
Par	Par
F→M	F→M
ND	D

If we compare questions 4 and 7, we find that the meanings attributed to the imperfect vary depending on whether the question is directive or nondirective. When the question is nondirective, twenty informants out of twenty recognized the imperfect as expressing a real event; with a directive question, the same informants admit other semantic values. Eighteen informants out of twenty accepted the 'real' meaning, two

Figure 7 Imperfect in French: 'real' vs. 'hypothetical'.

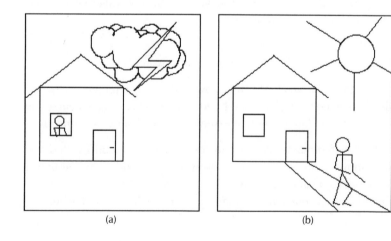

(a)   (b)

informants accepted the 'hypothetical' meaning, but none of them admitted that the imperfect could mean either 'real' or 'hypothetical'.

From this, one can conclude that of the two semantic values, the meaning 'real event' is more closely attached to the verbal syntagm 'imperfect'. This is why, without any hint from the survey, 'real event' is the meaning that comes to the user's mind, unlike the meaning 'hypothetical event', which needs to be suggested to informants for it to be accepted by some of them.

These experiments and many others show that the meaning of linguistic elements has a complex structure consisting of multiple layers. Different techniques may be used to bring the meaning to light, but no single technique can highlight all aspects of that meaning.

Empirical studies supply an adequate solution to other problems encountered in semantics, among them the question of whether a word has a meaning out of context. Singy and Oberlé (1987) carried out a series of surveys to reveal the semantic properties of grammatical and lexical items. In one of the surveys, informants were asked to give the meaning of isolated lexical items: *congé* 'time off', *chien* 'dog', *idée* 'idea', *sens* 'meaning', *fourchette* 'fork', and *raison* 'reason'. It should be remembered that the semantic variants are not distributed randomly; for each word, one variant heads the list. The meaning 'mental operation' was given for *idée* by thirty-five of the forty-two informants. In the same way, the variant 'instrument for food' was given forty times for *fourchette*. This corroborates results obtained by a pilot survey.

In my view, the results seem to invalidate the thesis that items only have a meaning in context. Not only can meanings be attributed to monemes out of context, but also a hierarchy among their semantic potentials appears. Below, the meanings of *idée* and *fourchette* are presented in descending order within their respective hierarchies.

> *idée:* (a) = mental operation
> (b) = discovery, origin, project
> (c) = opinion
> (d) = dream, chimera
> *fourchette:* (a) = instrument for food
> (b) = statistical instrument (deviation)
> (c) = part of a hair (split end)
> (d) = mechanical part (belt-guide)

(e) = soldering of two pieces (bracket)
(f) = trencherman

Other quantitative data from the same series of surveys show that this is not specific to the lexical field but is also valid for grammatical items. So, meanings obtained for grammatical items also reveal a clear hierarchical structure. For example, each of the following monemes has a central semantic variant: 'instrumental' is mentioned twenty-seven out of thirty times for *avec* 'with', and '*locative*' twenty-four out of thirty times for *à* 'to'.

These results also show that the degree of rigor in the structure of grammatical monemes is related to the number of variants a signifié has: the higher the number of variants for a signifié, the greater the hesitation and dissension in semantic intuition. This is valid for both grammatical and lexical items.

Thus, the moneme French *avec* 'with' and its three variants—'comitative' (*avec toi* 'with you'), 'instrumental' (*avec un marteau* 'with a hammer'), and 'manner' (*avec rage* 'in anger')—causes significantly less hesitation and dissension than the moneme *à* 'to', which has six variants: 'locative' (*à Paris* 'to Paris', 'in Paris'),[61] 'possession' (*il est à moi* 'it is mine'), 'linkage' (*il se prépare à partir* 'he is getting ready to leave'), 'goal' (*machine à écrire* 'typewriter'), 'manner' (*à pied* 'on foot'), and 'dative' (*donne à Paul* 'give to Paul').

Philippe Bossel's research (cf. Bossel, 1986) shows that lexical monemes like *bébé* 'baby', *enfant* 'child', *adulte* 'adult', and *vieillard* 'old man' have hierarchized meanings both out of context and within the context of a sentence. I am citing this work to illustrate grammatical-lexical interrelations. Consider the sentence *cette mère a eu deux bébés* 'this mother had/has had two babies'. It could mean that she gave birth twice or that she had twins. What is the reason for this ambiguity? Perhaps it is to be imputed to the passé composé which can refer to a recent past or a perfect. But this ambiguity is only effective as long as the number of babies does not make their simultaneous births improbable or impossible.

Bossel submitted the following sentences to survey.

Cette mère a eu deux bébés (Q. 14)
'This mother had/has had two babies'

Cette mère a eu huit bébés (Q. 17)
'This mother had/has had eight babies'

and asked twenty-two informants to give their meanings. These are their replies:

Q. 14		Q. 17	
(a) two births	17	(a) eight births	18
(b) twins	14	(b) octuplets	10
		(c) small animals	7

It can be seen that the number of replies referring to simultaneous births decreases with the increase in the number of babies. This is because the user finds it difficult to imagine that a mother could give birth to eight children at the same time. This tends to rule out the meaning 'recent past' for the verbal syntagm and to favor the meaning 'perfect'. Two alternative solutions suggest themselves: either the mother is thought to be an animal (and not human), or the eight births are considered to be successive. This interpretation of the informants' responses can be presented as a conflict between meaning features in the sentence. I take for granted that the French monemes passé composé and *mère* possess, among others, the following features:

Moneme	Meaning features
a eu passé composé	'recent past'
	'perfect'
	. . .
mère	'human'
	'nonhuman'
	. . .

If 'recent past' is actualized, then the parent must be nonhuman. The feature 'human' cannot be actualized unless the event is deemed to be not recent (hence 'perfect'). This is why the feature 'nonhuman' is more probable in the case of octuplets. Naturally, an explanation must be given as to why eight out of the twenty-two informants accept the meaning 'octuplets, human'. It is highly likely that such a meaning leads to situating the sentence in a fantastic universe. This is a hypothesis that ought to be verified.

To come back to classical debates, this survey provides an answer to the question of whether grammatical meaning is independent of lexical meaning and experience of the world. The interdependence of the two orders of facts emerges clearly from this survey.

Type and rank: two aspects of semantic heterogeneity. The experiments cited above bring out the structural heterogeneity of phenomena of meaning and show that multiple methods should be employed for any fully developed semantic study.

A closer examination of the heterogeneity of meaning reveals two aspects: types of meaning and levels or layers of structure. On the one hand, the way the average user knows linguistic meaning is multiple: a given signification might be known mainly because it is applicable to an extralinguistic experience, whereas in another case the meaning is essentially grasped by circumlocution. On the other hand, not all semantic variants are equally closely bound to a linguistic item—that is, some meaning phenomena are more rigorously structured than others and are thus situated on a higher level in the structural hierarchy.

These two aspects must not be confused, although they are somewhat related. A higher grade in the hierarchy, for instance, might have an effect on the type of semantic knowledge; if I know the meaning of a word perfectly I can use it for the appropriate thing and propose an adequate paraphrase for it. Thus there will be no difference between a referential type of semantic knowledge and a paraphrastic one. In this case, the user can specify the meaning of an item—say, French *quatre roues indépendantes* 'independent four-wheel suspension' as a technical characteristic of a car—by pointing to the things it does and does not apply to. He can also use a circumlocution such as: 'the axle is articulated (in three parts) so that when one wheel slips, the other is not pulled as well'. In such cases, a higher rank in the hierarchy implies a lack of distinction between the meaning types. But this is neither necessary nor generally the case: one can handle a linguistic item quite accurately with reference to things and yet not be able to describe its meaning (paraphrase), and *vice versa*.

One of the inadequacies of current semantic studies seems to be attributable to this confusion between type and rank. Reducing semantic phenomena to two kinds—grammatical and lexical—is a case of such confusion.

As for rank, semantic analysis is concerned with the internal structure of a signifié and its interrelation with other signifiés; the problems raised here are of the following kinds.

—How many variants does a signifié have? How wide or narrow is their scatter?
—How are different variants ranked relative to each other?
—What are the relations between the meanings manifested by one item compared with other items (i.e., homonymy, synonymy, polysemy, antonymy)?
—How are different signifiés or variants integrated in the system? How frequent are they in discourse?
—And so on.

Much of this has been discussed in classical works.[62] Type distinction, on the contrary, has been neglected in pure linguistics. The matrix above emphasizes this aspect of semantic heterogeneity. The experiments reported above reveal discrepancies between phenomena of meaning that are related to the dimensions of mode, role, and interference (or adherence). A theoretical reflection on meaning should explain the causes of such discrepancies and propose testable hypotheses. My conviction is that the way we acquaint ourselves with phenomena of meaning is relevant with respect to both the synchronic functioning of semantic structure and its diachronic evolution. Moreover, this explanation induces an interdisciplinary view of semantic problems.

Thus, if the user knows a given meaning mainly by the referent mode, this has certain effects on its uses and evolution. Consider the French word *canapé* 'settee, sofa': a description based on the paraphrase mode may bring out the following features: 'seat for two or three', 'made of hard material', 'with (four) legs', 'with a back-piece', and 'with arms' (cf. B. Pottier, 1963 and 1965). Yet on a synchronic plane, the average user will identify a seat without legs and made of soft material—for example, an inflatable plastic seat—as a *canapé* if certain conditions are satisfied (e.g., 'seat', 'comfort', etc.). Also, from a diachronic point of view, the evolution of such a moneme depends much less on the evolution of adjacent items than on the evolution of the things to which it refers. The appearance of new items—for instance, French *canapé-lit* 'sofa-bed'— is thus due to the appearance of new things. This is not indiscriminately true for all linguistic items. There are items for which the meaning is basically known by the paraphrase mode (e.g., words relating to art, intellect, virtue, etc.). In this case, what is relevant is mainly the semantic interrelations of words, semantic field theory (for both synchronic and diachronic aspects). As Trier showed (cf. Trier, 1973), the functioning and evolution of either words such as *Wîsheit, Kunst, List,* and *Wizzen* can best be explained within an interrelational framework.[63] Likewise, the limitations of semantic field theory demonstrate the relevance of the mode distinction: as Mounin showed, the delimitation of semantic fields raises serious problems in the case of domestic animals and habitat (cf. Mounin, 1965a and b). In my view, these difficulties relate at least in part to the fact that the items under study are essentially known by referent mode.

The experiments I have mentioned confirm the heterogeneity of semantic facts and the twofold distinction of rank *versus* type. However, these are my personal conclusions. They are not self-evident and remain questionable. For instance, certain of my conclusions about modes would collapse if it were shown that the techniques used are not adequate. Consider the experiment on 'comitative' versus 'instrumental'. Several objections are possible, among others, how do we know that our drawings represent 'instrumental' and 'comitative' respectively? can we be sure that our paraphrases interpret these relational meanings? in the survey, where the referent question precedes the paraphrase question, does this not affect the informants' responses? and so on.

From a technical point of view, these questions are to be examined seriously and tested experimentally. While preparing the questionnaire, care was taken to ensure that nondirective questions were not placed after directive questions. One might presume that presenting a question like "does the item *i* have the feature *f*?" might influence the informants in their answers to a question like "what features does the item *i* have?" *A priori,* such an influence between a referent question and a paraphrase question does not seem plausible.

From a theoretical point of view, one should note that regularities have been observed in the relation between modes of access and informants' responses. Any serious reflection has to explain the reasons this is so. I do not construe my explanation as a definitive one. We should abandon it if a more satisfactory one (for instance, one with greater plausibility or generality) is found.

I would like to return to one point in order to stress precisely where I believe experimentation should be placed within semantics. There are certainly sentences whose meanings are obvious to anyone, but there are also cases where the meaning is not evident at first sight. Does the sentence *colorless green ideas sleep furiously* have a meaning? Instead of referring to the authority of a Chomsky or a Jakobson, another way— and a far more judicious one—is to refer to the behavior and intuition of the users. This simple idea constitutes the foundation of experimentation in linguistics.

(iii) The entailments of semantic experiments

What do semantic experiments like those reported here entail for other areas of linguistic research?

In order to answer this question, I should mention that the matrix given in (VII.3.iii) is based on a fundamental principle: the relation be- tween signifiant and signifié as a constitutive function of language signs and, more generally, of semiotic systems. From this it follows that such experimental devices are, *mutatis mutandis,* applicable outside the area of semantics—in syntax, morphology and phonology, as well as in non- linguistic sign systems.

In semiotic systems, for example, it is altogether possible to use the same procedures to demonstrate the user's knowledge of such signs as a flashing amber light (for road traffic) or an index finger pointing at someone or something (gestural behavior). But a difference appears here which is due to differences in the semiotic power of languages on the one hand and of nonlinguistic systems on the other: the omnipo- tence of languages means that although any nonlinguistic message can be translated into languages, the converse is not true. The consequences of this disparity can easily be imagined; however, we will not discuss the point here.

As to the application of these survey techniques in other areas of lin- guistics and the modifications they must undergo for this purpose, it should be noted that apart from the constitutive function of the sign, semantic surveys resort, as we stated in the preceding discussion, to other presuppositions without which the objectives of a survey would be too limited and surveys would lose a great deal of their interest. In what follows we want to make the assumptions for both semantic and phonological surveys quite explicit.

A comparison of the two seems rich in lessons about the scope and limits of surveys; it could show if (and to what extent) the limits of surveys are dependent on the characteristics of the objects under study, or if these limits have been set by accident (i.e., if a finer study of a given phenomenon is not available, it might be due to the fact that no researcher has judged the problems beyond certain limits to be of sufficient interest).

Identity of elements. By confining oneself to the problems connected with the identity of elements, it would be reasonable to expect a survey to provide solutions to the following problems (among others).

–An isolated element: To what extent can an element be identified in isolation? What features can be assigned to it?
–An element in context: How do reciprocal influences (i.e., those exercised by an element, or those affecting it through contact with other elements) contribute to identifying this element?
–An element in the system: How does an element's place in the system (i.e., its relations of opposition and resemblance to other elements) contribute to its identification?

If the linguist resorts to a survey to solve these problems, it is because he supposes that the language user has a certain knowledge of the phenomena under study. This supposed knowledge can be formulated as follows.

(A) an isolated element: The language user has some intuitive knowledge of the element and its properties.
(B) An element in context: The language user knows the influence an element has on neighboring elements and the influence these have on the element under study.
(C) An element in the system: The language user is aware of the resemblances and differences of an element with respect to other elements in the system. He makes use of them to identify the element.

Transposed to semantics, points (A), (B) and (C) concern what a language user knows of the signifié, but by this wording I have in mind a much more explicit thesis than the vague phrase "knowledge of the signifié." It has the advantage of showing (as we will see later) the difference between the prerequisites underlying semantic and phonological surveys. Indeed, as long as we confine ourselves to generalities—for example, knowledge of the signifié and signifiant—the prerequisites are the same for both types of survey. Clarified in this way, these hypotheses can be confronted with the results of surveys. The confrontation helps in realizing the extent to which these hypotheses are of value for both semantics and phonology.

It should be noted that the object considered here is a single element, not a sequence of elements. This limitation has been fixed for the practical purposes of comparison; it is not at all—needless to say—a consequence of the theoretical framework, nor of the inherent properties of language phenomena. The elements considered are the phoneme for phonology and the signifié of a free moneme (or morpheme) for semantics.

Semantic awareness versus phonological awareness. What does the language user know of the signifié of a moneme? We will restrict ourselves here to the type of knowledge he can recall to his consciousness; it is in fact knowledge of the type under consideration which makes linguistic surveys possible as those reported here.

(A') An isolated moneme. Does the language user know the signifié of an isolated moneme (i.e., one not inserted in a sentence and not opposed to a paradigm of elements)? I believe we can answer this in the affirmative, on the evidence of the results of existing surveys. This knowledge may be revealed by the way the language user talks about the meaning of words. From this emerge the semantic properties the language user attributes to words, that is, the relevant features of the signifié (or sememes).

(B') A moneme within a context. Does the language user know of the influence of context on an element? It seems so. The proof is that in order to define the meaning of a word, the language user often resorts to exemplification, which is nothing other than putting the moneme into a context. It is not rare for the language user to explain the reason for this.

(C') A moneme within the system. Does the language user know of the relationship of one moneme to another? Yes. Strategies of definition like the following are frequent: "a glider, it is the same as a plane except that a glider doesn't have an engine."

When transposed to the phoneme, analogous questions do not receive analogous replies.

(A'') An isolated phoneme. Is the language user able to give a definition that parallels the one he gives of a moneme? It seems not. Without special training the language user is probably unable to give a definition of phonemes (e.g., in terms of their relevant features).

(B'') A phoneme within a context. Does the language user know of the relationship of a phoneme with its context? The answer seems practically to be in the negative. In any case, he does not use such knowledge naturally to identify phonemes, and rightly so, I believe. I do not see how putting a phoneme in a (phonematic) context can help in identifying it or in specifying its properties.[64]

(C'') A phoneme in the system. Does the language user know of the relationship of opposition between one phoneme and other phonemes? Yes. And this is, it seems to me, the most usual means of identifying phonemes and of characterizing them. Moreover, it is within reach of every language user, and it requires no special training for him to cite phonemes of his language.

The comparison we have just made between semantic and phonological awareness is so global that little experimental data have been given to support it. However, the comparison does have a certain interest, as it leads to conclusions that to my knowledge have not been stated very clearly. Thus, we have established that if the intuitive knowledge of the language user is taken as empirical data, great differences appear between the objects of semantics and those of phonology. Yet, the first proposals for a method of analysis were designed for and applied in phonology.

Consequently, it is sensible to give pride of place to oppositional relations in a phonological analysis, as it is mainly in this way that the language user knows phonemes. Nothing, on the contrary, would justify granting the same importance to relations of opposition in semantics; the intuitive reactions of the speaker show that he is also aware of the semantic properties of monemes out of context and that he knows how to use the elements of context to identify the signifié of a moneme. It appears that applying in semantics the descriptive tool designed for phonology was a hasty step, as it was not accompanied by any profound reflection on the adequacy of such a methodological borrowing.

It seems to me of great interest to underline the link between the linguistic function(s) of an element and the way the speaker knows that

.element. The fact that the user knows phonemes from the point of view of their oppositions is certainly not due to accident. My own conclusion is that awareness of the object—in this case a phoneme—is linked to the way the speaker uses it. If the phoneme serves above all a purpose of distinction, it is by its distinctive properties that the user knows and identifies it. Consequently, recourse to oppositions constitutes an adequate means of reconstructing the user's knowledge. This justifies the survey techniques used in phonology. The same techniques do not have the same value when the object under study does not have the same characteristics. The methodological conclusion is that any transfer of survey method must be justified by the common properties of the objects under study.

Meaning and frequency of monemes. Apart from the global comparison we have just made, it is also possible to make a more detailed study which would allow the limits of semantic awareness and their causes to be understood. Such a detailed study necessarily requires subdivisions at the level of both monemes and phonemes in order to account for the heterogeneity of the structures at each of these levels. Furthermore, these subdivisions must be sufficiently fine to lead to explanations which are both likely and verifiable.

As an example of limitation, one could cite the case of the French moneme *de* for which informants seem unable to attribute—in the context Noun + *de* + Noun—semantic properties showing up one or several common bases.[65] From this observation one might conclude that the users may be unaware of the meaning of a grammatical unit they currently use in everyday speech. This does not seem to be the case for lexical monemes.

Thus the distinction between grammatical and lexical monemes, however necessary, is not sufficient, if only because not all grammatical monemes have a signifié which is not accessible in the speaker's intuition. Results of surveys carried out on grammatical monemes like *avec* 'with' and *contre* 'against' show semantic regularities and hierarchies. This is what leads us to assume that beyond a certain level of frequency, grammatical monemes have a signifié which is inaccessible in the awareness of the language user. And finally, this also leads to many interesting problems, such as the following.

—The relationship between the frequency of a moneme and the status of its signifié in the intuition of a speaker: Does an increase of frequency entail laxity in the structure of the signifié?[66]
—The relationship between the frequency of a moneme and the range of its signifié: Does an increase of frequency have as an effect a widening of the distribution of its semantic variants?
—The relationship between the context-bound presence of a moneme and the status of its signifié in the intuition of a speaker: Does semantic awareness decrease as one increases the contextual constraints on its choice (i.e., on its presence or absence)?

Questions about the frequency of the signifié are certainly not new; but I have tried to state the problem in terms that make empirical verification possible. Semantic features, as well as their identity or difference, are conceived in such a way as to make research independent of the describer's arbitrariness or his *ad hoc* decision. From the same point of view, other experimental perspectives open up as well: for example, the role of high frequency or wide scatter in the process of desemantization, a process by which a moneme's signifié becomes weaker and tends toward zero, with the result that the moneme, which no longer has a signifié, ceases to be a moneme (cf. Lüdtke, 1977 and 1986).

The fact that in certain cases the signifié of a moneme is not accessible in the intuition of the language user is not specific to grammatical monemes. Cases can also be found in the lexicon. Thus, the man in the street might have no precise idea of what *nitrate* means. In the same way, a child of about four might not be able to explain the meaning of *hundred* or *thousand*. Here, the kind of explanation proposed for *de* is not applicable; rather, we shall resort to experiential limitation which we oppose to structural limitation, as, for example, the case of *de*. In the latter case, the experience reported by a linguistic element is very well known by the speaker: everyone knows the relation established by *de* between the elements of *ville de Paris* 'city of Paris', *huile d'olive* 'olive oil', or *maison de campagne* 'country house'. The difficulties the language user encounters when he tries to define a meaning come therefore from linguistic structure. It is quite different for *nitrate*: this moneme is linked to a concept which is not too familiar to the average person. In the same way, *hundred* and *thousand* denote concepts a little outside a child's experience and his environment (cf. Tabouret-Keller, 1972–73).

By context-bound presence, we refer to cases where a moneme is the only one that can occur once the preceding and following monemes have been chosen. For instance, in French *huile d'olive* 'olive oil', the choice of *huile* 'oil' and *olive* 'olive' determines the presence of the preposition *de,* so that no other preposition can figure in the context *huile—olive*. This amounts to the assumption that the freer the choice of a moneme in a context, the higher the user's awareness of the richness of its signifié.

This assumption may be subsumed under a more general hypothesis, namely, that the way the speaker-hearer uses the elements of his language conditions the way he knows them.

Thus, the problems encountered in our attempts to gain access to semantic intuition lead to the statement that not all aspects of meaning can be attained by the same technique; furthermore, these problems lead to the advancement of hypotheses that can be tested on the cases of the inaccessibility of meaning.

Conscious knowledge and operational knowledge. In what precedes, I have only considered one type of awareness that the language user has, that is, what he can consciously recall. This choice does not mean that other types of awareness are worthless or of little importance. The opposite is in fact true, as I believe that all forms of knowledge must be taken into account in a full-fledged study, and it was with this aim (i.e., widening the scope of the data examined) that we proposed the matrix for the survey on the signifié. Thus, an operational knowledge can be distinguished from conscious knowledge; it is also knowledge, although of a different type. It is often[67] this operational knowledge which is referred to in affirming the language user's awareness of phonemes. This affirmation is based on the observation that the user is able to distinguish *pad* from *bad* or *cod* from *god*. This kind of knowledge, important as it may be, does not exhaust the variety of angles from which the speaker knows the elements of his language. Yet because of a postulate (often implicit) in many linguistic theories, knowledge was conceived as monolithic and reduced to operational knowledge. Such a conception and the reduction to which it led have had practical and theoretical consequences which need to be examined.

One of the consequences of this conception was to expect only one thing from the informant: he was to deliver evidence of his operational knowledge to the describer. Thus, techniques were created which enabled the linguist to manipulate linguistic materials, the role of the language user being limited to passing a judgment on the product of the manipulations, for example, is the sequence *xyz* possible? and is it equivalent to or different from *wyz*?

For instance, in commutation tests (termed substitution tests in American linguistics), the describer varies an element and submits the result of the operation to the intuitive judgment of the language user. (Examples could be cited from descriptive techniques of generative grammar, but I won't dwell on them here.) Limiting the role of the informant in this way is based on the hypothesis that beyond this he cannot provide us with any relevant information. Even if this limitation is valid to a certain extent in phonology,[68] nothing permits it to be considered equally valid for meaningful elements. If certain grammatical monemes are considered, there is definitively an analogy with phonemes from this point of view: for instance, bound morphemes, which by definition cannot be used in isolation and whose semantic identity cannot be revealed out of context. This is the case with French /-r-/-r- 'future' and Fr. /-i-/-i- 'imperfect'. For French /numarʃrō/ *nous marcherons* 'we will walk' and /numarʃiō/ *nous marchions* 'we walked', on the contrary, it is much easier to determine the meaning. The exaggerated role attributed to context is due in part to these two factors: the semantic model was inspired by the phonological model, and the first studies concentrated mainly on grammatical monemes (especially on those which present rigorous constraints from the point of view of syntactic construction). The result was that only the grammatical domain—or rather a part of it—was considered to be structured.

It should be noted that in most linguistic theories, semantic studies started relatively late. This seems attributable to the limiting conception of a speaker's knowledge. If we consider our hypothesis about the linguistic knowledge of users, we have no reason to maintain such indefensible assumptions. That grammar and lexicon are distinct seems obvious; but this does not imply that grammar must serve as a model for the lexicon, nor that it enjoys a logical priority. Consequently, the observation that constructional constraints are stronger in grammar than in the lexicon does not lead to the conclusion that the lexicon is less structured or not structured at all; the only judicious conclusion that can be drawn is that constructional constraint is virtually unusable in the lexicon and has a convincing application in only part of the grammar. This means that a method used in a phonological analysis and efficacious for this purpose can hardly be so for the analysis of the signifié of monemes. Such a statement leads to the question of what the properties of the signifié are which create an obstacle to the application of such methods.

The answer to this question points the way to an alternative solution. One could examine the different roles that oppositional and contextual properties play in the two domains; one could also show that lexical meaning is more immediately accessible in the intuition than grammatical meaning. This statement enables us to understand why theoretical reflection about the word and meaning is much older than reflection about phonological elements. One of the reasons seems to be that access to meaning is more direct, on the one hand, and may follow multiple paths (as we tried to show in the matrix on access to meaning); whereas to gain an understanding of phonological mechanisms it was necessary to wait for sophisticated theories to show the preponderant role of a system of opposition in the identification of elements. I cannot present here an exhaustive treatment of the differences between semantic and phonological structures from the triple point of view of isolated element, element in a context, and element in the system. The aim of my discussion has been to show the interest of the varieties of knowledge possessed by language users in the quest for solutions to certain problems in linguistics.

Syntax versus phonology and semantics. To conclude, a short comparison with syntax seems useful, on account of the problems that it reveals; what makes it easy to compare signifié and phoneme is the fact that they are the terms of the constitutive function of the linguistic sign: signifiant ↔ signifié. An attempt to understand the meaning of a form (for example, the meaning our French-speaking informant attributes to the phonic sequences /furʃet/ 'fork') does not come up against any major difficulties; nor does understanding the form that corresponds to a meaning. The problems are more intricate when the sign is considered in its entirety. For example, when the informant reacts to our question about phonic sequences—such as French *la pluie n'a pas cessé de la journée* 'the rain hasn't stopped all day' and *il a plu toute la journée* 'it has rained all day'—as equivalent (or different), the linguist cannot say if the judgment bears on their syntactic or semantic identity. Introducing technical concepts such as signifiant, signifié and sign in order to decide this is inconceivable; at best, the informant would be transformed into a describer. I do not think other solutions to this problem can be envisaged; in this case the distinction between sign and signifié cannot be based directly on the user's conscious knowledge. This distinction does not appear firsthand in that it is supported by concepts the linguist has created within the framework of his model or theory. From this concept come the variable boundaries which are dependent on the theoretical perspective of the describer. There is no need to stress further the importance of determining the extent to which, and the viewpoint from which, the speaker identifies the sign, the signifié, and their limits. If it is not possible to gain access to this identity by resorting to some sort of conscious knowledge, the alternative is to resort to his operational knowledge, and that is precisely the kind of criteria used in structural linguistics to set up the hierarchy between phonology, morphology, syntax, and semantics. Yet this hierarchy often suffers from a great shortcoming: the criteria used to appreciate the levels are not the same. When it is affirmed that phonology is more structured than syntax, the degrees of structuration are evaluated differently. Indeed, structuration is determined in syntax solely in terms of operational knowledge of the speaker, whereas in phonology it calls on both conscious knowledge and operatory knowledge; this is comparing incomparables. In the same way, to say that semantics is less structured than syntax is to compare one domain in which the knowledge of the speaker is above all operational (i.e., syntax) with another in which the speaker's knowledge is mainly conscious. The problem of the boundaries between syntax (domain of the sign) and semantics (domain of the signifié) is thus reduced to the problem of the relationship between the two types of knowledge. One interesting question is raised here: to what extent do the two types of knowledge go hand in hand or come into conflict? In terms of the behavior and intuition of the speaker, the problem comes back to this: to what extent does the speaker, in order to identify a sign, resort to the positive properties of the sign, and to what extent to its relational properties (in contexts or in the system)? To what extent do the two types of property complement each other or come into conflict?

Once these questions about the sign and the signifié have been asked and answered, it will be easier to envision the links between syntax and semantics. Interesting problems still remain in this area. I will restrict myself to two diachronic problems: which factors must come into play in order for a single moneme to fragment and become a sequence of monemes, and what are the respective roles of combinatory and semantic properties in these processes? An adequate solution to these problems seems impossible unless the multiple facets of the user's linguistic knowledge are taken into consideration.

The common feature of all the problems discussed here is that we have an established survey technique which we attempt to apply to new facts. Each time we fail in our attempt, we question ourselves about the causes of this failure, and this leads us to advancing new hypotheses. It is this simple idea which is at the root of the dialectic links between hypothesis and experimentation.

Speaking of experimentation, up to this point I have invoked data coming almost exclusively from sample surveys. This is due neither to a culpable ignorance of former inquiries, nor to a cheap quest for authenticity, nor to the belief that it is the only means of access to empirical data; these three misunderstandings I want to avoid.

I am fully aware that recourse to a questionnaire type of survey is nothing new to linguistics: as early as 1902, Gilliéron and Edmond published the *Atlas linguistique de la France*, the data of which had been gathered through surveys. Since then, linguists have not ceased to use this technique in different forms and more or less felicitously, even if the uncompromising formalism of some threw discredit on it—for instance, discredit of those who would take an interest only in *langue,* structure or competence.

The originality claimed by the theoretical positions defended in the present work rests in the fact that the collected data are situated within the to-and-fro movement between hypotheses and observations, and in aiming at a progressively closer adequacy of hypotheses and higher precision of observations. It is within this movement to and fro that one can realize that a technique is efficient only for a certain range of phenomena, and that past a certain point, it has to be reexamined, reshaped, readapted, or even abandoned and replaced by other techniques that are more able to explain and foresee the reactions of the object under study. With such a view, the exclusive recourse to the survey technique does not imply that the other experimental techniques are uninteresting—for instance, corpus, interviews, devices perfected by psycholinguists such as perception tests, measuring the reaction speed to stimuli, observation of the neurovegetative system, and so on. On the contrary, we assert that confronting results obtained by different techniques will give us the opportunity to shed new light on problems inadequately resolved by a single technique. This is provided that a thorough examination be made of the reasons for the greater efficiency of one technique versus another; merely stating the success or failure of one technique compared to another would of course not be sufficient. Furthermore, the implications of such efficiency for our conception of the linguistic structure must be pursued.[69] Thus it is possible not only to understand more completely the object of study, but also to have the opportunity to grasp the structure of other phenomena. The studies made by Thomas Lahusen illustrate how reflecting thoroughly on the goals and methods of experimental research on phonology and syntax can lead to insights in the field of the semiology of the literary source. Starting from the idea that language and literature both have a social dimension, Lahusen formulates the hypothesis that they share certain characteristics as to their relationship to social phenomena and as to the way they follow from and reflect social discrepancies (cf. Lahusen, 1979, 1982). Lahusen's study shows that the relevance of the distinction between "rigorous" and "lax" zones in the linguistic structure, together with its individual and collective correspondence, can be verified through its being confronted with the extralinguistic. The quantitative study of the systematically recorded forms of address in a Polish novel from the nineteenth century and in five Russian works from the same period—four novels and a cycle of short stories—demonstrates the absence of a discrete allocutionary structure of a *tu/vous* dichotomy type. Even though two poles undoubtedly exist (the reciprocity-solidarity relationship and the nonreciprocity-power relationship), this bipolarity affects only part of the examined interactions and only symbolizes already polarized social relationships (aristocracy/servants, bourgeoisie/ manual workers, etc.). Furthermore it expresses the rigidity of an important and still feudal part of society. A third relationship, called "indecision," is situated between both poles; fuzzier than the other two, it is a kind of transitory zone between a power relationship and one of solidarity. It significantly concerns intermediary social groups (the petty bourgeoisie, for instance) whose status precarity corresponds on the symbolic level to an indecision of the "social self," or, in other terms, the euphemization of the objective power relationships. On the collectivity level, the "fuzzy" relationship is nothing but the expression of the social mobility and the other great changes connected with Poland's and Russia's entering the industrial revolution era. As for the forms of address, they belong to the "central structure" when they express polarized relationships (nominal paradigm). The indecision relation is connected with the "marginal structure": more subtle (more euphemized) use of the first name, of the last name, of the title, of the terms of kinship, and so forth.

VIII Conclusion: Language, Its Structure and Use

VIII.0 Purpose of this Work

This book is dedicated to the explanation of language phenomena. The fundamental problem is the examination of the way the speaker-hearer uses and knows his language. The issues raised are: What is language? What is its structure like (i.e., its makeup and constitutive parts)? Is language structure formal (i.e., homogeneous and invariable) or random? What characterizes language variations? How is intercomprehension possible despite language variations? What is the relation between language structure (in synchrony) and language evolution (in diachrony)? And so on. This book has aimed at examining these questions. Let us now summarize the answers. Note that the same problems can be raised about our field of study itself, for instance, what are the object and the method of linguistics?

Let us forget for a while that there is no unanimity concerning the notions mentioned above,[70] and let us summarize the problems the way I have conceived them in this book.

VIII.1 Language Structure

Languages—conceived of as systems of universal communication—are characterized by two types of properties that specify (a) their constitutive parts and (b) the nature of their system.

(a) Constitutive parts

The system of a language includes signs made up of signifiant and signifié. Each of these sides of the sign is in its turn a complex, composed of smaller elements. The signifiant of a minimal sign (the moneme) is made up of phonemes and sometimes of prosodemes. The signifié of a moneme is also a combination, one of semantic elements (features, particles, etc.).

(b) Nature of the system

Languages have a complex and hierarchized structure, in the sense that their constitutive elements (units, sequences, classes, and rules)—nonfinite in number—are distinguished by continua to which they assume different degrees of relevance.[71]

Here is another formulation, as a way of showing this conception of language in contrast with the classical point of view.

(b') Nature of the system

Languages have a nonformal structure, complex and hierarchized in the sense that they are made up of elements which themselves are not formal in nature and thus cannot be reduced to a finite number of absolutely rule-governed discrete items.

VIII.2   Structure versus Usage

To illustrate this conception of language and of its use, and also to underline the kind of ability and knowledge it supposes on the language user's part, let us consider again the following example.

(1) *Baby Jack finished his scotch broth and french fries.*

To utter this sentence, the speaker starts from an experience that he articulates (cuts up, divides, segments . . .) into significant units (words, monemes, morphemes . . .) to which he assigns the corresponding signifiants, in their turn articulated into phonemes. The process can be represented as follows:

Speaker: experience→monemes→phonemes→speech (*parole*)

The hearer then follows the same path backwards to reconstruct the experience.

Hearer: speech→phonemes→monemes→experience

This schematic sketch[72] illustrates the characteristics listed under (a), which are found (with slight differences) in most structuralist and post-structuralist theories. These characteristics take in a certain number of fundamental properties of language. Thus they allow the determination of the phonological units that constitute an utterance. For instance, the above example is manifested by the following phonematic sequence.

/bejbi dʒæk finiʃt hiz skɔtʃ brɔə ænd frentʃ frajz/

They make it possible to bring out the significant units (monemes or morphemes) that form the utterance. Using these principles, one can establish, besides the units themselves, the relations these units have within the sequence (syntagmatic relations) as well as the ones they have within the system (paradigmatic relations). These relations make it possible to establish relatively explicit criteria and procedures that circumscribe concepts such as *classes* (*categories* or *paradigms*), *syntactic properties* or *rules* (*function, subordination,* and *coordination*), and so on. These relations also permit us to go beyond the traditionally vague and *ad hoc* definitions which often become worthless when one simply changes the examples that accompany them. Consequently, structural linguistics, while retaining certain terms and/or categories from former traditions, redefines these relations by basing them on clear criteria. Categories—for example, those of *noun* and *adjective*—are thus no longer opposed on the level of their semantic content; it cannot seriously be upheld that the adjectives *scotch* and *french* are exclusively quality indicators, nor that the nouns *broth* and *fries* only refer to beings. If one makes a distinction between noun and adjective, it is above all because of their differing structural relationships: syntagmatic ones on the one hand (nouns and adjectives appear in distinct surroundings), and paradigmatic ones on the other hand (the elements with which they are interchangeable are not the same for nouns as for adjectives). Let us now consider another utterance.

(2) *Tough guys built a small house and a huge barn.*

It is above all the choice and sequence ties that make *scotch, french, small,* and *huge* (or *broth, fries, house* and *barn*) belong to the same class.

In other respects, certain language features follow by implication from characteristics (a). The existence of phenomena such as *paradigms* (*choice, categories* or *class*), syntagms (*sequence* or *combination*), and *rules* or *syntactic properties,* far from being an *ad hoc* assumption, is thus a condition and a consequence of the function of language as a communication tool of universal extent. One can hardly imagine that any language devoid of these properties could be employed. By way of proof, judicious use of these concepts permits the establishment of analysis procedures—such as the commutation test—the results of which are widely confirmed by empirical facts.

All this constitutes enormous progress in the knowledge of language and presents unquestionable advantages. Thanks to this acquired knowledge, it is now possible to grasp and describe the structure of language without being grossly influenced by one's own cultural and linguistic systems.[73]

The (rather classical) characteristics (a) have a broad scope of relevance, but nevertheless they are subject to application restrictions and constraints, which seriously question their acknowledged absoluteness. Were one to adhere strictly to these properties, language production and perception would be submitted to absolute rules, the validity of which is more than problematic if one refers in the matter to empirical evidence. The more recent characteristics (b) state the relativity of characteristics (a).

Let us try to illustrate the difficulties that principles (a) encounter by applying them to example (1). Given the notion of moneme class, *scotch* and *french* both belong to the adjective class and are likely to determine (i.e., to be subordinated to) a noun, respectively *broth* and *fries.* Strictly speaking, each class includes a set of monemes characterized and defined by the same syntactic properties, among others to take on the same functions. How then do the other members of the adjective class behave? Are *wooden, Muslim, disgusting, Catholic, delicious,* and *metaphysical* adjectives? If so, are they all supposed to assume the same functions as *scotch* and *french*? If not, to what class(es) do they belong? Difficulties will not fail to appear whichever the adopted solution may be. In the first case (in which all belong to one class), the describer has to look for the causes accounting for the fact that some of the following sentences are more or less normal (i.e., correct or grammatically acceptable) than others.[74]

(1a) *Baby Jack finished his scotch broth and french fries*
(1b) *Baby Jack finished his wooden broth and french fries*
(1c) *Baby Jack finished his Muslim broth and french fries*
(etc.)

In the second case (i.e., if *Muslim, disgusting,* etc. are not assigned to the same class as *scotch* and *french*), one will be tempted to refine the classification and to establish adjective subclasses. Yet this is not a better solution since there is no end to such a subclassification, as shown by theoretical or empirical research (cf. Gross, 1975, 1976; Mahmoudian, 1980; Ross, 1972, 1973).

This kind of problem requires reflection on the theoretical foundations of descriptive practice. What is the significance of the difficulties encountered in the forming of classes? And more generally, what is the status of classes in language structure? Two solutions have been proposed to the question of moneme classes, yet neither seems satisfactory. The first one consists of setting apart structure (competence, *langue*) from use (performance, *parole*). But in the end, this causes theory to miss its goal and object at the risk of losing control of the process of theory construction. The second solution questions the legitimacy or even negates the existence of any concept of class. This conception has one important drawback: the principle of semiotic omnipotence (or universality) cannot be maintained, given the fact that it presupposes the existence of classes and rules (among others, syntactic ones).[75]

Examining these attempts and mistakes inspires me with the conclusion that classes are a necessary element of every language structure, yet do not take on the formal structure that most structural theories have assigned them. That is to say that classes do indeed exist, but they are entities governed by complex and hierarchized regularities.

Syntactical classes do not build a particular case. Each linguistic notion—on the level of the model as well as on the theoretical level—demonstrates the same relativity of structure, for each characterizes a complex phenomenon which includes conflicting, ill-balanced, perpetually readjusting factors.

Characteristics (b) follow from this, pointing to the relativity rather than to the invalidity of these concepts. These more recent features have been less thoroughiy developed and discussed, and their consequences have not all been brought to light. They will be emphasized in the following sections.

VIII.3 Object and Method of Linguistics
If we take again the question raised at the beginning of this chapter about the object and the method of linguistics, we are now able to summarize the answer.

—The object of linguistics is to view human languages as communication tools.

—The method consists in starting from postulates (axioms or premises) concerning languages, to draw from them the consequences for the behavior and the intuition of the language user, and to evaluate the postulates in and by their confrontation with empirical data. If the hypotheses do not correspond—at all or in part—to observable data, one returns to the postulates to reshape or replace them. This will constitute the starting point for a new run: hypotheses→empirical confrontation (not to use the term verification, which is too heavily loaded with connotations), and so on.

The example of phonological units is particularly enlightening as an illustration of the duality between theory and model: the linguistic theory states axioms such as the following.

(1) Axiom: Every linguistic system includes phonemes.

But it is not verifiable nor falsifiable. By way of compensation, the model states hypotheses, these being susceptible of empirical control. Thus:

(2) Hypothesis: (a) /ə/ is a phoneme by French-speaking individuals who satisfy precise age, geographical, social, and other conditions. (b) the postvocalic and tautosyllabic phoneme /r/ is pronounced as a constrictive retroflex consonant by upper middle class New Yorkers under forty (this in 1964).

It is important to say that the movement back and forth between hypothesis and data does not develop in a closed circle; at the end of his experimenting, the linguist is not returned to his point of departure. A better image for the procedure presented would be that of a spiral, given the fact that every new experiment starts from a raised level, since the basic linguistic knowledge has been enriched with elements acquired from the preceding experiment.

Two types of postulates are needed to ensure our moving back and forth between conception of language and observable phenomena:[76] a general theory of the human language and particular models concerning pinpoint problems. These models provide one with sufficiently explicit hypotheses so that they can be subjected to the verdict of observable facts. Theory, which enunciates the fundamental properties of language, is too general to allow for a confrontation with empirical data.

The observable object is not identical with raw facts but is a strictly defined part of them. It is only under such conditions that the model gains precision; the price paid for this is that the validity of the model remains limited to local, pinpoint facts, as well as to a given theoretical framework. Since the object delimitation and its observation are determined by the searcher's choices—at the level of theory as well as at the level of the model—the object remains dependent upon them. For instance, to value the phonematic status of /ə/, one can access the language user's behavior and intuition,[77] but the results obtained become worthless in a theoretical framework denying any relevance to intuitive[78] and/or behavioral[79] data.

VIII.4 Theoretical Differences

Let us return to a problem we have just put aside (cf. VIII.1): the lack of unanimity about the object and method of linguistics.

Linguistics is not a *normal science:*[80] There is no consensus as to what linguists as a whole take for granted and as to the directions of research they view as valid. From there result the problems one encounters when trying to take stock of our current knowledge in matters of language. But these problems are not all of the same nature: they go under different levels: terminology, exposition, emphasis, point of view or conception.

First, there are *terminological differences,* which are not troublesome in themselves: it does not matter much for a linguistic unit to be designated by two distinct terms, as long as the concept to which they refer is the same (e.g., the Saussurians' *moneme* and Bloomfield's and the Bloomfieldians' *morpheme*).[81]

Secondly, one encounters *expository problems:* the adopted itinerary can differ from one linguist to another. Two ways are equivalent insofar as the phenomena they reveal are the same. Such is the case for the freedom and constraints that a language's syntax provides in the construction of utterances of different degrees of complexity. It is of no importance if one goes from complex to simple sentences (through the successive elimination of their constituents),[82] or in the opposite direction from simple to complex sentences (through the successive adding of new constituents).[83]

Certain differences are due to the fact that some currents *emphasize* a certain type of phenomena rather than another, for example, the way Chomsky privileges syntax, which he considers a generative component, as opposed to semantics, considered an interpretative component.

The investigation of linguistic facts can be made from two *points of view:* either from the language user's or from the describer's. In the first case, one considers what the subject (speaker-hearer) does with his language and the aspect(s) under which he knows it. The second point of view is centered on what the describer does to analyze and present linguistic phenomena.

One finally finds differences due to the very *conception of language,* of its structure, of its constitutive parts. Henri Frei considers for instance that errors are important for their disclosure of information on the functioning of languages,[84] whereas they are irrelevant for Chomsky.[85]

These differences—which often add up in linguistic texts—make any comparison between the different linguistic theories difficult, and any attempt to take stock of the situation tricky. It goes without saying that the essential problems which deserve a careful examination are to be found at the level of conceptual differences, the ones that can be considered as theoretical differences proper. In the preceding chapters we have tried to elucidate conceptual identity or difference, once the secondary problems of terminology, emphasis, etc., had been resolved.[86] In the present chapter we have focused our attention on theoretical problems, hoping to reveal interesting problems and perspectives; real linguistic stakes.

VIII.5 Epistemological Positions

The comparing of two opposed theories does not lead to convincing conclusions; if there are conclusions they do not follow as logical consequences from the comparison, but are mostly supported by personal experience, which can vary from one subject to the other. For a comparison to be conclusive, it is necessary before anything else to discuss epistemological questions and to define precise evaluation criteria.

We have kept as a main criterion for the evaluation of a model[87] external adequacy, that is, the ability for the model to account for the language user's behavior and intuition, thus pushing internal adequacy criteria into the background. Such a choice is based on the established fact that internal adequacy criteria—coherence, exhaustivity, simplicity, etc.—often assign to the object properties which are not decidable or which are not proven to be constitutive of the object (cf. below at VIII.8). To aim for external adequacy is to look for the confrontation of hypotheses with empirical data, with a view toward confirming or invalidating the model. Our efforts have been centered on this. Now it appears that such a confrontation is possible only through the integration of experimentation into the model. Given the complexity of the object and the multiplicity of its possible observational conditions, it is not certain that the results of any experiment—obtained under specific conditions—remain valid under different observational conditions. Thus any experimental model must include hypotheses (about how the object of study behaves) and observational procedures (also called protocol of experimentation).

VIII.6 Integration of Experimentation into the Model

Empirical research—rightly or wrongly—often gives rise to negative reactions. One is certainly entitled to question the validity of the conclusions drawn from empirical research for manifold reasons (even when the collecting of data is not subject to caution). It can be that the argumentation leading from observation to conclusion lacks rigor; for instance, different conclusions could be drawn from the same set of data. It can be that in his interpreting the data, the researcher leaves part of the data out of consideration by throwing it away into the dustbin of exceptions. Or it can be that overly *general* principles are inferred from observations made under *specific* conditions; it is then no wonder that other observations, made under differing conditions, lead to different results. Still, it can be for many other reasons.

But such criticism, however justified it may be, cannot lead one to conclude that experimental research is impossible within the domain of linguistics, if not within that of human facts. It would be more judicious to attempt to discover in what respect a hypothesis can be ill-adapted to an object. Its inadequacy can be due to the fact that the conception of the object is too simple. In many cases, the object of study receives an overly complicated structure which includes conflicting factors. These are conflicts in which sometimes one, sometimes the other of the contradictory tendencies wins.

Attention should be paid here to the concept of explanation. A model explains a set of data if it can be applied to this set, that is, if it makes it possible to predict how the object behaves under specific conditions. The predictability of the object reaction from the model guarantees that one indeed controls the factors at work, and that it can be said with certainty that every time such conditions combine, such events occur. In a way, the researcher hence enters a bet.

In the opposite case (that is, when one does not conceive of the object behavior as predictable even under specific conditions), one cannot speak of a model proper, but rather of more or less vague, more or less precise ideas or impressions about the object of study.

Linguistics has long been at issue on the question of showing that of two or several models, one was true (or good, or adequate), and the other(s) wrong (or bad, or inadequate).[88] Were it not for the precept of formal structure and of discrete units, nothing would justify the quest for one and only one procedure to apprehend a given linguistic phenomenon.

VIII.7 Object Complexity and Model Multiplicity
Quite a number of other conclusions can be drawn from the fact that an object observed under certain conditions (let us say the semantic features a language user attributes to isolated words) demonstrates properties which are not totally identical with the ones obtained under other observational conditions (for instance, the semantic features revealed by the user's intuition toward the same words as above, but presented within sentences); cf. VIII.2. I adhere for myself to the following theses.

(i) Linguistic structure includes variation and dynamics.
(ii) The diversity of linguistic behaviors can be explained by the concordant or conflictual working of the variational factors.

Although (i) is a rather old thesis, (ii) has been looked at only recently.[89] Trying to explain the regularity and the variability of linguistic phenomena requires preliminary conditions and entails consequences which are rich in implications for our knowledge of language. Below I present some of these implications.

(a) As soon as one seriously tackles confronting hypotheses with the data, the question comes up of where to look for data. Since a corpus is not sufficient as the only source of data—a classical solution of structuralism—one can access the user's intuition. Such recourse is of course only legitimate if the user's *psychical dimension* is acknowledged as part and parcel of the linguistic object. In another connection, and since communication necessarily has a social framework, the collecting of data makes it obvious that the *social dimension* is an indefeasible feature of language phenomenon.

(b) When linguistic materials are presented to users for evaluation, it is frequently to gather opinions given with more or less hesitation or certainty; on the level of the collectivity as well, the judgments passed are marked with more or less dissension or consensus. The sorting out of what is relevant and what is not thus calls for quantified data. This leads to acknowledging a *statistical dimension* to the linguistic structure.

(c) There is a *correlation between psychic and social dimensions* of language: the more certain the status of a language phenomenon in the user's psyche, the more important is its degree of consensus within the speech community. Conversely, a fact which is not certain in the user's intuition finds a corresponding dissension within the collectivity.[90]

(d) The structural phenomena of language thus belong to a continuum of hierarchy ranging from a central zone (where certainty and consensus are maximal) to a marginal zone (where hesitation and dissension are maximal).[91]

In such a conceptual framework—that is, one of relativity—the image of the language object appears to be considerably more complex than the one proposed by classical structuralism. On the other hand, such a conception makes it possible to account for certain facts through the elaboration of a multiplicity of models which are not explainable in a formal structuralist framework.

VIII.8 Descriptive Simplicity versus Empirical Adequacy
Even if this relative conception of structure lacks simplicity, it has definite advantages as far as the adequacy to the object is concerned and for the prospects for explanation and empirical evaluation it offers. Among other things, it sheds new light on acquired knowledge and the limits

of the classical structural tenet in linguistics. The problems raised in the study of semantic phenomena will provide us with an example about these remarks.

It is a well-known fact that semantic studies made within the framework of structural linguistics between the 1930s and the 1960s were at a dead end. A simple structure was sought for (i.e., a single set of elements and rules valid for the whole of semantic systems). Now different observational techniques lead to different results; what is more, there were not any really convincing reasons to choose one technique over another for the collecting of data and for the description of matters of meaning. From this originated the idea that semantics was not structured.[92] Such ideas can be supported by a formal conception of language as background (as long as a structure exempt of any variation is pursued).

As soon as one resorts to a different conception and adopts that of relative structure (i.e., a structure including rules and rule-governed variations, or structured variations) apprehension of the semantic structure becomes possible: then one only needs to look for the factors determining the variations, to classify the different types of semantic realizations, and to rank them on a hierarchy. One then has an adequate model for semantic phenomena, similar to the one proposed by Labov,[93] Rosch, or else the one we have presented in this book in chapters VI and VII. What permits us here to qualify and value such a model as appropriate is that it does not entail any arbitrary reduction of empirical data, and that it offers solutions and prospects for grasping the functioning of meaning and the factors conditioning its variations.

Let us now take as an example the following question: what meaning can one assign to words such as *to run, dog, idea,* or *fork*? One would easily admit (and the empirical works quoted in chapters VI and VII show this) that on the one hand, each of these elements does not refer to a single concept, and, on the other, that certain mechanisms exist that compensate for the fuzziness of words. This explains how a vague utterance can refer to a precise situation. *To run* may thus designate a 'rapid', or 'not rapid movement', 'with the help of legs', or 'without the help of legs', and can even point to an event involving no movement at all: *he runs for parliament.* It is our taking into account of the extralinguistic situation and/or of the linguistic context that enables us to understand the speaker's intention as he utters *the baby runs fast* or *the baby runs on all fours.* The idea that context and situation influence meaning realizations is not new in itself; but the contribution of recent works is highly significant in that they have revealed the sources and the targets of the interaction between a linguistic unit and its context, or between linguistic and situational elements. Furthermore, they have made it possible to evaluate the scope of this interaction in definite cases. One of the general conclusions that can be drawn is that the realization of the semantic features of a linguistic unit follows precise constraints, and that the variability of semantic facts is actually nothing but the result of numerous asymmetrical regularities, the complexity of which made any satisfactory explanation impossible within the overly narrow framework of classical structural theories.

The complexity specific to the semantical structure results from the fact that several asymmetries are at work in the process leading from a virtual signifié to its actual semantic realizations (and *vice versa*). For instance, what the hearer does is not an exact inversion of what the speaker does (see VIII.2 above). There is, as well, no relation of equivalence between the explanation of meaning by utilizing the (extralinguistic) referent and the one made by means of (linguistic) circumlocutions. Also, the subjects' semantic judgment varies according to the degree and nature of the inquirer's intervention. The basic idea is that each of these intuitive reactions is revealing for certain aspects of the linguistic reality of meaning and thus has to be examined in earnest. Such an examination is promising and, according to the results we know, shows that not all semantic features vary when one changes the inquiry technique, and also that the phenomena that most resist variation in terms of inquiry techniques are also most constant within the same technique. To put it otherwise, such an examination reveals what builds the central zone of the semantic structure and allows us to separate it from the marginal zones.

A description based on such premises and made by means of such observational procedures is evidently much more complex than the one obtained by following the procedure advanced in a formal conception of language matters.[94] Is this sufficient reason to abandon it? I do not think so, for I am convinced that the descriptive tool must be adapted to its tasks. If the object is complex, then the describer has to shape the tool accordingly. The criterion of simplicity raises more problems than it resolves. What justifies, for example, the quest for descriptive simplicity if not the fact that it corresponds to economy in human behavior? Now, it is questionable whether the utilization of simple, even rudimentary, tools is economical; furthermore, there is much to be said for the idea that the quest for economy leads man to create tools that are more and more sophisticated in order to make tasks less and less difficult. Why should it be otherwise for languages, man's communication tool?

It seems to me that the criteria of internal adequacy all raise analogous problems. Let us take consistency. How is it to be valued? As long as the model is not fully developed, nothing guarantees that there will not be any contradiction between two statements S^n and S^m. In other respects, what allows us to assign the feature of consistency to the user's behavior in the way it is conceived in formal logic? It is much more likely that speech follows another kind of logic, a more flexible, more economical, more complex logic. Such a logic is likely to be closer to language processes and more capable of explaining them.[95] The effort of the logicians and linguists who study the problems of natural logic or of discursive logic is promising;[96] it also allows us to lay the foundations for a fruitful cooperation between logic and linguistics.

VIII.9 Achievements and Current Issues

When trying to close in on actual problems and resolve them, it is useful to determine what former research has accomplished and what might have hindered it in its development. I shall still keep within the domain of semantics to do so.

Quite generally,[97] structural linguistics admits the existence of one kind of regularity within the scope of meaning and judiciously underlines the asymmetry between phonology and semantics. Yet this established fact does not make possible any progress in the structuralist investigation of meaning structure. It seems to me that the reason for this lies in the ambiguity of the concept of structure itself. On the one hand, it is explicitly stated that languages are structured; what is meant by that is that they are organized insofar as any utterance—a whole divisible into parts (monemes, morphemes or words)—is rule-governed. To put it otherwise, the combining of units is not free.[98] On the other hand, any field in which variations are attested is considered nonstructured. A shift thus occurs in the conception of structure: the only type of structure taken into consideration is formal structure. From this it follows that any regularities accompanying variations or bearing statistical properties are put aside or neglected. Since the semantic structure is not formal in nature, it is not at all assimilated to structure; semantics remains therefore outside the concerns of structural linguistics.[99] The shift in the concept of structure and the displacement of the object of linguistics are doubtless due to the antecedence of phonological studies. The success of the application of formal methods in phonology has given rise to two different positions: on the one side, some have hopes of finding the means to transpose methods utilized in phonology over to semantics. On the other, owing to the flagrant differences in the results of semantic analyses and those obtained in phonological analyses, some go so far as to deny any structure to the signifié. It is obvious that both positions are to be criticized as excessive, but I will not insist on this here. I would rather stress the causes of such mistakes, the analysis of which seems rich in consequences for current research.

VIII.10   Phonological Structure versus Semantic Structure

Are the concepts and methods of phonology adequate for semantics? There is *a priori* nothing wrong with borrowing concepts and methods developed within the study of a connected field. It is nevertheless true that the two domains involved—source and target—must have sufficiently numerous properties in common for the use of borrowed tools to be conclusive. There are most certainly analogies between the object of phonology and that of semantics: both are systems operating on substances (phonic for one, semantic for the other), and both produce structures *sui generis*. But can these analogies justify a mechanical transfer? I believe not. In my opinion, semantics has arrived at a deadlock, which is due to the fact that no serious thinking has been done about the similitudes and differences between both fields before applying the new analysis and description techniques to semantics. Many questions have been either wrongly posed, or have remained unanswered. Here are some of them.

(i) If the language user's intuition is at all included in the object of linguistics (namely, the knowledge he has of his language), one must consider from this viewpoint the similitudes and differences referred to above. For instance, how does the user know the phonic elements of his language? And how does he know the semantic elements? Is he able to recognize some and/or the others in isolation? Does he only recognize them in relation with other elements of the system? If he resorts to the relations one element has with the others to recognize it, of what type are these relations? Are these relations of an oppositive type (within the system or paradigm)? Are they of a contrastive type (within the syntagmatic chain)?

(ii) Inasmuch as phonological structure was considered as typical structure (or structure *par excellence*), and as variations were the stumbling block of semantic analyses, it would seem proper to ponder the status of variations in phonology. For example, what is the fate of such elements in phonological descriptions? If one considers these analyses without indulgence, one will notice that the positions adopted in phonology in relation to the elements' variability leave much to be desired: either the variability of an element is ignored on grounds that are mostly *ad hoc* and the phonic element concerned is viewed as a full phonological unit (i.e., it rightfully belongs to the phonological structure); or else the element is dismissed of the structure because of its variability.

(iii) Given the fact that any structure—semantic as well as phonological—has been based on the concept of relevance, it would seem proper that this very concept be sufficiently clarified to make the solving of pending problems possible. In this respect, problems remain such as: is phonological relevance determined by the role the phonic elements have within communication? Or by the constancy they show? There is after all no reason for both criteria always to go together (i.e., communicative role and lack of variability).[100]

The critical examination of these problems during the last two decades has led to a radical questioning of the principle of formal structure and to its conception as relative. Such a conception has contributed a great deal to the progress realized in semantics as well as to the development of models capable of explaining meaning phenomena. The effects of this new conception of structure are not restricted to semantics; even at the level of phonology it brought significant results, making it possible to grasp more fully the complex processes of linguistic functioning and language change.

VIII.11   What the Relative Conception Changes in our View of Language

What does this change in viewpoint imply for linguistic research? It goes without saying that the attribution of a relative nature to structure entails the reconsideration, if not the reevaluation, of all concepts and of all categories admitted in the past. In the classical conception, the linguistic analysis is supposed to meet three requirements: (i) to propose a single description of linguistic processes, (ii) to resort to a limited number of discrete factors (i.e., units or relations), and (iii) to base linguistic analysis on a binary division of functionality (i.e., relevant vs. nonrelevant).

A relative conception of structure invalidates all of these requirements. Let us take again the example given above to show how these requirements make a classical structural analysis unsatisfactory. I will examine some of their implications here.

(1) *Baby Jack finished his scotch broth and french fries.*

(i) Should one aim at a single description of linguistic processes? I have already remarked that not every adjective can substitute itself with equal ease for *scotch* and *french* (cf. VIII.2 above); this is due to the fact that a combination of monemes can—according to communication circumstances, the experience referred to, and the person addressed— have one meaning or another, or even no meaning at all. The syntagm *wooden fries* is thus meaningless if the referent, the object referred to, is situated in the most current, most frequent practice of everyday life;[101] the same syntagm barely raises any problem when the speech refers to an imaginary world (a children's tale, a play production, etc.). Besides, it is not the only case in which the constitutive elements of a sentence refer to one aspect of experience in a certain situation and to another aspect in a different situation; the same goes for *finish* in (1), which means 'absorbing food' under "normal" conditions, but which could refer to *'making'* if speech were shifted onto a context of stage setting, production, play accessories, and so on. The same moneme *finish* would refer to 'writing' or 'reading' if in the object function appeared as something like *first tale, new book,* and so on.

This is just to show that if we want to make our analysis capable of accounting for the various usages which a sentence admits, we must offer a range of descriptions (not one single description) including what each of these implies as to their relationship with the world of extralinguistic experience. This can be realized by assigning multiple and hierarchized properties to each moneme or moneme sequence.

(ii) A description based on a limited number of elements is necessarily inadequate if it is to reflect the great diversity that actual concrete realizations of a given abstract structure are susceptible of showing. To account for the fact that *wooden fries* can either be nonsense or mean 'of ligneous aspect', 'having a quality likened to the hard consistency of wood', or 'consisting of wood', the semantic description of *wooden* must entail an open and hierarchized set of elements (and not only one element such as 'consisting of wood') including the potentialities of assimilation and of dissimilation of each element. Then it will be possible to explain how and under the influence of what communication circumstances a given word *W* manages to convey the meaning *m*. If we agree that a semantic description is all the more adequate if it is capable of setting out the most complete range of semantic realizations, it then follows that the best possible description is not the one composed of the fewest semantic features. On the contrary, the more numerous the features (even so far as to form an open set), the more able the description is to represent the semantic mechanisms. This is on the condition that the features kept in the description be hierarchized. Without hierarchy, one runs the risk of presenting, without any idea of order, a mass including the most probable meanings together with the most far-fetched ones.

(iii) The fundamental concept of relevance calls for a drastic reshaping. In the formal conception, the analysis is supposed to reveal whether an element, a feature, or a relationship is relevant or not (i.e., whether it is of value for the chosen viewpoint), without any kind of middle stage. Now, such a dichotomy is not proven theoretically.[102] Empirically, convincing arguments speak for a continuum of relevance. Thus, the features 'consisting of wood', 'of ligneous aspect', or 'having a quality likened to the hardness of wood' are all bound to the signifiant *wooden* and are therefore all relevant, but not to the same extent. To put it otherwise, their *degree of relevance* is not the same.

It is perhaps appropriate to insist on two points: first, the three requirements or principles discussed here are not worthless and have been of great use; but the progress made demands that these be reshaped and above all made relative so that they can still be useful in linguistic research. The second point is that the inadequacies of these principles have been illustrated with a single example borrowed from the syntactico-semantic field. The conclusions drawn here are valid not only for other semantic facts but also for the whole of semantic phenomena. Considered under this triple viewpoint, what I call relative structure counterbalances formal structure; every linguistic element is conceived of as including multiple properties, all of which do not have the same degree of relevance (i.e., the same value), nor are all of them realized in the element occurrences as a whole.

One of the consequences of this conception is that a description is not exhaustive in itself but can be considered to be so only according to a given *degree of approximation*. The notion of approximation seems to play an important role in language description as well as language use. The informant (or the describer) who deems unacceptable a sentence such as *Baby Jack finished his Muslim broth and wooden fries* initiates a gross approximation in which every utterance refers to "normal" situations. The same informant (or the same describer) would not exclude the possibility for this utterance to be acceptable under circumstances outside of everyday life. By doing so, he shifts from one approximation level to a sharper one in which less relevant features are taken into consideration. Concurrently, the relationship between units on the one hand and relevant features on the other becomes relative. From the classical viewpoint, one considers that at the end of a description it should be possible, firstly, to list for each unit all of its relevant features, and secondly, to tell if a given feature does or does not take part in the making up of such or such unit. One of the inevitable consequences of the degrees of relevance is that one must define an approximation level prior to answering both of these questions, for a unit does not have any absolute composition. That is to say, a unit includes features only to diverse degrees, and a feature is constitutive for a unit only to variable degrees, which must be specified in each case.

No single notion or principle can escape the effects of such a change of conception. Thus, syntactical functions also become complex notions, with multiple properties to be found at various hierarchical levels. So it is not possible to give once and for all a clear and forever operational definition of a function. To reach a precise definition of a function such as 'subject', 'predicate complement' 'object', and so on, one must take into account the level of approximation aimed at by the description.[103]

Numerous other consequences can be foreseen. For instance, the boundaries between the different chapters of linguistics, viewed as a no-man's-land, become gradual transition zones (between phonetics and phonology, phonology and morphology, morphology and syntax, or syntax and semantics). Following this idea is the concept of equivalence between two elements of a language undergoing the same changes. Two phenomena—such as active and passive voice—can be equivalent under certain conditions while remaining distinct under others. That is to say, even equivalence or difference cannot be valued in an absolute manner but by taking into account the various degrees of approximation.

This is a far more complex conception than the formal one. It certainly makes the analysis and description of language phenomena more difficult; on the other hand, it has the advantage of explaining certain facts that hitherto have remained unexplained as far as usage, the evolution of languages, and their interrelations are concerned. It also makes it possible to understand why numerous attempts inspired from diverse linguistic currents have failed. If no satisfactory solution has been found to problems such as *"one or two classes?," "one or two functions?,"* it may be due to the fact that the question has been wrongly posed, in the sense that the clearly delineated boundary that was sought does not exist as such in the facts. From there it follows as well that problems such as the distinction between homonymy and polysemy, or the limitation and the significance of a sharp classification of the significant units, must be reconsidered from their very conception.

Is the analysis of the successes and mistakes in linguistics of some interest? Is it anything greater than an intellectual pastime? I believe it is. I see in such an analysis two major interests: for one, it allows us to avoid mistakes of the past (even though it will not prevent us from making other, new mistakes in the future!). For the other, it points toward new prospects and reveals new paths to be explored which are themselves suggested in the analysis. My remarks and thoughts about the successive or parallel linguistic currents are impelled by this hope. The latter might also be used as a justification—or as an excuse—for the wealth of details in the examination of linguistics' acquired knowledge and of its mistakes, especially in the second part of the book. Are such processes fruitful? It is up to the reader to judge.

Notes

1   As far as the opponents of universals are concerned, the idea to elaborate distinctive phonetics itself (Pike, Martinet) shows a possible partial structuration of sound patterns independently of the individual language systems, which thus leads to a limited arbitrariness—nothing else than a limited universalism. As to the defendants, see Greenberg (1978), who develops in his introduction the idea of *relative* universals.

2   Cf. Mulder and Hervey, 1980, who bring the object of semantics on the denotational level down to a finite number of relevant features and thus show phonology and semantics to be parallel.

3   Cf. Chapter VII.

4   Assumption 6 says: "Every form is made up wholly of phonemes."

5   Vinay and Darbelnet (1967, §131) think that in this context, the 'mood' opposition *a fait/ait fait* cannot be maintained in English unless we change lexical items; they suggest the following translations.
    Je ne dirai pas qu'il l'a fait exprès
    'I won't tell anyone he did it on purpose' and
    Je ne dirai pas qu'il l'ait fait exprès
    'I won't go so far as to say he did it on purpose'.

6   For more detail, see Henry G. Schogt, 1988, Chapter 2.

7   One could raise as an objection that the signifié of the moneme *fille* includes a relevant semantic feature which has as realization one or the other of the semantic properties 'nonadult' or 'in lineal descent'. These properties would find themselves in partly complementary distribution; the feature 'in lineal descent' would occur in the exclusion of 'nonadult' in *ma fille est mariée et mère de deux enfants* 'my daughter is married and the mother of two children'; whereas only the feature 'nonadult' is actualized in *à seize ans, les filles rêvent toutes d'un monde idéal* 'sixteen-year-old girls all dream of an

ideal world'. Such a description is indeed more complete than the former one, but it does not change at all the conclusion which we drew from the former analysis: it is indeed still possible to show that the feature 'in lineal descent' is neither necessary nor sufficient; nor is this the case for the other features of the signifié of *fille*. One only has to consider a sentence such as *c'est une fille qui ne doute de rien* 'she is a girl who doubts nothing': the feature 'in lineal descent' is not taken into account, and, besides, the feature 'nonadult' may here very well not be actualized either, since this sentence can be spoken about a fifty-year-old person.

8 See *Le Petit Robert* (under *figuier*): "tree or shrub from areas with Mediterranean climate, with lobate leaves, whose flowers are attached to the inner wall of a fleshy pear-shaped receptacle that, after fecundation, bears figs." Note that, in the definition given to the students, I replaced *figs* with *fruit*. The definition given by *Le Petit Larousse* is: "tree from warm countries whose fruit is the fig."

9 (3.6) These are the three definitions given for *beech, oak,* and *teak* by *The Concise Oxford Dictionary* (4th ed., 1951):

> *beech,* n. Smooth-barked glossy-leaved mast-bearing forest tree; its wood
> *oak,* n. Kinds of tree and shrub, of which the best known is a forest tree yielding hard timber and acorns and having jagged leaves (Dyer's, Holm, Scarlet, etc.,—, other species; Dwarf, Ground, etc.,—, plants named from some resemblance to—); wood of the—(HEART of—), (poet.) wooden ships.
> *teak,* n. (E.-Ind. tree with) heavy durable timber that does not warp or shrink or corrode iron, much used in ship-building.

10 The definition given by Katz and Fodor is represented in figure 8.

11 The term "*primitive premise*" is not used in its current meaning but refers to the hypotheses concerning the collection and observation of data.

12 "Hierarchical" does not refer to the same concept as in my terminology.

13 I have tried, where possible, to give a translation of the examples in French. Needless to say, the translations cannot reproduce the syntactico-semantic complexity of the data under study; they are to be regarded as an aid to the reader unfamiliar with French.

14 Morphological problems are partly assigned to the transformational component, partly to the distributional component, and partly handled as in Martinet's phonological description, which is presented here. In traditional grammatics, part of the variations of the signifiant are studied within the frame of word analysis and part of them within the study of sentences (e.g., syntactical agreement).

15 Cf. Harris, Hockett, Gleason, and others.

16 Cf. Hjelmslev, Martinet, and others.

17 One would be tempted to coin a term such as "*objectness*" or "*objectitude*" to express this idea (*roman*).

18 This example is borrowed from Mahmoudian et al., 1976.

19 This context does not present the same syntactic constraints in English. In

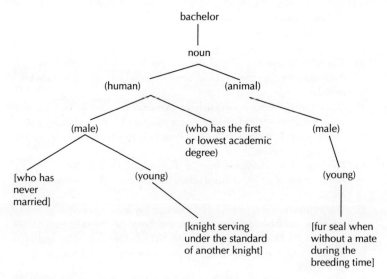

Figure 8 Semantic analysis of *bachelor*.

French, *obéir* is intransitive in most contexts, except in the passive, where it is used in an indirect (prepositional) construction (with the preposition *à*), which explains the agrammaticality of forms in 4(a), 4(c), and 4(d), as well as the grammaticality of 4(b).

20 Cf. the building of syntax on combinatory properties, Fries, 1952.

21 See for instance *"parasynthematic complexes"* in Martinet, 1985, §3.10.

22 As a matter of fact, I can see little force in the suggestion, commonly made by certain linguists, that *sur-* is significative in *surprendre*.

23 This example is borrowed from Mahmoudian, 1975.

24 Cf. Prieto, 1968, in which he states that the contents are not analyzable. What he explicitly states has been applied by other structuralists without any theoretical explanation. Such a tactical attitude is also obvious in the introduction of Martinet, 1960.

25 *"Relevant"* and *"relevance"* are not used here in the same acceptation as by Grice or by Sperber and Wilson (cf. footnote on relevance in VI.13).

26 Cf. *Le Petit Larousse,* 1968, under *courir.*

27 As the expression *aller vite sans précisément courir* 'to go quickly without actually running' shows. This was taken from the *Petit Robert,* 1967, under *courir,* as were most of the examples and definitions.

28 One could also be tempted to conclude that there are several homonymic units with the signifiant /kurir/. This would raise problems such as the following: how can the user decide which one of the homonymic units is represented in a given occurrence? This is much the same as asking to which one of the

semantic fields the unit under study belongs in a given occurrence. See below §5, ss., for discussion.

29 Cf. Mounin, 1972, and Schogt, 1976.

30 This scheme does not give all the semantic features for the lexemes; only the features that are the source or target of contextual influences have been included.

31 This interdependence is valid only for an overall structure; in finer structural zones disagreement and partitioning are observed. Cf. V.7 and Chapter VII.

32 This is, it seems to me, what the *Petit Robert* means when it characterizes this meaning as "special."

33 This example was borrowed from Denise François, 1974, p. 764.

34 Partial results of an unpublished survey seem in the main to sustain this hierarchy.

35 This conception of a hierarchized structure has been expounded by myself (Mortéza Mahmoudian, 1980). It has also been the object of applications in syntax (cf. Maryse Mahmoudian and Nina de Spengler, 1980, and Rémi Jolivet, 1980) and in phonology (cf. Marianne Schoch and Nina de Spengler, 1980).

36 Cf., for example, Thomas Bever, 1975.

37 Only to consider European linguistics, post-Saussurians such as Trier, Weisgerber, and others developed only lexical semantics, while Jespersen (1924) and Tesnière (1959) go through a description of the signifié to study syntax.

38 Syntax is considered an independent part of language structure in theories as distant as Martinet's structuralism and Chomsky's transformationalism (cf. Chomsky, 1972, Chapter 1: Deep Structure, Surface Structure, and Semantic Interpretation).

39 Both '*general*' and '*global*' meanings stand here for German *Gesamtbedeutung*.

40 Cf. Jakobson, 1984, pp. 79–82.

41 I use this term as defined by Bloomfield (1933, p. 162): "the meaning of a morpheme is a *sememe*."

42 My concern is to give an illustration of the theses about the structure of the signifié, and not to sketch the work and evolution of linguists considered individually. This is the reason Martinet is cited twice: once as an example of implicit work on semantics, and once as an example of explicit theses on it.

43 Other conditions are the answering of the following questions: when may/must one have recourse to semantics? and is it legitimate to state the syntactical equivalence between two sequences such as *the rain has stopped* and *it doesn't rain any more,* and if not, why? One could easily think of other problems concerning the connections between syntax and semantics.

44 That is to set anew the problem of the semantic universals without the polemic about the absolute characteristic of the universals.

45 The contribution of the speaker-hearer's knowledge (about his partner in the communication act and/or the dialogue's object) to the meaning perception process forms the object of interesting studies, among them Sperber and Wil-

son's. A general outline of their book can be given as follows, formulated in our terminology: starting from Grice's theses, their purpose is to examine the connections that meaning conveyed by utterances has with the linguistic context and/or the extralinguistic situation. The closer this link (i.e., meaning—context and meaning—situation), the more significant is the contribution of the context and/or of the situation in the communication act. This contribution is designated by the term *relevance*. Yet this concept is not the same one as relevance in our terminology. Ours follows from the sign's constitutive function. From this viewpoint, the more intimately a feature of the signifié is bound to the signifiant, the more relevant it is. And *vice versa:* the relevance of features of the signifiant is measured by their more or less close link with the signifié. It follows that in certain cases, what appears relevant from one viewpoint is not considered to be so from the other. From this it appears that the issue is not merely terminological. Another sizeable difference also distinguishes the two research directions: for Sperber and Wilson, relevance affects certain aspects of semantic phenomena, while for us pertinence is a concept that can be applied to all linguistic elements whatever the level they come under may be (phonological, syntactical, semantic, etc.). The general concept of relevance has the advantage of offering a unified view of language and of its partial systems. Thus, by examining the economy of semantic mechanisms, Prieto (1966) and Herrmann (1983) underline the tendency toward maximum differentiation that diachronical phonology brought to light on its part. That searchers working decades apart and in different directions come to the same conclusion confirms the importance and the interest of relevance as a general principle.

46 Or *bound forms,* as they are termed by Bloomfield (1933, §10.1).

47 Cf. for example in European structuralism, one will notice that Martinet (Martinet, 1960) devotes no chapter to semantics; neither do Hockett (Hockett, 1968) or Gleason (Gleason, 1961).

48 Cf. among others Ruwet, when he criticizes the concept of syntactical autonomy in his introduction to generative linguistics (Ruwet, 1964, Chapter 2, §3.3); even though his criticism is founded, one cannot conclude straightaway that the criticized concept is erroneous; it is one of the possible conclusions, but it is not self-evident. One can well mean that the concept is ill-formed, but also that it is the application which is wrong (of a concept which itself is adequate), or else that the concept has limitations that the theory did not foresee, for instance.

49 Cf. Theo Herrmann (1983) for a criticism of the competence/performance dichotomy. Cf. also Katz (1964), who says in substance that he does not know the actual process of uttering and understanding speech, but that the concepts he defends are necessary. A more judicious argument would be: what he knows of the speech process supports the necessity of these concepts.

50 In certain cases, statistical studies are made on linguistic material without being linked to theoretical considerations.

51 Cf. Hamburger, J., ed. (1986), p. 10, in which René Thom gives scientific

experimentation a four-point definition. I have retained only three of these defining characteristics, leaving out the first about the definition of laboratory.

52 This definition corresponds to the one given by Claude Bernard (1865): "The thorough scholar is the one who covers theory as well as experimental practice. 1. He observes a fact; 2. about this fact, an idea comes to his mind; 3. with respect to this idea, he argues, sets up an experiment, imagines and realizes its material conditions. 4. From this experience, result new phenomena to observe. And so forth." (pp. 43–44). While opposing experimentation to observation, he points out that "the only difference is that the phenomenon that the experimenter should observe not being naturally offered to him, he has to bring it to light, i.e., to provoke it for a particular reason, with a given aim. It ensues that one can say: in the main, experiment is nothing but an observation provoked with a certain aim. . . . experiment is an observation with the aim of control" (pp. 35–36). One can see here the concept of, if not the term, perturbation. This idea is evident in other passages, such as on p. 40.

53 I refer here to J. Hamburger, dir. (1986), in which not only the problems and acquired knowledge of these disciplines are exposed but also diverging positions and evaluations that are sometimes opposed.

54 Recent research carried out thanks to financial support from the Swiss National Science Foundation shows the accessibility and hierarchy of meaning of isolated monemes. Cf. P. Singy and G. Oberlé (1987).

55 When translated into British
    A: Well! Well! You've had your hair cut. Me too.
    B: No! You've had your hair cut. I cut mine myself.
    it can be seen that unlike French, the causative can carry the two meanings. *B* uses this syntagm, contrasting it with the causative, whereas *A* uses it in a nondifferentiated context.

56 The exaggerated questioning of received knowledge and innovation at all costs are also criticized in the physical sciences. Cf. the "well-moderated evolution" extolled by Bernard d'Espagnat, "Approfondissement et création," in H. Atalan (1986), *Création et créativité*.

57 Except for minor differences which have no bearing on the issue raised here. The matrix is given in table 5.

58 Note that this application of the questionnaire was designed for French and cannot be transposed to English without readjustment, given that the syntactico-semantic constraints are not the same as in French. For instance, it seems that in this context, *with* is unlikely to be 'instrumental', and that 'instrumental' is almost obligatorily expressed by *on*. For a precise evaluation of the survey, see the original version with French example, shown in table 6.

59 Here is the questionnaire:

    1) Pouvez-vous mettre en scène par un dessin le sens de la phrase suivante?
       IL FAISAIT BEAU, JE SORTAIS
    2) Les dessins suivants représentent une situation qui s'est passée hier, où j'ai dit "il fait beau, je sors"   .

Table 6 *Etude du signifié*: illustration des techniques proposées.

Procédés	Stimuli	Réactions
ND F > S Par.	On donne une phrase comme: Jean arrive avec son cheval (ou: la sorcière avec son balais, etc.)	On demande de donner par une paraphrase la signification de cette phrase
D F > S Par.	On donne la phrase: Jean arrive avec son cheval	On demande de choisir la paraphrase qui lui correspond: (i) Jean arrive en compagnie de son cheval (ii) Jean arrive sur son cheval (iii) Jean arrive sur ou en compagnie de son cheval
ND S > F Par.	On donne deux phrases comme: (a) Jean arrive, et il est à cheval (b) Jean arrive, et son cheval l'accompagne	On demande de paraphraser (a) et (b)
D S > F Par.	On donne deux phrases comme: (a) Jean arrive, et il est à cheval (b) Jean arrive, et son cheval l'accompagne	On présente la phrase: Jean arrive avec son cheval, et on demande si c'est ce que veut dire (a), ensuite, même démarche pour (b)
ND F > S Réf.	On donne une phrase comme: Jean arrive avec son cheval	On lui demande de mettre en scène—avec des figurines ou en dessinant—la situation qu'elle représente
D S > F Réf.	On présente par une scène (figurines, ciné, dessin, etc.): (a) Un homme à cheval (b) Un homme à pied accompagné d'un cheval	On demande laquelle des phrases lui correspond (i) Jean arrive avec son cheval (ii) Jean arrive en compagnie de son cheval (iii) Jean arrive sur son cheval
ND S > F Réf.	On présente par une scène: (a) Un bonhomme à cheval (b) Un bonhomme à pied accompagné d'un cheval	On demande de raconter la scène (a), ensuite la scène (b)
D F > S Réf.	On donne la phrase: Jean arrive avec son cheval	On lui présente la scène (a) (bonhomme à cheval) en lui demandant si elle correspond à la phrase. Même démarche pour la scène (b) (bonhomme à pied accompagné d'un cheval)

ND: non directif; D: directif; F > S: du stimulus formel à la réaction sémantique; S > F: du stimulus sémantique à la réaction formelle; Par.: sens explicité par paraphrase; Réf.: recours au référent pour expliciter le sens.

Comment peut-on raconter la situation représentée par ces dessins?
a) /b)
3) Lequel de ces deux dessins représente le sens de la phrase suivante?
IL FAISAIT BEAU, JE SORTAIS
a), b), a) et b) sont possibles.
4) Que veut dire la phrase suivante?
IL FAISAIT BEAU, JE SORTAIS
Pouvez-vous exprimer la même idée d'une autre façon?
5) A supposer qu'il ait fait beau, je serais sorti.
Pouvez-vous exprimer la même idée d'une autre façon?
6) Quand il faisait beau, je sortais.
Pouvez-vous exprimer la même idée d'une autre façon?
7) Que signifie la phrase suivante?
IL FAISAIT BEAU, JE SORTAIS
1) Il a fait beau, et je suis sorti
2) S'il avait fait beau, je serais sorti
3) 1) et 2) sont possibles
8) Dans le passé, quand il faisait beau, je sortais.
Peut-on exprimer cette situation par la phrase suivante?
IL FAISAIT BEAU, JE SORTAIS
9) Ayant dit que s'il avait fait beau, je serais sorti.
Peut-on exprimer la même idée par la phrase suivante?
IL FAISAIT BEAU, JE SORTAIS

60   Here is the questionnaire:
1. *Soulignez celui des deux termes qui vous paraît le plus concret.*

sens—chien	chien—congé
congé—idée	fourchette—raison
fourchette—congé	congé—sens
idée—raison	sens—fourchette
fourchette—chien	chien—raison
idée—fourchette	sens—idée
raison—sens	congé—raison
idée—chien	

2. *Donnez au moins trois sens possibles pour chacun de ces termes.*
CONGÉ / CHIEN / IDEE / SENS / FOURCHETTE / RAISON
3. *Sur cette ligne graduée, placez dans un ordre allant du plus concret au plus abstrait les termes suivants.*
CONGÉ / CHIEN / IDEE / SENS / FOURCHETTE / RAISON

concret   abstrait

4. *Soulignez celui des deux termes qui vous paraît le plus concret.*

avec—par	avec—contre
de—à	par—sans
sans—contre	contre—à

de—avec   à—avec
avec—sans   contre—de
de—sans   par—à
par—de   par—contre
à—sans

5. *Donnez à l'aide d'exemples les divers sens de chacun de ces termes.*
   AVEC / PAR / DE / CONTRE / A / SANS
6. *Sur cette ligne graduée, placez dans un ordre allant du plus concret au plus abstrait les termes suivants.*
   AVEC / PAR / DE / CONTRE / A / SANS

concret |_____|_____|_____|_____|_____| abstrait

61 The question asked in the survey was: "Give the diverse meanings of each of the following terms with the help of examples." Thus the question was not designed to make a distinction between the locative and the allative.

62 Cf. for example Martinet, 1979; the paragraphs about axiology (i.e., the study of the signifié) are practically concerned with some of these problems. One could also pretend that certain transformational elements of generative grammar tackle this kind of problems.

63 See Germain, 1981, for example: "Trier's study shows that at the beginning of the thirteenth century, the German vocabulary of knowledge is made up essentially of the three words: *Wisheit* 'art?', *Kunst* 'Art' and *List* 'Artefact'. At this time, knowledge covers two large domains: material and spiritual. The material one is twofold: on the one hand, it refers to courteous society and its attitude toward knowledge (*Kunst*), and on the other to the non-courteous society and its way of apprehending (=perceiving) the knowledge (*List*). As for spiritual knowledge, it represents a common attitude of noblemen and commoners toward moral wisdom and divine knowledge (*Wisheit*). At the beginning of the fourteenth century, *List* is replaced by *Wizzen* 'knowledge', and at the same time the meaning of *Wisheit* and *Kunst* is changed (in Ecklhart's work for instance). Knowledge is now divided in three distinct parts: higher spheres (*Kunst*), knowledge in general and technical ability in particular (*Wizzen*); and spiritual wisdom (*Wîsheit*). About 1300, we see the beginning of a separation between science and technology and the disappearance of a social valuation of these domains" (pp. 42–43). Notice that even in this example, the sociocultural conditions (e.g., the way a society is cut into classes or the way science and technology are construed as being related, etc.) are not completely irrelevant.

64 In spelling proper nouns on telephone, phonemes are often identified by their environment: *S like Susan*. Notice that the environments called upon are generally fixed by convention. Such limited exceptions do not invalidate the general rule.

65 These difficulties may be due to the underlying hypotheses of and/or the techniques used in this survey. Under other conditions, surveys indicates regu-

larity and hierarchy of the meanings of *de* comparable to those obtained for other prepositions. Cf. Singy and Oberlé, 1987. Nonetheless, it is obvious that grasping the features of a signifié is particularly complex for some grammatical units. This complexity seems to have lead Martinet to consider that *de* has no signifié of its own, whereas he gives a definition for the signifié of *contre* 'against'. More generally, this complexity seems to be the origin of the concept "empty words." See Vendryès (1921), who considers that some units (called semantemes) have semantic content, in opposition to the morphemès, which have none.

66 The terms system and structure refer to a makeup and to constitutive parts; the assemblage of these elements to build the system can be more or less lax, or solid. "Laxity of structure" refers to this (cf. also Conclusion, VIII.1 and VIII.7).

67 Often, and not exclusively. By designing their questionnaires, certain phonologists aim at finding out what phonetic properties the users attribute to phonemes.

68 To a certain extent only. As we said above, surveys have shown that the users are aware of certain phonetic features of phonemes.

69 If I did not busy myself with other experimental techniques, it is only for personal reasons: indeed, such an examination inevitably goes through a minute control of the technical means. Now, sophisticated technical means, even though they have the advantage of being very accurate in the measure and observation of phenomena, have nevertheless the drawback that the controlling is more difficult. And the experimenter will not be allowed to hand over his responsibilities to the technician to be safe from raised risks of error. He must acquire the necessary technical competency and/or take care of an interdisciplinary cooperation, all things for which I do not have the required preparation.

70 We shall come back to this below in VIII.4.

71 The properties listed here are uneven in value; we think that some of them can be logically derived from others. We believe that the features of (a) and (b) can advantageously be subsumed under two fundamental principles: (A) semiotic omnipotence (or universality) of language and (B) its economical structure (cf. Mahmoudian, 1982, §3.6).

72 In reality, all theories implicitly or explicitly contain levels of analysis such as morphology, semantics, and others. This simplified picture is sufficient at this point of our discussion.

73 Cf., for example, Houis (1971), even if only subtle, insidious influences of the describer's language and culture remain in the structure he assigns to the languages under study.

74 This is an intuitive estimate for the time being; cf. VIII.7 and VIII.11 for a more objective judgment.

75 Cf. the virulent criticism TGG made of taxonomy in the 1960s and 1970s. Note that TGG could not avoid the concept of class but only established another taxonomy.

76 Those who start with one level only end up implicitly or explicitly with two: for example, with theory and metatheory.

77 As Martinet does when he interviews his informants (cf. Martinet, 1945, questionnaire, pp. 10–13).

78 As an example, Bloomfield rejects intuitive data as being irrelevant (cf. Bloomfield, 1933, §2.7 and §10.1).

79 As another example, Hjelmslev rejects any substance phenomenon including intuitive and social data as being irrelevant (cf. Hjelmslev, 1953, pp. 413–414).

80 Cf. Thomas Kuhn, 1962, chapters I and II.

81 It is indeed the case for moneme and morpheme. Cf. Martinet's definition of *monème:* "Monemes are the smallest segments of speech that have some meaning attached to them. According to Saussurean terminology, they are minimal "signs," with two faces: *signifiant* and *signifié*" (Martinet, 1962, p. 22). Cf. Bloomfield's definition of *morpheme:* "Thus a form is a recurrent vocal feature which has meaning" (§6.), and "A minimum form is a *morpheme;* its meaning is a sememe. Thus a morpheme is a recurrent (meaningful) form which cannot in turn be analyzed into smaller recurrent (meaningful) forms" (§9, Bloomfield, 1926).

82 Hockett, from complex to simple (cf. Hockett, 1958).

83 Martinet, from simple to complex (cf. Martinet, 1960, §4.30–4.33, and 1962, pp. 58–60).

84 Frei's aim is to "search in what respect errors are conditioned by the functioning of language and how these are an indication of it" (cf. Frei, 1929, p. 9). The title and subtitle of his work already state this: *La grammaire des fautes. Introduction à la grammaire fonctionelle* ("A Grammar of Errors. An Introduction to Functional Grammar").

85 Chomsky considers "errors (random or characteristic)" to be "irrelevant." Cf. Chomsky, 1965, pp. 3–4.

86 This clearing up has been taken for granted in the present chapter.

87 The matter is to value the models and not the theories, for empirical valuation of a theory is possible only indirectly, that is, through the empirical valuation of the models it allows to be constructed.

88 Cf. Bever (1975) and his acquisition study through comprehension; he does not envisage any possible complementarity between his model and the other models he rather severely criticizes.

89 Number (i) can be found in Martinet (1944, 1955), in which nothing has been undertaken as to the study of (ii). As far as we know, it was around the 1960s and 1970s that the first serious studies were made to explain behavior in terms of variation and dynamics. Cf. among other studies Labov (1972a), in particular chapters 8–9, and Rosch and Lloyd (1978).

90 The third section includes those parts of language structure that are effective in communicative use.

91 There are other aspects to structural hierarchy: on the intrinsic level, one can

observe variabilities (frequent vs. seldom, integrated vs. isolated) that seem to go hand in hand with extrinsic variations; from this follows that intrinsic hierarchy (=structure) and extrinsic hierarchy (=usage) condition each other. We will not dwell on this here; for further details, see Chapter IV.

92 This idea is expressed in currents as different as Harris' distributionalism and Martinet's functionalism; cf. Harris (1954, §1 and §3 and Martinet (1960, §2.8, where is expressed the idea that no study of meaning is possible without its taking into account its formal counterpart; and 1989, p. 136, where his reaction toward the models of meaning analysis is "not marked with optimism as to the possibility of going much further than what we know today"). Note that Martinet also expresses a different opinion when he introduces a linguistic study of meaning called *axiology* (cf. Martinet, 1975).

93 Cf. Labov, 1973.

94 For example, the procedure applied by Katz and Fodor (1963) which is in its findings really the same as the one followed by Hjelmslev (1953).

95 The problem of exhaustivity raises the same kind of questions, but we will not discuss them here. For a more detailed analysis of the coherence and exhaustivity criteria, see Mahmoudian (1982).

96 Cf. Borel, Grize, and Miéville (1983).

97 That is, in its majority, by a few exceptions such as Harris, who does not believe in the existence of any meaning structure, or such as Hjelmslev, who postulates isomorphism between the structure of the signifiant and the structure of the signifié.

98 Cf. Harris, 1954, beginning of §1.

99 Cf. Harris, 1954, §11.3.

100 It is in fact possible for a speaker-hearer ‹SH1› to use in his practice of speech a given element ‹E›, while being nevertheless aware that others ‹SH2, SH3 . . . › would use different elements instead of ‹E1›: ‹E2, E3, etc.›.

101 Does not one refer to this when speaking of *utterances out of context*?

102 In proof of this, many of those who start in this field with a principle of discreteness in mind finally admit the existence of a continuum; cf. Martinet (1960), §1.14 and §1.17, where he assigns a characteristic of discreteness to the linguistic units, as opposed to §V.1, where it is obvious that the reduction to discrete units is a pedagogical, if not a tactical simplification. See also Martinet (1965), Chapter X.1, "Réflexions sur le problème de l'opposition verbo-nominale," where he conceives certain grammatical categories to enter a bipolar opposition, as well as zones of transition. Cf. also Chomsky (1956), §2.1, where he asserts that there is no order of approximation between probability and grammaticality; he distinguishes between grammatical and agrammatical, leaving to grammar the decision whether a doubtful sequence is or not grammatical, as opposed to his proposal to establish "degrees of grammaticalness" between two poles; 1961, "Some Remarks on Generative Grammar" (in *Word* 17, reprinted in Katz and Fodor, 1964); and 1975, §32.2, pp. 131–132.

103 Cf. the functions 'subject' and 'predicate complement':

(1) Peter is John's colleague.

(2) John's colleague is Peter.

Is it legitimate to say that a syntactical pattern such as the one given here allows us to establish an equivalence between 'subject' and 'predicate complement'? In the affirmative, one supposes that the substituting of one for the other entails no modification of the sentence meaning. That is to say that all contexts or usages of (1) also work for (2). Now, it is not always true:

(1) is more likely to occur under the following conditions:

Peter is known to the speaker and the hearer.

Peter's function or job is not known to the hearer.

(2) is more likely to occur under the following conditions:

John's function and job are known.

Peter is not known.

The equivalence is not absolute on a semantical level either:

(1) Peter is John's colleague.

(3) John is Peter's colleague.

That (1) entails (3) and (3) entails (1) is not true in all cases. To put it otherwise, (1) and (3) can be said to mean the same thing. Now under certain circumstances, one could point to a certain antecedence of one element over the other, cf. the possible utterance:

(4) Peter is John's colleague, or rather John is Peter's colleague!

meaning *Peter is more influential than John.*

There is thus no absolute answer to questions such as the one asked above. Equivalence seems justified in both cases, at a level of gross approximation (at which only the identity of John's and Peter's activities is taken into consideration), but not at a level of finer approximation, at which other aspects come into play beside the identity of John's and Peter's activities, such as the importance of each person, his seniority, the degree of acquaintance of the protagonists taking part in the conversation, and so on.

References

Atalan, Henri (ed.), 1986, *Création et créativité*, Albeuve, Switzerland: Castella.

Bach, Emmon, and Robert T. Harms (eds.), 1968, *Universals in Linguistic Theory*, New York: Holt, Rinehart and Winston.

Bailey, Charles J., and Roger W. Shuy (eds.), 1973, *New Ways of Analyzing Variation in English*, Washington, D.C.: Georgetown University Press.

Bendix, Edward Hermann, 1966, *Componential Analysis of General Vocabulary; the Semantic Structure of a Set of Verbs in English, Hindi and Japanese*, The Hague: Mouton.

Benveniste, Emile, 1966, *Problèmes de linguistique générale*, Paris: Gallimard.

Bernard, Claude, 1865, *L'introduction à l'étude de la médecine expérimentale*, Paris: J. B. Baillières et fils.

Bernstein, Basil, 1971, "Linguistic Codes, Hesitation Phenomena and Intelligence," in *Class, Codes and Control*, vol.1, London: Routledge & Kegan Paul.

Berry, Margaret, 1975, *Introduction to Systemic Linguistics*, London: Batsford.

Bever, Thomas, 1975, "Functional Explanations Require Independently Motivated Functional Theories," in *Papers, from the Parasession on Functionalism*, Chicago: Chicago Linguistic Society.

Bloomfield, Leonard, 1926, "A Set of Postulates for the Science of Language," in *Language* 2, pp. 153–164 (reprinted in Joos, 1957).

————, 1933, *Language*, New York: Holt, Rinehart and Winston.

————, 1939, "Menomini Morphophonemics," in *Travaux du cercle linguistique de Prague* 8, pp. 105–115.

Bossel, Philippe, 1986, *Etude de la structure du signifié appréhendée à travers quelques unités lexicales du français délimitées dans le cadre du champ notionnel des ages de la vie humaine* (unpublished memoir), Faculté des lettres, Université de Lausanne.

220 References

Carden, Guy, 1973, "Disambiguisation, Favored Readings and Variable Rules," in Bailey and Shuy (eds.).

Carnap, Rudolf, 1968, *Logische Syntax der Sprache*, Hamburg, New York: Springer.

Chomsky, Noam, 1957, *Syntactic Structures*, The Hague: Mouton.

———, 1962, "A Transformational Approach to Syntax," in Archibald A. Hill, *Proceedings of the Third Texas Conference on Problems of Linguistic Analysis in English*, Austin: University of Texas (reprinted in Katz and Fodor [eds.], 1964).

———, 1965, *Aspects of the Theory of Syntax*, Cambridge, Mass.: MIT Press.

———, 1968, *Language and Mind*, New York: Harcourt-Brace.

———, 1972, *Studies on Semantics in Generative Grammar*, The Hague: Mouton.

———, 1975, *The Logical Structure of Linguistic Theory*, New York: Plenum Press.

———, 1977, "Introduction à la théorie standard étendue," in Chomsky *et al.*

——— et al., 1977, *Langue. Théorie standard étendue*, Paris: Hermann.

De Camp, David, 1973, "What Do Implicational Scales Imply?" in Bailey and Shuy (eds.).

Deyhime, Guiti, 1967, "Enquête sur la phonologie du français contemporain," in *La linguistique*, vol. 1, 97–108, Vol. 2, 57–84.

Ebeling, C. L., 1978, *Syntax and Semantics. A Taxonomic Approach*, Leyden: Brill.

Espagnat, Bernard d', 1986, "Approfondissement et création," in Atalan (ed.).

Fillmore, Charles J., 1968, "The Case for Case," in Bach and Harms.

———, 1972, "On Generativity," in Peters (ed.).

François, Denise, 1974, *Français parlé*, Paris: S.E.L.A.F.

François, Frédéric, 1977, *La syntaxe de l'enfant avant 5 ans*, Paris: Larousse.

Frei, Henry, 1929, *La grammaire des fautes. Introduction à la grammaire fonctionnelle*, Paris: Geuthner, Kundig & Harassowitz.

Fries, Charles C., 1952, *The Structure of English: An Introduction to Descriptive Linguistics*, New York: Harcourt, Brace.

Germain, Claude, 1981, *La sémantique fonctionnelle*, Paris: P.U.F.

Glason, Henry A. Jr., 1955, *An Introduction to Descriptive Linguistics*, New York: Rinehart and Winston.

Goffman, Ervin, 1959, *The Presentation of Self in Everyday Life*, New York: Anchor Books.

———, 1971, *Relations in Public: Microstudies of the Public Order*, New York: Basic Books.

Granger, Gilles-Gaston, 1967, *Pensée formelle et sciences de l'homme*, Paris: Aubier-Montaigne.

———, 1979, *Langages et épistémologie*, Paris: Klincksieck.

Greenberg, Joseph, H., 1978, *Universals of Human Language*, Stanford: Stanford University Press.

Grize, J.-B., M.-J. Borel, and D. Miéville, 1983, *Essai de logique naturelle*, Berne: P. Lang.

Gross, Maurice, 1975, *Méthodes en syntaxe*, Paris: Hermann.

Hamburger, Jean (ed.), 1986, *La philosophie des sciences aujourd'hui*, Paris: Gauthier-Villars.

Hamp, Eric P., Fred W. Householder, and Robert Austerlitz, 1966, *Readings in Linguistics II*, Chicago: University of Chicago Press.

Harris, Zellig S., 1951, *Methods in Structural Linguistics*, Chicago: University of Chicago Press.

————, 1954, "Distributional Structure," in *Word*, vol. 10 (2–3).

————, 1969, "The Two Systems of Grammar: Report and Paraphrase," in *Papers in Structural and Transformational Linguistics*, 612–692.

Herrmann, Theo, 1983, *Speech and Situation*, Berlin: Springer (German edition 1982).

Hiz, Henry, 1961, "Cogrammaticality, Batteries of Transformations and Grammatical Categories," in *Proceedings of Symposia in Applied Mathematics*, XII, 43–50.

Hjelmslev, Louis, 1944, "Linguistique structurale," in *Acta Linguistica* 4, pp. v–xi.

————, 1953, *Prolegomena to a Theory of Language*, Indiana University Publications in Anthropology and Linguistics, memoir 7, *IJAL* (Danish version published in 1943).

————, 1966, *Le langage*, Paris: Minuit.

————, 1968a, *Prolégomènes à une théorie du langage*, Paris: Minuit.

————, 1968b, *La Structure fondamentale du langage* (addendum to 1968a).

Hockett, Charles F., 1957, *A Course in Modern Linguistics*, New York: Macmillan.

Hoekstra, Teun (ed.), 1980. *Lexical Grammar*, Dordrecht: Foris.

Houis, Maurice, 1971, "Les effets de mirage," in *Anthropologie linguistique de l'Afrique Noire*, Paris: PUF.

Hughes, Arthur, and Peter Trudgill, 1979, *English Accents and Dialects. An Introduction to Social and Regional Variations of British English*, London: E. Arnold.

Ionesco, Eugène, 1968, *Présent passé. Passé présent*, Paris: Mercure de France.

Jakobson, Roman, 1936, "Beitrag zur allgemeinen Kasuslehre. Gesamtbedeutung des russischen Kasus," in *Travaux du cercle linguistique de Prague* 6, pp. 240–288 (reprinted in Hamp, Householder, and Austerlitz).

————, 1959, "Boas' View of Grammatical Meaning," in *American Anthropologist* 61/5, part 2, pp. 103 and 129.

————, 1984, *Russian and Slavic Grammar*, Berlin: Mouton. (Chapter 6, "Contribution to the General Meaning of Case: General Meanings of the Russian Cases," is the English translation of Jakobson, 1936).

Jespersen, Otto, 1924, *The Philosophy of Grammar*, New York: H. Holt.

Jolivet, Rémi, 1973, *Descriptions quantifiées en syntaxe du français*, Genève: Slatkine.

————, 1980, "La place de l'adjectif," in *La linguistique* 16/1, pp. 77–103.

Joos, Martin (ed.), 1957, *Readings in Linguistics*, Chicago: University of Chicago Press.

Katz, Jerrold J., 1964, "Mentalism in Linguistics," in *Language* 40, pp. 124–137.

Katz, Jerrold J., and Jerry A. Fodor, 1963, "The Structure of a Semantic Theory," in *Language* 39, pp. 170–210 (reprinted in Katz and Fodor [eds.], 1964).

————, 1964, *The Structure of Language. Readings in the Philosophy of Language*, Englewood Cliffs, N.J.: Prentice-Hall.

Kuhn, Thomas, 1962, *The Structure of Scientific Revolutions*, Chicago: University of Chicago Press.

Labov, William, 1972a, *Sociolinguistic Patterns*, Philadelphia: University of Pennsylvania Press.

————, 1972b, *Language in the Inner City*, Philadelphia: University of Pennsylvania Press.

————, 1973, "The Boundaries of Words and their Meanings," in Bailey and Shuy (eds.).

Lahusen, Thomas, 1979, "Allocution et société dans un roman polonais du XIXe siècle, Essai de sémiologie historique," *Wiener Slawistischer Almanach* 3, 167–195.

————, 1982, "Autour de 'l'homme nouveau,' *Allocution et société en Russie au XIXe siècle, Essai de sémiologie de la source littéraire. Wiener Slawistischer Almanach*, Sonderband 9.

Lakoff, George, 1968, "Instrumental Adverbs and the Concept of Deep Structure," in *Foundations of Language*, 4/1, pp. 4–29.

————, 1969, "Presupposition and Relative Grammaticality," in W. Todd (ed.).

————, 1970, "Linguistics and Natural Logic," in *Synthese* 22/1–2.

————, 1972, "Hedges: A Study in Meaning Criteria and the Logic of Fuzzy Concepts," in *CLS* 8, pp. 183–228.

Lamb, Sydney, M., 1966, *Outline of Stratificational Grammar*, Washington, D.C.: Georgetown University Press.

Lazard, Gilbert, 1978, "Eléments d'une typologie des structures d'actance: structures ergatives, accusatives et autres," in *BSL* 73, pp. 49–84.

————, 1985a, "A Few Remarks on Actance Gradients," in Seiler and Brettschneider (eds.).

————, 1985b, "Les variations d'actances et leurs corrélats, in *Actances* 1.

Li, Charles N. (ed.), 1976, *Subject and Topic*, New York: Academic Press.

Lockwood, David G., 1972, *Introduction to Stratificational Linguistics*, New York: Harcourt, Brace, Jovanovich.

Lüdtke, Helmut, 1977, "Epistemological Remarks on Language Change and Language Universals," in *Journal of Maltese Studies*, 2, pp. 3–18.

————, 1986, "Esquisse d'une théorie du changement langagier, in *La linguistique* 22/1, pp. 3–46.

Mahmoudian, Maryse, and Nina de Spengler, 1980, "Constructions pluripronominales dans les syntagmes verbaux complexes," in *La linguistique* 16/1, pp. 51–75.

Mahmoudian, Mortéza, 1970, *Les Modalités nominales en français, Essai de syntaxe fonctionnelle*, Paris: Presses Universitaires de France.

————, 1975, "A propos de syntagme et synthème," in *La linguistique* 11/1, pp. 51–73.

————, 1980, "Unité et classe en syntaxe," in *Actes du VIème Colloque International de Linguistique Fonctionnelle*, Rabat: Publications de la Faculté des Lettres et des Sciences Humaines.

References **223**

———, 1980, "Structure linguistique: problèmes de la constance et des variations," in *La linguistique* 16/1, pp. 5–36.

Mahmoudian, Mortéza, et al., 1976, *Pour enseigner le français, Présentation fonctionnelle de la langue*, Paris: Presses Universitaires de France.

———, 1982, "Elaboration formelle et subjectivité," in *Bulletin de la section de linguistique de l'Université de Lausanne* 5 (1982), "Axiomatisation et description linguistique," pp. 33–61.

Martinet, André, 1945, *La prononciation du français contemporain*, Genève and Paris: Droz (repr. 1971).

———, 1955, *Economie des changements phonétiques*, Berne: Francke.

———, 1960, *Eléments de linguistique générale*, Paris: Armand Colin.

———, 1962, *A Functional View of Language*, Oxford: Clarendon Press.

———, 1965, "Arbitraire linguistique et double articulation," in *La linguistique synchronique*, Paris: PUF.

———, 1967, "Syntagme et synthème," in *La linguistique* 2, pp. 1–14.

———, 1975, "Sémantique et axiologie," in *Revue roumaine de linguistique* 20/5, pp. 539–542, Bucarest: EARSR.

———, 1985, *Syntaxe générale*, Paris: Armand Colin.

———, 1989, "Réaction aux quatre exposés," in *La linguistique* special issue, *Sens et signification* 25, fasc. 1, pp. 133–136.

Martinet, André (ed.), 1968, *Le langage*, Paris: Gallimard ("Encyclopédie de la Pléiade").

Martinet, André, et al., 1979, *Grammaire fonctionnelle du français*, Paris: Hatier.

Martini, François, 1968, "Le cambodgian (khmer)," in Martinet (ed.), *Le langage*.

McCawley, James D., 1968, "The Role of Semantics in a Grammar," in Bach and Harms (eds.).

Miller, George A., 1969, "A Psychological Method to Investigate the Verbal Concepts," in *Journal of Mathematical Psychology* 6, pp. 169–191.

Moulton, William Gamwell, 1968, *The Sounds of English and German*, Chicago: University of Chicago Press.

Mounin, Georges, 1965a, "La dénomination des animaux domestiques," in *La linguistique*, 1; reprinted in Mounin, 1972.

———, 1965b, "La structuration du lexique de l'habitation," in *Cahiers de lexicologie*, 6/1, 1965; reprinted in Mounin, 1972.

———, 1972, *Clefs pour la sémantique*, Paris: Seghers.

Mulder, Jan W. F., 1977, "Postulates for Axiomatic Functionalism," in Mulder and Hervey (first published in French in *La linguistique* 13 [1977]).

Mulder, Jan W. F., and Sandor G. J. Hervey, 1980, *The Strategy of Linguistics*, Edinburgh: Scottish Academic Press.

Oberlé, Gabriella, 1988, "Monèmes grammaticaux: une enquête," in *Bulletin de la Section de linguistique de l'Université de Lausanne* 9, "Sens et traits de sens: Etudes empiriques," pp. 75–90.

Petit Larousse, 1968.

Petit Robert, 1967.

Peškovskij, A., 1934, *Russkij sintaksis v naucnom osvescenii* (cited in Jakobson, 1936).

Peters, Stanley, 1972, *Goals of Linguistic Theory*, Englewood Cliffs, N.J.: Prentice-Hall.

Piaget, Jean, 1967, "L'épistémologie et ses variétés," in Piaget (ed.), 1967.

Piaget, Jean (ed.), 1967, *Logique et connaissance scientifique*, Paris: Gallimard ("Encyclopédie de la Pléiade").

Pike, Kenneth L., 1967, *Language in Relation to a Unified Theory of the Structure of Human Behavior*, The Hague: Mouton.

Popper, Karl R., 1973, *Objective Knowledge: An Evolutionary Approach*, Oxford: Clarendon Press.

Postal, Paul, 1968, "Epilogue," in Roderick A. Jacobs and Peter S. Rosenbaum, *English Transformational Grammar*, Waltham: Xerox College Publishing.

Pottier, Bernard, 1963, "Recherches sur l'analyse sémantique en linguistique et en traduction automatique," in *Publications de la Faculté des Lettres et Sciences humaines de Nancy*.

———, 1965, "La définition sémantique dans les dictionnaires," in *Travaux de linguistique et de littérature*, tome 3, 1ère partie, Strausbourg: (entre de Philologie et de Litteratures Romanes de l'Université de Strausbourg.

Prideaux, Gary Dean (ed.), 1979, *Perspectives in Experimental Linguistics: Papers from the University of Alberta Conference on Experimental Linguistics*, Amsterdam: John Benjamin.

Prideaux, Gary Dean, Bruce L. Derwing, and William J. Baker (eds.), 1980, *Experimental Linguistics: Integration of Theories and Applications*, Ghent: Story—Scientia.

Prieto, Luis J., 1966, *Messages et signaux*, Paris: PUF.

———, 1964, *Principes de noologie. Fondements de la théorie fonctionnelle du signifié*, The Hague: Mouton.

———, 1968, "La sémiologie," in Martinet (ed.), 1968.

Reichstein, Ruth, 1960, "Study of Social and Geographic Variation of Linguistic Behavior," in *Word* 16, p. 55.

Rosch, Eleanor, and Barbara B. Lloyd, 1978, *Cognition and Categorization*, Hillsdale, N.J.: L. Erlbaum.

Ross, John Robert, 1972, "The Category Squish: Endstation Hauptwort," in *CLS* 8.

———, 1973, "A Fake NP Squish," in C.-J. N. Bailey and R. W. Shuy, *New Ways of Analyzing Variation in English*, Washington, D.C.: Georgetown University Press.

Ruwet, Nicolas, 1964, *Introduction à la grammaire générative*, Paris: Plon.

Schoch, Marianne, and Nina de Spengler, 1980, "Structure rigoureuse et structure lâche en phonologie," *La linguistique*, 16/1 (1980), pp. 105–117.

Schogt, Henry G., 1976, *Sémantique synchronique: synonymie, homonymie, polysémie*, Toronto: University of Toronto Press.

———, 1988, *Linguistics, Literary Analysis, and Literary Translation*, Toronto: Toronto University Press.

Seiler, Hansjakob, and Gunter Brettschneider (eds.), 1985, *Language Invariants and Mental Operations*, Tübingen: Gunter Narr.

Singy, Pascal, 1988, "Enquête sur la modalité imparfait," in *Bulletin de la Section de linguistique de l'Université de Lausanne* 9, "Sens et traits de sens: Etudes empiriques," pp. 59–74.

Singy, Pascal, Christine Lusseau, and Gabriella Oberlé, 1986, "Syntaxe et sémantique," in *Bulletin de la Section de linguistique de l'Université de Lausanne 7*.

Singy, Pascal, and Gabriella Oberlé, 1987, "Enquêtes sémantiques: grammaire versus lexique," in *Bulletin de la Section de linguistique de l'Université de Lausanne 8*.

Sperber, Dan, and Deirde Wilson, 1986, *Relevance*, Oxford: Blackwell.

Tabouret-Keller, Andrée, 1972–1973, "A propos de l'acquisition du langage," in *Bulletin de psychologie* 304, tome 26, 5–9, pp. 321–331.

Tesniere, Lucien, 1959, *Eléments de syntaxe structurale*, Paris: Klincksieck.

Thom, René, in Hamburger, 1986.

Todd, W., 1969, *Studies in Philosophical Linguistics*, ser. 1, Evanston, Ill.: Great Expectation.

Trier, Jost, 1973, *Der deutsche Wortschatz im Sinnbezirk des Verstandes. Von dem Anfang bis zum Beginn des 13. Jahrhunderts*, Heidelberg: C. Winter (first published in 1931).

Vendryes, Jules, 1923, *Le langage. Introduction linguistique à l'histoire*, Paris: La Renaissance du livre (reprint, Albin Michel, 1968).

Vinay, J. P., and J. Darbelnet, 1967, *Stylistique comparée du français et de l'anglais*, Paris: Didier.

Wagner, R. L., and J. Pinchon, 1962, *Grammaire du français classique et contemporain*, Paris: Hachette.

Weinreich, Uriel, 1964, *Languages in Contact*, The Hague: Mouton.

Index

system: center and margins of, 56;
economy of, 95; and experimentation, 151; formal, 6, 157; nature
of, 186; relative, 20; and unit, 3,
172, 186

Tabouret-Keller, 176
taxonomy: conceptions of, 5; new, 66
technique: adequacy of, 154, 170;
choice of, 57; descriptive, 19; for
experimentation, 43; observational,
46, 119, 139, 157; science as, 12
terminological differences, 191
Tesnière, 70
theory: comparing 's, 192; and empirical facts, 149; and model, 13, 103,
190; and object, 12; simplicity of, 39

Thom, 151
traffic code, 15
Trier, 170

unit: and features, 203; frequency of,
56; in formal system, 6; grammatical,
103, 121, 137; integration of, 54;
lexical, 103, 121; linguistic, 3, 4, 12,
20, 53, 70, 138; minimal significant,
81; number of 's, 36; phonological,
35, 187; significant, 24, 122, 187; vs.
rule, 62
universals, 7, 25

Wagner and Pinchon, 16
Weinreich, 43

Mortéza Mahmoudian is Professor of General Linguistics at the Université de Lausanne. He is the author of *Les modalités nominales en français* and *La Linguistique*.

Library of Congress Cataloging-in-Publication Data
Mahmoudian, Mortéza.
Modern theories of language : the empirical challenge / Mortéza Mahmoudian.
p.   cm.—(Sound and meaning)
Includes bibliographical references and index.
ISBN 0-8223-1278-6 (alk. paper)
1. Linguistics, Experimental. I. Title. II. Series.
P128.E94M35   1992
410—dc20   92-13538 CIP